HEALING LABO

HEALING LABOR

Japanese Sex Work in the Gendered Economy

Gabriele Koch

Stanford University Press
Stanford, California

Stanford University Press
Stanford, California

Printed in the United States of America on acid-free, archival-quality paper

Parts of this manuscript were previously published in *Critical Asian Studies* as "Willing Daughters: The Moral Rhetoric of Filial Sacrifice and Financial Autonomy in Tokyo's Sex Industry," 48 (2): 215–34, copyright ©BCAS, Inc., reprinted by permission of Taylor & Francis Ltd, http://www.tandfonline.com on behalf of BCAS, Inc.

Library of Congress Cataloging-in-Publication Data

Names: Koch, Gabriele, 1984- author.
Title: Healing labor : Japanese sex work in the gendered economy / Gabriele Koch.
Description: Stanford, California : Stanford University Press, 2020. | Includes
    bibliographical references and index.
Identifiers: LCCN 2019019680 | ISBN 9781503610576 (cloth : alk. paper) |
    ISBN 9781503611344 (pbk. : alk. paper) | ISBN 9781503611351 (electronic)
Subjects: LCSH: Prostitutes—Japan—Tokyo. | Sex workers—Japan—Tokyo. |
    Prostitution—Japan—Tokyo. | Sex-oriented businesses—Japan—Tokyo. |
    Women—Employment—Japan—Tokyo.
Classification: LCC HQ247.T6 K63 2020 | DDC 306.7095/1352—dc23
LC record available at https://lccn.loc.gov/2019019680

Cover design: Susan Zucker

Cover photo: iStock

Typeset by Westchester Publishing Services in 10/14 Minion Pro

Für meine Eltern

Contents

Acknowledgments

So many individuals have contributed to this book in myriad forms. Foremost, I am deeply indebted to the women in the sex industry, activists, journalists, lawyers, police officers, researchers, and others who spoke with me, allowed me to accompany or spend time with them, and told me about their lives and their work. Their generosity and patience made this research possible, and their words bring life to these pages. I have done my best to "get it right," and any errors herein are entirely my responsibility.

When I first began thinking about the topics that eventually led to this project, Kären Wigen and Anne Firth-Murray were important early mentors, and classes with Beth Berry, Estelle Freedman, Setsu Shigematsu, and Matthew Sommer helped to clarify my academic interests. Time spent at the Kyoto Center for Japanese Studies and a summer internship at the Iwate Nippō newspaper proved to be formative experiences, which led to a year working as a coordinator for international relations on the Japan Exchange and Teaching Programme in beautiful Shimane Prefecture.

I am indebted to many colleagues and friends from the University of Michigan. Jennifer Robertson encouraged this project from the beginning. Her formidable intellect continues to influence me in important ways, and I am humbled by her fierce support and boundless hospitality. Gayle Rubin has indelibly shaped both this project and my broader intellectual commitments. Many lively and energizing conversations with Liz Roberts challenged me to think about the larger theoretical implications of an argument or an idea.

Kiyo Tsutsui pushed me to think through human rights politics in Japan, and Bridgette Carr provided a grounded legal perspective on human trafficking, sex, and labor. The keen eye and sharp wit of Liz Wingrove continually challenge me to clarify and refine my arguments. I have also benefited greatly from the mentorship of David Akin, Sarah Besky, Webb Keane, Stuart Kirsch, John Mitani, Holly Peters-Golden, Eric Plemons, and Elisha Renne. Thank you, also, to Debbie Fitch, Darlinda Flanigan, Yuri Fukazawa, Laurie Marx, Jane Ozanich, Margaret Rudberg, and Ann Takata.

The camaraderie of a talented and generous group of friends in Ann Arbor and beyond nurtured my spirit alongside the development and completion of this project: Dan Birchok, Jen Bowles, Hillary Brass, Shannon Brines, Ali Chetwynd, Dimitris Economou, Nick Emlen, Ariel Fleming, Katherine Fultz, Nora Hauk, Janet Holt and Lucas Arribas Layton, Adam and Kaeko Liff, Janelle Jimenez, Jieun Kim, the Kwaiser family, Scott MacLochlainn, Lamia Moghnieh, Bruno Renero-Hannan, Jess Robbins, David Saeger, Perry Sherouse, and Andrea Wright.

In Tokyo, the Fulbright Japan staff at the Japan-United States Educational Commission—especially Junko Brinkman—made sure that my stay for long-term fieldwork was a pleasant one. Muta Kazue at Osaka University hosted me for a summer of preliminary research in 2009. Glenda Roberts graciously provided me with an institutional home at Waseda University during long-term fieldwork and welcomed me to her weekly *zemi*, while Omori Ryoko at the International Office facilitated my affiliation. The Asia-Japan Women's Resource Center and the Tokyo Women's Plaza have always been welcoming and hospitable spaces. I am thankful, too, for stimulating conversations with Aoyama Kaoru, Kainō Tamie, Nagai Yoshikazu, Saitō Yuriko, Tsunoda Yukiko, and Yoshida Yōko. My stints of fieldwork were immensely enriched by the friendship of Jake Adelstein, Horie Aimi, Courtney Howell, Elaine Hung, Ishiyama Akiko, and Renee Riddle. In particular, I will always remember the camaraderie that Elaine, Aimi, and I shared in the uncertain hours after the March 11, 2011, disaster, and I thank Aimi for taking us in. Jake deserves particular thanks, as well, for providing me with a place to stay numerous times and for his generosity in sharing with me interesting and unusual materials.

At the Edwin O. Reischauer Institute of Japanese Studies at Harvard University, I had the good fortune to be part of an exciting community of Japan scholars. In particular, Ethan Bushelle, Michelle Damian, Tristan Grunow, Sachiko Kawai, and Ryo Morimoto provided a supportive and collegial environment for thinking and writing. I am particularly grateful for wonderful conversations with Ted Bestor, Vickey Bestor, Mary Brinton, Ian Condry, Andy Gordon, Susan Pharr, and Ellen Schattschneider. Stacie Matsumoto provided excellent support and structure to my research experience; Ted Gilman offered astute advice; and Catherine Glover, Yukari Swanson, Fun Lau, and Jennie Kim made sure everything ran smoothly.

At Yale-NUS College, I am blessed with a set of wonderful colleagues, including Nienke Boer, Steve Ferzacca, Kevin Goldstein, Erik Harms, Zachary Howlett, Marcia Inhorn, John Kelly, Shian-Ling Keng, Neena Mahadev, Brian and Robin McAdoo, Nozomi Naoi, Anju Paul, Matthew Schneider-Mayerson, Stuart Strange, Cecilia Van Hollen, Christine Walker, and Robin Zheng. Marcia Inhorn, in particular, is a mentor extraordinaire. I am thankful, too, to John Driffill, Jeannette Ickovics, Jane Jacobs, Joanne Roberts, and Naoko Shimazu for their guidance and support, and to Renee Lau, Vicky Poon, and Jolene Tan for administrative assistance. The Gender Research Cluster (supported by grant number IG16-RCS101) has been a stimulating environment for writing. Cluster members Nienke Boer, Zachary Howlett, Marcia Inhorn, Joanne Roberts, Christine Walker, and Robin Zheng read an early version of Chapter 5 and participated in a book workshop, providing excellent feedback for revising the manuscript. Nicole Constable deserves monumental thanks for coming such a long distance to participate in the workshop. Her intellectual engagement made important interventions in the manuscript, especially in terms of thinking about the bigger picture. Finally, I thank the fantastic and intrepid students who challenge me so much, especially those who have taken part in the Sexual Economies seminars.

Outside of my institutional homes, I have been fortunate to benefit from conversations with Allison Alexy, Anne Allison, Joe Alter, Elana Buch, Nicole Constable, Emma Cook, Kate Goldfarb, Ofra Goldstein-Gidoni, Joseph Hankins, Arthur Kleinman, ann-elise lewallen, George Paul Meiu, Casey Miller, Glenda Roberts, Doug Rogers, Lisa Stevenson, Miriam Ticktin, Carole Vance, and Kimberly Walters. Josh Reno shared his book prospectus as the outlines of the manuscript were just coming into focus. Sabine Frühstück, in particular, deserves heartfelt thanks for her many thoughtful engagements with my work. I have benefited greatly from her expert advice and am continually inspired by her scholarship, generosity, and wisdom.

It has been a privilege to share and receive feedback on earlier versions of portions of this manuscript with audiences at Brandeis University, Harvard

University, MIT, Nanyang Technological University, the National University of Singapore, Santa Clara University, Southern Methodist University, Union College, the University of Michigan, and Yale University. Productive collaborations at the annual meetings of the American Anthropological Association also helped me to refine my arguments.

Parts of this manuscript were previously published in *American Ethnologist* as "Producing *Iyashi*: Healing and Labor in Tokyo's Sex Industry," 43 (4): 704–16; and in *Critical Asian Studies* as "Willing Daughters: The Moral Rhetoric of Filial Sacrifice and Financial Autonomy in Tokyo's Sex Industry," 48 (2): 215–34.

Funding for the research and writing of this manuscript has come from many sources: the Fulbright Institute of International Education, the National Science Foundation's East Asia and Pacific Summer Institutes Program, numerous sources at the University of Michigan (including the Department of Anthropology, the Center for Japanese Studies, the International Institute, the Institute for Research on Women and Gender, and the Rackham Graduate School), the Edwin O. Reischauer Institute of Japanese Studies at Harvard University, and Yale-NUS College. I am particularly grateful to the Institute for Research on Women and Gender's Community of Scholars at Michigan for a summer fellowship, which allowed me to engage with a dynamic and attentive group of colleagues. At Yale-NUS College, a faculty startup grant has provided crucial funds for follow-up trips to Tokyo. The final touches to this manuscript were added during a semester of study leave, for which I am very thankful.

At Stanford University Press, Marcela Maxfield and Sunna Juhn have provided encouragement, excellent advice, and crucial support, while Gigi Mark, Deborah Grahame-Smith, and Stephanie Adams ushered the book through the production process and Paul Vincent provided careful copyediting. I would also like to thank the two anonymous readers, whose astute observations and suggestions helped me to see where my argument needed sharpening.

Finally, my thanks and my heart go out to my family, who make all things possible. Anne and Keith Strange have provided great support throughout the writing of this book. Alexander and Malou bring curiosity and irreverent humor to everything. My parents, to whom this book is dedicated, offer unconditional love and unflagging support. They unknowingly fostered their daughter's future in anthropology through providing a bilingual upbringing, a home overflowing with books, and the great fortune of living and traveling abroad from a young age. They have visited me wherever I have gone. Without their influence, the idea that I might pursue a career in anthropology would have been unimaginable. My canine companion Tosca hates computers but puts up with them nevertheless. She has experienced perhaps the greatest trials during the writing of this manuscript, which has at times taken us away from the good things in life: parks, treats, and play. She is a very good girl. Stuart Strange has read every page of this manuscript several times and our conversations have pushed me toward bigger and bolder ideas. The seemingly endless expanse of his intellectual interests, curiosity, adventurous spirit, and generous nature continuously astonishes me. What a joy to be able to travel through life together! I thank him for his love.

Author's Notes

All Japanese names will be given following the Japanese convention of family name first followed by personal name (unless they are scholars based outside of Japan who publish in English). For example, Prime Minister Abe Shinzō.

Although currency rates fluctuated throughout the period of my fieldwork (2008–13), ¥100 can be considered to be roughly equivalent to US$1.

All translations of Japanese sources are my own unless otherwise indicated.

HEALING LABOR

Introduction

ON SEPTEMBER 18, 2006, two days before the scheduled election of the new leader of Japan's ruling Liberal Democratic Party—a position that, then as now, led to the prime ministership—the frontrunners appeared on a special television program entitled "Ask Japan's Next Leader."[1] The host played prerecorded voiceovers with questions from the public, which were put to the three male politicians on stage: Chief Cabinet Secretary Abe Shinzō, Foreign Minister Asō Tarō, and Finance Minister Tanigaki Sadakazu. One question came from a twenty-four-year-old female office worker, or "office lady," who said that she was barely making ends meet on her monthly salary of ¥140,000. Although she had clearly defined plans for her future, she saw no way of pursuing the qualification she needed and realizing her intended career. Her parents were unable to help her. Would it, she wanted to know from Japan's next prime minister, be immoral to begin working in the sex industry (*fūzoku*) several days a week?

Finance Minister Tanigaki, the first to be prompted, agreed that the woman's salary was very low.[2] "It's a tough salary to live on," he said. "But," he continued, "isn't it a bit hasty to immediately look to the sex industry? There is the issue of whether it goes against morals to consider, but, well, what is the sex industry? To use an older word, it's prostitution (*baishun*), after all." Tanigaki warned that the stigma around the work could do significant harm to the woman, signaling potential damage to her social relations, marital prospects, and laboring future. "Of course, there are many kinds of work in the sex industry," he qualified, to audience laughter. But Tanigaki made his opinion clear: "I do not recommend it."

But where the finance minister was unequivocal, his counterparts were far more ambivalent in their advice. Secretary Abe, who would be elected party leader, explained, to further laughter, that the forms of sex industry work are diverse.[3] "The law legally permits these businesses. There are people in this industry who take pride in what they do, and the industry also includes 'traditional' Japanese occupations"—a reference to how commercial sex has long been recognized as part of the economy. Abe suggested that the woman carefully consider the potential effects of the work on herself and perhaps consult with the government-run unemployment agency, "Hello Work," first.

The third politician, Foreign Minister Asō, likewise observed that sex work was a broad category.[4] "The sex industry includes everything from prostitution to other things, so I'd like to ask the woman what, exactly, she's considering." Asō reasoned that "fundamentally, if she can have a conversation with her parents about it—if it's something she can talk about with them—that's a good indicator of what she should do." If the woman had a guilty conscience, on the other hand, she should give the idea up.

When the program host tried to elicit further commentary from his guests, pointing out that he thought there were many young women in similar situations, the female moderator impatiently cut him off and moved on to the next voiceover.

Working Women

A young woman, struggling on the feminized wages of an office lady and wondering whether she will ever achieve her dream job, asks three powerful men—one of whom is about to lead the country—about entering the sex industry. The sex industry has a visible, public presence and is known for its high earnings. But the woman is concerned about the possible moral implications of the work and asks for advice. If behind her question is a critique of a limited labor market for women and young people—or of the political party responsible for the recent restructuring of the economy and the welfare system—none of the politicians engage with it. All three men appear at ease and smile when they draw audience laughter at their apparent familiarity with the varieties of sexual commerce. One politician sternly advises the woman against the work, yet offers no alternatives, while the future prime minister speaks of the positive feelings of many sex workers and of the sex industry's long-standing role in Japanese life. The lone woman on stage is the only one who seems uncomfortable and rushes on to the next topic.

What is noteworthy about both the politicians' responses to the anonymous woman's question and the fact that it is asked at all is how they signify an acceptance of commercial sex as part of social life and, by extension, of the economy as always being sexual. The recently retired sex worker Sachiko captured this sense of the industry's basic importance. Sachiko could not keep herself from laughing when I asked her about the state of Tokyo's sex industry in the aftermath of the March 11, 2011, earthquake, tsunami, and nuclear disaster—an event that occurred in the midst of my fieldwork. Across the nation, cherry blossom–viewing parties, festivals, and other celebrations were canceled following the "triple disaster," in an exercise of *jishuku* (self-restraint), which calls for sobriety out of a collective sense of solidarity in the face of national loss.[5] But Sachiko assured me that this collective disciplining stopped short at the sex industry: "Commercial sex will outlive every other industry," she explained, suggesting she believed that while the satisfaction of some desires was optional, male access to sex was not. Sachiko understood the male search for intimacy and gratification—and for the feminized care of sex workers—as an exception even to calls for restraint in other areas of leisure and enjoyment.[6]

Contemporary Japan is home to one of the world's largest and most diversified markets for heteronormative sex. Widely understood to be socially necessary, the sex industry operates and recruits openly, with messages about the availability of commercial sex—and its attractiveness as short-term work—circulating throughout public space. A diverse group of young Japanese women staff this industry, attracted by its high pay and by the autonomy they see it as offering. Although some women engage in sex work only for a brief amount of time, others may spend years in their twenties and/or thirties—when their youth may translate to substantial earnings—working in different genres of the industry.[7]

The work of these women, however, remains stigmatized and unmentionable. In spite of the acceptance of male consumption of commercial sex, women's participation in sex work transgresses widespread norms of respectable feminine behavior. Moreover, in many ways, the same things that make sex work appealing to some young women are also those that make it problematic as work. Women's experiences of pride and satisfaction in their work may go hand in hand with stinging social isolation; as Sayaka, a veteran sex worker, told me, "The good days can be very good, and the bad days can be very bad." Although sex workers' lack of formal recognition as laborers engaged in an "ordinary" category of work shapes their lucrative and flexible working conditions, women in the sex industry also face vulnerabilities and abuses due to this reality. Despite the skill that many women develop at the work, they define themselves as amateurs rather than as professionals. And, although they labor in risky and insecure conditions, largely to public indifference and apathy, sex workers show little interest in or engagement with the rights rhetoric and interventions of either an anti–human trafficking or a sex workers' advocacy campaign aimed at addressing conditions in the sex industry.

This book explores how adult Japanese women working in Tokyo's sex industry experience and understand these contradictions in their work and in its social value. It argues that these contradictions matter because they reveal the socially and historically specific dynamics of how the concept of gender remains fundamental to the economy. Thinking about what the simultaneous importance and marginality of female sex workers in Japan exposes about the nature of women's work more generally, in other words, helps us to understand the processes by which the gendering of the economy is continually reconstituted.

What I call *healing labor* centrally illustrates many of the contradictions that define female sex work in Japan. Healing labor refers to how sex workers articulate what it is that they offer to their customers as a reparative, feminized care that is necessary for restoring both the well-being and productivity of men. Specifically, women working in Tokyo's sex industry narrate their contribution to Japanese society in terms of *iyashi* (healing), a carefully constructed performance of intimacy that commingles maternal care with sexual gratification. Sex workers invest considerable effort in making their care emotionally authentic, but the value of this labor rests on their successful enactment of the very assumptions of naturalized femininity commonly used to justify women's exclusion from the professional economy. Even as women in the sex industry view their intimate encounters with customers as socially and economically essential, the value of their labor depends on their marginalization.

Collectively, these various contradictions offer a view onto the gendering of the economy through manifesting the relationship between how sex workers think about what sex is and what it does and the roles and possibilities that they imagine for themselves. Women in Tokyo's sex industry must engage with distinctions—their own and others'—between the kinds of work they participate in and the valorized and protected areas of the economy that are implicitly gendered male. How they do so illustrates the political and economic consequences of sex workers' care for everything from how they constitute themselves as moral persons to the kinds of futures they envision and to the rights claims that they choose to make. In this way, focusing on sex workers—a group of women that might at first seem marginal to the economy—offers us a way to consider the gendered interdependencies and inequalities that shape the Japanese economy more generally.

The economy is not a natural entity but a rhetorical object and a set of relationships that are enacted and reenacted.[8] Although in Japan (and elsewhere), the national economy is imagined as a genderless abstraction, in practice male labor comprises the default idea of what constitutes productive work. And yet, such imaginings conceal both the public secret of (some) men's reliance on the sex industry and the crucial role of the underrecognized feminized labor that produces the contemporary Japanese political economy more broadly. This book thus underscores the relationship between erotic life and how people understand the gendering of the economy—or, to be more precise, the ways in which people think about the linkages between women's work, sex, and the economy. Ultimately, paying attention to these linkages exposes underlying ideas and assumptions about how people think they should relate to one another and how that reproduces social life, in ways that inevitably rely on gendered performances and expectations.

Tokyo's Sex Industries

According to the most recent statistics published by the National Police Agency, there are approximately 22,200 legal sex industry businesses across Japan today.[9] Although there are no official data on the number of women working in the sex industry, an estimate of at least ten women working at each business yields upward of 222,000 female sex workers employed in legally registered businesses nationwide—and this is surely a considerable underestimate.[10] Customers, of course, as the unmarked category, are much harder to tally, and any man is potentially a customer.[11]

The history of commercial sex as an organized institution in Japan dates back at least to the late sixteenth century, when the first instantiation of what would develop into a system of licensed prostitution was established in Kyoto. In 1956, Japanese members of parliament—including a coalition of the nation's first female elected parliamentarians—passed the Prostitution Prevention Law (*Baishun Bōshi Hō*), against the protests of prostitutes themselves.[12] But although the anti-prostitution law, which took full effect in 1958, prohibits prostitution, the law's narrow definition of "sex" as penile-vaginal intercourse has allowed for the gradual proliferation of a sex industry offering any and every service short of this act.[13] Today, the Law Regulating Entertainment Businesses (*Fūzoku Eigyōtō no Kisei oyobi Gyōmu no Tekiseikatō ni Kansuru Hōritsu*) recognizes and oversees businesses in which women offer male clients a range of explicitly sexual services under the legal category of *seifūzoku* (colloquially often shortened to *fūzoku*). Many of these businesses are owned by corporations that standardize services among their holdings and set prices in relation to market demand. Moreover, employment and promotional media serve as important sources for recruiting women into commercial sex and advertising businesses to consumers. The cohesiveness and degree of organization at play with regard to commercial, labor, and regulatory practices warrants the use of the term *sex industry*.[14]

Today, cisheteronormative commercial sexual services are available throughout urban Japan via both brick-and-mortar businesses that are highly integrated within the dense urban landscape and escort services accessible through the phone or the Internet. Physical storefronts exist in every major urban center as well as in many prefectural capitals and in regional towns that rely heavily on tourism. Streets or areas with high concentrations of sex industry businesses are known as *fūzokugai* (sex industry area or street), but more often sex industry businesses are only one form of entertainment or nightlife among many in a *kanrakugai* (entertainment area or street). Until a nationwide crackdown in the mid-2000s, the sex industry asserted its presence through flashy or gaudy store signs, touts who aggressively pursued passersby while bearing albums filled with photographs of sex workers, and advertisements placed in phone booths, public bathrooms, and mailboxes. Since the early 2000s, however, the industry has overwhelmingly shifted to a "delivery" (*deribarī*), escort-based model and restrictions on advertisements and touting have considerably increased.

Numerous other forms of sexual commerce exist around or outside of the margins of the mainstream sex industry. Some women engage in a form of amateur prostitution through monetized "one-night stands" (*warikiri*) with men whom they meet through "encounter-type" (*deaikei*) websites or "encounter cafés" (*deai kafe, deai kissa*).[15] Street solicitation by Japanese women is rare—and criminalized under the anti-prostitution law.[16] Sexual services (including intercourse) may be purchased from non-Japanese women working illegally in underground businesses.[17] At the time of my fieldwork (2008–13), Chinese and South Korean women constituted the two largest non-Japanese populations in the sex industry.[18] A diverse and diffuse male same-sex sex industry as well as a transgender (*nyū hāfu*) sex industry operate nationwide.[19] Women seeking to purchase sexual services have few options, limited to male escorts (who may be known as *shutchō hosuto, deribarī hosuto*, or *rentaru kareshi*), gay male sex workers who accept female clients (*urisen*), and informal arrangements with male hosts off-premises of their clubs.[20]

More generally, the mainstream sex industry exists at one end of a spectrum of a larger market for eroticized intimacy in Japan, in which cisgender women and men as well as transgender women provide affective labor and sexualized services. For example, the proliferation since the 1990s of host clubs, where female customers pay for intimate conversations and romance with young men, shows that Japanese men may also be affective-erotic laborers.[21] Although these host-customer relationships mostly stay in the realm of romantic fantasy, they can occasionally involve sex. Many host club customers are themselves hostesses or sex workers.[22] The diverse range of nightlife businesses that include, among others, host clubs (*hosuto kurabu*), cabaret clubs (*kyabakura*), snack bars (*sunakku*), girls' bars (*gāruzu bā*), and S&M show pubs (*SM shō pabu*) are collectively known as the *mizushōbai*.[23]

In this book, I follow the convention of my field site in distinguishing the explicitly sexual services on offer in the sex industry from the forms of flirtation, sexualized banter, and intimacy available in the *mizushōbai*. For my interlocutors, this is a meaningful and socially significant distinction—when Chie told me about how she had worked at a cabaret club before entering the sex industry, for example, she emphatically added, "But that's not the sex industry," peering closely at me to make sure I had understood. Legally, these businesses are also subject to different forms of oversight by the Law Regulating Entertainment Businesses. In practice, there is certainly some ambiguity and overlap between these two industries, despite regulatory and social distinctions: both exist in *yoru no sekai* ("the night world") and are not considered to be respectable forms of labor—although hostess work has recently become more normalized through a range of media that portray it as glamorous and exciting, and hostesses as a source of lifestyle inspiration.[24] Women working in both industries share a male gaze and offer forms of feminized care. Moreover, as with Chie, it is not unusual for a woman who has worked in the *mizushōbai* to enter sex work. Critically, however, not only are services in the *seifūzoku* explicitly oriented around sexual gratification, but the effects of working there also differ both in degree and in kind, from the forms of social stigmatization and isolation that women may experience to the kinds of violence and risks to their health and safety they may encounter. It is women working in the sex industry who are the subject of rights rhetoric and intervention by activists focused on Japanese women. Given the much deeper degree of stigma associated with the sex industry, women in the *mizushōbai* themselves draw a line between themselves and women in the *seifūzoku*.[25] Thus, for clarity's sake, in these pages, when I refer to sex work, commercial sex, or the sex industry, I am referring specifically to the *seifūzoku*—even while recognizing that the bounds are not always so clearly defined. In cases in which I refer to both the sex industry and the *mizushōbai*, I will refer to these collectively as the sex and entertainment industries.

Labor Markets

With the development of a strong postwar male breadwinner ideology, employment experiences in the Japanese labor market have long been heavily gendered.[26] In the period of high economic growth in the 1960s and 1970s, women were subject to pervasive expectations that they leave the workforce at marriage and commit themselves to caring for their husband and children before returning to part-time positions years later—thereby constituting a striking "M-curve" of labor market participation.[27] In 1963, Ezra Vogel provided the first ethnographic portrait of what would become the paradigmatic Japanese middle-class household, anchored by a housewife whose reproductive labor freed her husband for total dedication to his workplace.[28] Women largely formed a reliable source of cheap and expendable labor, allowing Japanese firms to devote considerable resources to their (male) full-time employees.[29] The economic restructuring of the 1990s, however, led to a dramatic expansion in irregular labor overall. In the recession that followed the bursting of the asset bubble in 1990, corporations moved to protect the job security of middle-aged employees by freezing the hiring of new high school and university graduates into full-time positions and filling their labor needs with part-time and temporary workers.[30] As such, insecure labor in Japan is no longer the domain of women alone but of young people generally. As labor sociologist Mary Brinton has observed, "The increasing peripheralization of young people in Japan's labor market is indicative of the trend toward ever-greater dualism in the employment structure—the increasing polarization of labor into 'core' and 'noncore' jobs in one of the world's most important postindustrial economies."[31] These shifts in employment status among the young have had a seismic effect on Japanese society, affecting marriage and childbirth rates and leading to a wide-ranging discourse on social insecurity, alienation, and inequality.[32] As young people in particular struggle with what Anne Allison has described as "a sense of being out of place, out of sorts, disconnected,"[33] they have questioned long-standing assumptions about the meaning and purpose of work to individual identity.[34]

However, even as economic restructuring has degendered nonregular employment among the young, female workers are still typically the first to be downsized and constitute the bulk of flexible labor.[35] For example, in 2011 a staggering 54.6 percent of all female workers were "nonregular," meaning part-time or temporary workers, in contrast to 20.1 percent of male workers.[36] At large companies, where a two-track system separates employees into career (sōgōshoku) and noncareer (ippanshoku) tracks, women constituted only 6 percent of total career employees in 2010 (up from 2.2 percent in 2000) and only 12 percent of new career-track employees hired that year.[37] The feminization of poverty—long the overlooked norm—has become increasingly apparent.[38] The situation is particularly unstable for women outside of normative family forms, especially single mothers, 80 percent of whom are divorced.[39] Welfare restructuring, for instance, has diminished the already minimal financial assistance given to single mothers, even at a time when the number of female-led households is on the rise.[40]

Even as Japanese women have increased their participation in the full-time, professional labor market, any number of indicators signal the enduring strength of norms valorizing women's primary identity as wives and mothers. A few examples will suffice. From 2010 to 2014, 23.6 percent of first-time (married) mothers were already unemployed when they became pregnant, while 33.9 percent of first-time (married) mothers had quit their jobs by the time their child was one year old.[41] Despite the fact that the largest Japanese firms (those with over one thousand workers) have widely implemented generous parental leave policies, few professional women make use of them due to their lack of legitimacy within the workplace.[42] Discriminatory workplace practices—including demotion, salary reduction, and pressure to retire— often compel newlywed women who attempt to balance career and family to quit. In 2014, the Supreme Court of Japan ruled for the first time on a "maternity harassment" case, deciding in favor of a physical therapist who said that she had been unfairly demoted from her managerial position after taking a year of maternity leave.[43] The lack of adequate childcare facilities likewise remains a pressing political issue across Japan. The assumptions underpinning such workplace struggles are reflected in the responses to a 2016 government survey, in which 44.7 percent of male respondents and 37 percent of female respondents agreed that "husbands belong at work and wives belong at home."[44] Finally, many women are simply not hired into career-track jobs—a stubborn reality exemplified by the scandalous August 2018 discovery that Tokyo Medical University had for years systematically discriminated against female applicants due to assumptions about their future priorities (for example, that they would quit working upon marriage and childbirth).[45]

Thus, women are largely not seen as economic actors in the formal labor market in their own right, but as caretakers of children, husbands, and the elderly. Although occupational roles for women have greatly expanded, women who pursue careers are still burdened by assumptions about where their true commitments lie, and many women are not encouraged to consider themselves as having a "professional" identity in the first place. It is against the backdrop of this labor market in which many of the jobs available to women are low wage and nonregular that women make decisions about working in the sex industry.

The Gender of the Economy

Since the 1970s, scholarship across the social sciences has demonstrated how socially and historically constituted ideologies of gender deeply shape notions of who should or should not properly be engaging in what kinds of activity and how individuals imagine, experience, and value those roles and their possibilities. Early feminist anthropologists observed that, across societies, men's activity is consistently represented as more socially significant than women's activity, thereby turning women's work into an important site of inquiry.[46] Although women and men everywhere participate in creating economic life, women's labor is often made invisible through its circumscription to particular ideological domains.[47] When women's labor contributes to men's projects, feminized productivity may be "eclipsed" by the forms of male prestige it generates without this being understood as exploitation or alienation[48]— even as this may be hard to account for through the assumptions of liberal feminism.[49]

Discussions of gendered labor under capitalism rest on the basic conceptual framework given by Friedrich Engels of how industrial capitalism constituted the modern family as defined by the ideological differentiation between a public and private sphere and, subsequently, between the valuation of the paid (waged) labor of the former and the unpaid labor of the latter.[50] Marxist feminist approaches have examined how women's work is "marginalized by, but nonetheless fundamental to, capitalist valorization processes."[51] Within this tradition, the international Wages for Housework campaign called for wages to be paid for women's domestic labor as recognition that it is work obscured by a rhetoric of love and feminine "nature." As Silvia Federici has written, "It is the demand by which our nature ends and our struggle begins because just to want wages for housework means to refuse that work as the expression of our nature. . . . When we struggle for wages we struggle unambiguously and directly against our social role."[52]

Women's labor in the sex industry, however, both shares continuities with and is crucially different from other forms of reproductive labor—which I use here in the Marxist sense to mean all work that reproduces labor power, including housework, the care of family members, and procreative labor. Sex makes it different, and not just sex itself but the specific context and relations of sex.[53] That is, the fact that participation in sex work engages Japanese women in a stigmatized sexual activity and thereby removes them from the dominant accepted standard of female sexual morality in Japan distinguishes it from other kinds of women's work and requires that we conceive of it in alternate ways.[54]

How, then, can we think about the healing labor of sex workers as work? The interrelated concepts of emotional, intimate, caring, affective, and performative labor account for the nature of production in (feminized) service sector work and can help us to make sense of the labors involved in generating healing labor. *Emotional labor* refers to how workers manage their emotions so as to generate a particular state of mind in their customers.[55] *Intimate labor,* of which *caring labor* is one manifestation, "entails touch, . . . bodily or emotional closeness or personal familiarity, . . . or close observation of another and knowledge of personal information."[56] *Affective labor* refers to how the ability to make human relationships itself has become a primary site of labor in postindustrial economies.[57] More than just "selling personality," affective labor facilitates the well-being of others, sustains personhood, and reproduces sociality.[58] And, finally, *performative labor,* as theorized by Gregory Mitchell, refers to how sex workers, in catering to customers' desires, stage relational aspects of their identities, especially race and gender.[59]

These analytic concepts address the question of how to expand the category of labor to account for feminized affective and caring labors, a question that has long concerned feminist theorists of the gendered division of labor under capitalism.[60] With the recent mass movement of middle-class women into the full-time workforce in many postindustrial contexts, the identification of unacknowledged forms of women's work remains pressing, as unpaid reproductive labor previously relegated to the domestic sphere—itself a culturally and historically specific phenomenon of capitalist relations[61]—is increasingly subject to the market and filled by a global supply of flexible workers.[62] As Melinda Cooper and Catherine Waldby note, "Domestic tasks, sexual services, care provision, and . . . the process of biological reproduction itself have migrated out of the private space of the family into the labor market and are now central to post-industrial accumulation strategies."[63] At the same time, despite these changes, conventional gender norms and ideologies of intimacy from the private sphere—especially the naturalization of care as feminine—continue to be reproduced via their movement to the marketplace, thereby obscuring the roles of sex workers and others as skilled professionals.

As with other forms of feminized labor, the qualities that make the healing labor of Japanese sex workers effective rest precisely on its being downplayed as labor. Women working in the sex industry go to great lengths to produce something understood by their customers as based on an effortless and intrinsic femininity, even as its successful achievement obscures the labor involved in their work. What is notable about *iyashi*, then, is how Japanese sex workers' discourses about the importance of their work for male productivity are related to their own insecure and unstable laboring conditions. Sex workers themselves believe that there is a connection between their healing labor and male white-collar productivity. The goal of supporting male workers who labor in "important" areas of the economy is privileged in ways that naturalize feminized forms of economic productivity and that reflect gendered hierarchies of the value of labor.[64]

Economic and Erotic Life

What does it mean to see sex as socially productive? Productive of what, and for whom? This entails attending to the specific things that sex—setting aside for the moment the question of definitions—is understood *to do*. Early anthropologists treated the structures of relatedness created through sex as central to forms of social organization and as indicative of a society's "stage of development."[65] Claude Lévi-Strauss famously argued that the exchange of women between men in marriage is the most basic form of reciprocity in kin-based societies. "Because women have an essential value in group life," Lévi-Strauss wrote, indicating their reproductive capacity, "the group necessarily intervenes in every marriage. . . . Where relationships between the sexes are concerned, *a person cannot do just what he pleases.*"[66] Gayle Rubin took up Lévi-Strauss's model of the sexual economy to argue that marriage produces gendered persons and that kinship—as the system that organizes "obligatory sexualities"[67]—is thus at the basis of an oppressive sex/gender system.[68] Rubin's critique implicitly raised the question of how female sexuality is valued within kinship structures and who gets to realize that value—an issue that feminist anthropologists have addressed through examining women's value via kinship in different sexual economies.[69]

To examine what sex does—its effects—is simultaneously to challenge the notion that sex simply *is*. This has been critiqued as "sexual essentialism"— that is, "the idea that sex is a natural force that exists prior to social life and shapes institutions" and that "consider[s] sex to be eternally unchanging, asocial, and transhistorical."[70] Sexual essentialism maintains that, because we allegedly already know what sex is, there is no reason to think about it further, justifying a lack of curiosity and, due also to its associations with the private, the dismissal of sex and sexuality as irrelevant to supposedly more significant domains of social life. Through feminist and queer scholarship, it is abundantly clear that sex has a history.[71]

Likewise, thinking about widespread notions in Japan of the basic social necessity of commercial sex, or about how sex workers narrate their industry's contribution to society, means seeing sex as part of social life and not as divorced from it, or as narrowly circumscribed only to the "private" domain. Instead, it compels us to recognize how sex is directly implicated in the central institutions of human life and may have enormous public consequences. "Sex" and "the economy" are not separate categories but overlap and mutually constitute one another. Here, I focus specifically on the economy as a rubric for thinking about productive activity of all kinds and its valuation. The *sexual economy* is a useful term for thinking about this mutually constitutive relationship. By this term I mean all the exchanges that happen around sex, and the subjective meanings associated with them.[72]

Sex is also productive of intimacy. As with any other form of intimacy, the intimacies provided by sex workers are socially and historically contingent and emanate from particular political-economic moments.[73] In this ethnography I approach the sexual services provided by women in Tokyo's sex industry as a form of feminized care offered against the backdrop of shifts in family life and a globalizing service industry.[74] The healing labor of these women is a specific kind of care particular to the postbubble-economy Japanese sex industry. Importantly, this healing labor is understood to *do* things—to repair the well-being and productivity of men against what sex workers regard as the harsh and exhausting conditions of male work in postindustrial capitalism. Sex workers' healing labor is thus deeply implicated in regimes of precarity in contemporary Japan. In providing this intimacy, Japanese sex workers rely on both normative, middle-class family tropes of nurturing—especially the reified mother-child relationship within the nuclear family unit—and on forms of feminine care linked to relations that are possible only outside of households and domestic units.

At this juncture, it is important to note that it is not only women who offer this sort of feminized care via commodified intimacy. Akiko Takeyama has shown how male hosts face stigmatization because they offer emotional labor, care, and, sometimes, sex to their female clients—what is typically coded as women's work.[75] Takeyama does not discuss *iyashi* either in relation to how hosts describe their services or to what customers desire. This is not a maternal care and is also not theorized in terms of productivity, as that is not a valued association with femininity. What is similar, however, is how the emotional labor of hosts provides a gendered recognition of the mainly middle-aged women Takeyama describes, which allows them to recoup their feelings of vitality as youthful and attractive subjects.

Although the healing labor and other contradictions that define sex work that I describe in this book are specific to the postbubble-economy sex industry, more generally, postwar Japanese corporate settings have long relied on forms of commodified erotic intimacy to motivate or reward male productivity. In 1981, anthropologist Anne Allison worked at an elite hostess club in Tokyo's Roppongi area and detailed how corporate after-hours entertaining in such a *mizushōbai* site was understood as fostering social attachments within and between companies.[76] Hostesses' feminized and often highly sexualized conversations facilitated lively group banter and flattered male egos, catalyzing a corporate masculine bonding that produced committed workers for Japanese companies and nourished business relations. According to Allison, "The hostess's role is to help create a *group* out of a table of individuals. To restate, the role most basic to her is to change and vitalize the relations among men by her act of serving."[77] Allison underscored that this institutionalized practice is simultaneously relaxation and work—that men "get away from work, and they get together in ways essential for work."[78] Highlighting how women's sexualized labor is understood as economically productive, the Japanese government created favorable corporate tax laws that facilitated this corporate entertainment.[79]

In other ways as well, in Japan, male sexuality has long been seen as something that should be managed so as to productively direct the energy of men, whether in the service of wartime empire or the postwar economic "miracle."[80] For example, the 2013 blustering of Osaka governor Hashimoto Tōru, who suggested to a US military commander that US troops stationed in Okinawa would be more easily managed if they were permitted to patronize local sex industry businesses, was just one episode in a long history of ideas about how to productively canalize men's energy by controlling their sexuality.[81]

Work and Rights

What is the relationship between rights and how people assess the value of their work? How do specific understandings of work lend themselves to—or disengage individuals from—ideas and articulations of rights?

When Carol Leigh coined the term *sex work* around 1980 as a reaction to hostility and discriminatory attitudes toward prostitutes from within the North American feminist movement, she did so in order to provide new language through which to think about the value of commercial sex and the dignity of those engaged in it.[82] *Sex work* was not only a move away from derogatory terms and euphemisms for prostitution but a gender-neutral alternative that foregrounded that diverse kinds of transactional sex are a means of supporting oneself. As Leigh writes, "It acknowledges the work we do rather than defin[ing] us by our status."[83] Work becomes a basis from which to point out the inadequacy of the conditions under which commercial sex typically occurs and to call for better ones.[84] Since the early 1980s, an international sex workers' rights movement has adopted this approach of treating sex work *as* work.[85]

Although a number of Japanese activists have taken up the international rhetoric of sex work as work and sex workers' rights as human rights,[86] the vernacularization of these ideas has not yet had broader impact.[87] Within Japan, sex industry work is widely regarded as disreputable, shameful labor, even if, as I will discuss, women's participation in it may be viewed sympathetically under certain circumstances.[88] Women working in the sex industry are not politicized and, for the most part, disassociate themselves from their work. Although in this book I will use the term *sex worker* interchangeably with the much bulkier phrase, "woman (working) in the sex industry," the latter is truer to the Japanese term for women engaged in sex industry work—*fūzokujō* (sex industry woman), an apolitical female-gendered term that, in contrast to the rarely used transliterated term *sekkusu wākā* (sex worker), does not imply a consciousness of a particular laboring identity.

Questions of work and rights in relation to sexual commerce have been raised prominently in recent scholarship on women's international migration.[89] In response to a vigorous global anti–human trafficking discourse that casts all migration into diverse forms of sex work as exploitation, ethnographers and others have highlighted the forms of agency that migrant women have—and their desires to pursue adventure, travel, and romance—while also underscoring how the circumstances of their migration and the informal and (usually) underground nature of the work leave women vulnerable to abuse and exploitative labor. Rhacel Salazar Parreñas, for example, has forcefully challenged blanket depictions of migrant Filipina hostesses in Japan as victims of human trafficking.[90] Instead, Parreñas characterizes their labor migration in terms of an "indentured mobility"—"a middle ground that recognizes the agency of migrants without dismissing the severe structural constraints that could hamper their freedom and autonomy."[91]

The circumstances of the adult Japanese women working in the mainstream sex industry who form the focus of this ethnography are not those of foreign migrant women in an underground industry. Nevertheless, as nonregular workers in stigmatized labor that is formally differentiated from "ordinary" categories of work, women in the Japanese sex industry have little control over the frequently risky and insecure conditions of their labor. This book therefore tracks the strategies of two competing rights campaigns to draw attention to forms of vulnerability and abuse in the sex industry and remake laboring conditions. The first is an anti–human trafficking campaign, which seeks to reframe the normalization of short-term employment in the sex industry as exploitation. The second is a sex workers' advocacy campaign that uses a labor rights framework to demand legal protections and benefits and that works to improve the everyday conditions of sex workers. The activists behind these campaigns define what they consider to be problematic about sex industry labor in very different ways that hinge on their respective understandings of the relationship of sex to a gendered economy.

Women working in the Japanese sex industry are deeply preoccupied with navigating the risks of an industry with few protections. And yet, these same women are largely uninterested in the rights rhetorics that seemingly might address such problems. Many women in the Japanese sex industry, that is, do not engage with or even recognize themselves in the advocacy of either this human rights or labor rights campaign. Why not? The contradictions that define female sex work in Japan offer us a way to understand sex workers' lack of politicization in this context insofar as they illuminate how a willingness to see oneself as a politicized subject of rights may rely on the content of what one imagines oneself as offering and how it fits into a particular moral universe.

A Typology of Sex Work

In the vignette that opened this Introduction, each of the three senior male politicians notes, in his response to the anonymous woman asking for advice, that there are many kinds of work in the sex industry. As I have already mentioned, the anti-prostitution law narrowly circumscribes sex as penile-vaginal intercourse. Thus, legally, the services of the sex industry do not include this act—although, of course, just because heterosexual intercourse is prohibited certainly does not mean that it is not being transacted. With the overwhelming transition of the sex industry to "delivery"-based services, which remove the sex worker and customer from the oversight of management, this is perhaps particularly true, as I will discuss in Chapter 6. More significant, however, is how the existence of a large and diverse cisheteronormative sex industry organized around such a prohibition directs our attention *away* from intercourse as the referent of *sex*.[92] How, then, is sex constituted in this industry? Here I will provide a brief overview of some of the major genres of business within the legal sex industry and the standard services associated with them—although it bears mentioning up front that there is also stratification within and across different genres of sex work, from high-end to low-end businesses, and from lesser and more stigmatized forms of work.

Soaplands (*sōpurando*) were the first type of sex industry business to appear after the Prostitution Prevention Law took effect. Originally referred to as "Turkish baths" (*toruko buro*), these are businesses at which a sex worker bathes and massages a customer. Due to a legal loophole, these businesses are widely known to include (illegal) intercourse (*honban*) as a standard feature, as well as oral sex and/or manual stimulation.[93] *Hotetoru* and *mantoru* businesses involve soapland services but at a hotel or an apartment, respectively, instead of at a brick-and-mortar sex industry business. Strip theaters (*sutorippu gekijō*) followed the proliferation of soaplands, although they have faced a steep decline recently, due to a lack of customers and sporadic police enforcement of public indecency laws. Some dancers perform sexual acts on stage with paying customers (for example, allowing a customer to touch and penetrate them with a vibrator). Many more permit customers to take a polaroid photo of or with them, in a desired pose, for a small fee.

In the early 1980s, the sex industry diversified heavily. Among the new types of businesses emerging, many were characterized as representing a *nyū fūzoku* (new sex industry) organized around role-playing, arousal, and what sociologist Miyadai Shinji has called "changing one's day-to-day frame."[94] These businesses included *fasshon herusu* ("fashion health," often abbreviated as *herusu*), at which a sex worker provides the customer with oral sex and/ or a hand job. An *imekura* ("image club") is a *fasshon herusu* business that offers costumes (for example, school girl uniforms, office lady uniforms), role-play, and rooms designed to cater to fantasy scenarios (for example, a clinic, a train). *Kaishun massāji* and *seikan herusu* (also known as *seikan massāji*) are both types of *fasshon herusu* that include a prostate and anal/perineal massage. *SM kurabu* (S&M clubs) involve bondage and sadomasochism. At pink salons (*pinku saron*), sex workers offer customers oral sex or hand jobs in a partially cordoned-off area, while the customer can order drinks (for example, coffee, alcohol).

Finally, *deribarī herusu* ("delivery health," commonly abbreviated as *deri-heru*, and also known as *shutchō herusu*), are escort businesses in which a sex worker is dispatched to a hotel, rental room, or private home. The standard service is the same as at a *fasshon herusu*, and includes oral sex and hand jobs.

Studying Sex

In Euro-American film, literature, and news media, Japan is often portrayed as radically alter, especially on the subjects of sex and sexuality.[95] Sensitive to these problematic depictions, in this book I take care to ground my claims in the experiences of Japanese sex workers and others as articulated to me by them directly and in the diverse and long-standing Japanese-language debates and writings on the sex industry.

The analysis in this book is based on twenty-one months of ethnographic fieldwork that I conducted in Tokyo from 2008 to 2013, in addition to several short return trips in 2016 and 2017. My fieldwork took me to sites in and around the sex industry, including diverse establishments where women offer sexual services to male customers, a training session for new employees, a sex industry exhibition show for customers, and venues on the peripheries of this industry (for example, swingers' clubs, "encounter-type" cafés), where I observed and spoke with sex workers and others. In addition to spending time with adult Japanese women working in the sex industry when they were not at work, I conducted formal and informal interviews with sex workers, sex industry business managers and support staff, sex industry journalists, police officers, lawyers, activists, the staff of nongovernmental organizations (NGOs), and scholars and researchers. For comparison, I also conducted a handful of interviews with male and *nyū hāfu* (transgender women) sex workers. I also attended public events hosted by grassroots organizations and NGOs, closed-door police conferences, "opinion exchange" meetings between government bureaucrats and anti–human trafficking advocates, and hearings at the National Diet.

I met the sex workers who took part in my study in several ways. Many of my interlocutors were initially introduced to me through the prolific networks of two sex worker advocates, one of whom I consulted with throughout my fieldwork. As my contacts expanded, I used some snowball recruiting and, in other cases, met women who agreed to speak with me about their experiences simply by socializing with sex workers. I met numerous of my interlocutors several times; others I only met once. My interviews with women in the sex industry typically took place at a café or restaurant of their choosing. Some women carefully selected a secluded site or asked to meet at times when a particular venue would be relatively empty, but others seemed unconcerned over being overheard by strangers at a neighboring table—once they had ascertained that no acquaintances were present. A few interviews took place at individuals' homes or at the home of a mutual acquaintance. My interviews with managers, male staff, journalists, and others also typically took place in cafés or restaurants. One unusual interview—with a soapland manager who evidently suspected that some ulterior motive lay behind my questions—took place entirely in a van parked on the side of the road.

From March to August 2011, I conducted a six-month internship at the anti–human trafficking organization that I refer to by the pseudonym Let's Fight Slavery Japan (LFSJ). During this time, I worked at the LFSJ office for twenty hours a week and participated in all normal staff activities. At the time that I began the internship, I had already been acquainted with LFSJ's activities for some time, having first attended a talk by the director in August 2008 and interviewing her shortly thereafter. In the summer of 2009 and autumn of 2010, I regularly attended LFSJ events and met numerous staff and supporters. When I applied for the internship in January 2011, the director and I had already discussed the possibility several times, although the relatively brief nature of my previous research trips had made me an unattractive candidate. On the six-page application form, I wrote that I hoped to learn firsthand about the daily operations of an anti–human trafficking organization that deals with exploitation in the sex industry and is trying to reshape attitudes about what constitutes commercial sexual exploitation. In a separate research request letter that I sent with my application, I explained the nature of ethnographic research (including participant observation) and my project in greater detail. Throughout the internship, I was transparent about the fact that I was also doing fieldwork with sex workers, managers, and others. The staff and I sometimes discussed these research experiences while doing office work. Following the conclusion of my internship, I stayed in contact with LFSJ staff and supporters and continued to follow their activities.

As a woman in my mid- to late twenties during fieldwork, I was roughly the same age as—or slightly younger than—many of the women working in the sex industry whom I spoke with and roughly the same age as—or slightly older than—many of the supporters and staff of LFSJ. Being unmarried and not tied to a formal workplace (as a graduate student), I also shared a similar social status with many of my interlocutors in not being regarded as having quite achieved social adulthood yet. These similarities eased my entry into the relatively young and highly feminized circles of both sex workers and the anti–human trafficking advocates of LFSJ. Being non-Japanese, moreover, I was also situated in relation to my interlocutors in particular ways that, I believe, ultimately aided my research. Given the concerns of women working in a stigmatized industry in maintaining privacy and protecting their identities, my status as an outsider seemed to grant me access to hear from women who otherwise may have been much more reluctant with a Japanese peer. Although I do not doubt that the sex workers with whom I spoke carefully managed what information they shared with me, it also seemed to me that many of my interlocutors enjoyed being able to speak relatively freely about their work—work that most of them hid from their loved ones—with an attentive listener. One woman told me during our interview that she was having the "strangest feeling, like being in a dream" at being in the unlikely scenario of talking about her work openly with an American woman informed and knowledgeable about the Japanese sex industry. Many women were very curious to hear about my experiences conducting fieldwork in Japan and interested in hearing an outsider's view on their industry.

Finally, my analysis is also informed by the prolific Japanese-language commentary on the sex industry and related topics. In addition to reading contemporary publications, I also conducted archival research at the Tokyo Women's Plaza, the National Women's Education Center, the Tokyo Metropolitan Library, and the National Diet Library, as well as through the online archives of numerous Japanese newspapers.

Overview of Chapters

Chapter 1 considers how ideas about the social value of the sex industry drive its regulation as an organized sector of the economy in contemporary Japan. Despite widely held assumptions about the basic necessity of providing men with access to particular kinds of gratification, regulatory strategy has reflected a reluctance to fully sanctioning commercial sex. This contradiction manifests in the common description of the sex industry as occupying a legal "gray" area that mirrors the social position of sex workers and that creates an uncertain environment for those working in this industry. This chapter argues that the grayness of regulation reflects ambivalence about the importance of women's commercial sexual labor to the organizing logic of the economy.

Chapter 2 explores the diversity of those in the sex industry and what attracts them. In the context of a limited labor market for women, sex workers foreground the highly remunerative earnings and the forms of autonomy and flexibility offered by sex industry work. Many of the same aspects that women in the sex industry find appealing about sex work, however, also reflect its marginalization from the dominant norms that structure the male-gendered economy. This chapter examines how this contradiction reveals how sex workers imagine what "work" can and should be.

Chapter 3 examines how sex workers manage a problem central to their work: it is both uniquely lucrative *and* stigmatizing, opening up possibility while simultaneously being unmentionable. Sex workers go to great lengths to separate their working lives from their "real," socially legitimate identities. The stigma of working in an illicit industry contrary to normative notions of feminine respectability is always on women's minds as they maneuver the moral conflicts that accompany their entry into and departure from the sex industry. This chapter argues that the sexual economy is always also a moral economy, and that how women talk about their work is shaped by moral ideologies of whom and what women's labor should be for.

Chapter 4 looks at how sex workers themselves understand the services that they offer to their customers in terms of healing labor. Women working in Tokyo's sex industry value the care they provide for what they see as its contributions to the well-being and productivity of male white-collar workers. Their services center on *iyashi* (healing). Sex workers regard *iyashi* as a form of women's socially necessary care of men and centrally assess the value of their work in terms that foreground its contributions to men's work. Although sex workers may devote considerable effort to cultivating their skill at providing *iyashi*, they conceal this labor so as to engender the appearance of a naturalized femininity.

Chapter 5 follows the advocacy of an anti–human trafficking organization that seeks to reframe the normalization of women's work in the sex industry as exploitation. The individuals involved in this organization are deeply concerned with the vulnerabilities of adolescents and young adults in Japanese society and with how forms of neglect, marginalization, or lack of social connection may lead them into situations in which they can be taken advantage of by others. As with the healing labor of sex workers, the human rights advocacy of the organization's staff and supporters is also a form of feminized care set against the backdrop of a restrictive female labor market. This chapter contrasts the organization's anti-prostitution rhetoric with the responses of sex workers who describe these activists as fundamentally misrecognizing who they are and what they do.

Chapter 6 explores the issues that women working in the sex industry themselves identify as subjects of concern and how these derive from sex work's place in the gendered economy. Sex workers' rights advocates maintain that women in the sex industry should have access to the same dignity afforded by legal protections and benefits as individuals in other categories of work. These advocates recognize the social value of sex workers' healing labor and argue that the sex industry should be treated as a quotidian sector of the economy. Women working in the sex industry, however, regard themselves as transient workers and are largely uninterested in defining themselves as professionals. This chapter argues that the contradictions implicit to healing labor create an impediment for labor rights in this particular context.

1   Sex in Gray Spaces

"WITHOUT THE SEX INDUSTRY, sex crimes would skyrocket," Chie, a thirty-three-year-old *deriherujō* (woman who works at a *deriheru*), told me as she applied adhesive to a pair of fake eyelashes. Focusing intently on her reflection in a folding mirror she had set up on the table between us, she began to carefully place the lashes. "I don't mean to justify the industry but there are lots of essential elements to it. If it didn't exist, lots of people would be negatively affected. The jails would be full because of the crimes men would commit." Providing a sexual outlet for men in the form of commercial sex, Chie suggested, is a way to maintain social order.

The sentiment that the sex industry fulfills a basic social necessity was one that I regularly heard articulated throughout my fieldwork. Whether voiced by individuals within the industry or outside of it, its expression was remarkably similar in its imagining of male sexual desire as an irrepressible and potentially dangerous force in need of management. Notably, the same people who generally ignored the sex industry seemed most assured of its social function. Women such as my hair stylist, an apolitical woman in her mid-thirties working at a salon in the glamorous Omotesando shopping district, generally changed the subject to a more respectable topic of conversation when my research came up. But when I asked her what she thought of the sex industry, she, like others, immediately replied, "I think it's necessary." That necessity, she explained, had to do with keeping down crime. Beliefs in a connection between low crime and the existence of a legal sex industry are widespread enough that the speaker at a public anti–human trafficking lecture—a lawyer—interrupted her talk to explain that they are unsubstantiated.[1] The former manager of a *fasshon herusu* similarly recognized such ideas as belief and not fact, commenting: "People often say that the number of sex crimes will go up without the sex industry, but the industry has always been there, so no one knows if that's true." Distressingly, the discourse about the dangers of unmet male sexual needs shapes law enforcement practice in favor of men accused of sexual assault. The former police officer Makino Masako describes how the police often interpret the behavior of perpetrators in terms of *honnō*, an essentialized (male) "natural instinct" for sex capable of overpowering rational thought—leading to sympathetic treatment and, ultimately, lighter sentencing for assailants.[2]

These ideas, which take for granted a social imperative to provide men with access to particular kinds of gratification, bear echoes of twentieth-century wartime rationales for state-organized sexual violence.[3] More basically, however, they signify widespread acceptance of commercial sex as a part of social life. This chapter explores how ideas about the social value of the sex industry drive its regulation as an organized sector of the economy in contemporary Japan. I argue that, despite seemingly unambiguous acceptance of the industry's existence, regulatory strategy has reflected ambivalence, and even reluctance toward fully sanctioning commercial sex. This contradiction manifests in the common description of the sex industry as occupying a legal "gray" area—a position of ambiguity that creates an uncertain environment for those working in the industry. Effectively, authorities can crack down on the sex industry at any time. Recent regulatory changes, however, have also led to a transformation in the form of commercial sex, shifting it from a visible, public presence to dispersing it across public space—and changing the role that sex plays in local economies. I suggest that the grayness of regulation reflects, ultimately, ambivalence about the importance of women's commercial sexual labor to the organizing logic of the economy.

Separation, Containment, and Control

The contemporary regulatory context of Tokyo's cisheteronormative sex industry has emerged out of long-standing attitudes that take the significance of commercial sex for granted. Here I provide a brief historical overview. The regulatory model for sexual commerce was established at the outset of the early modern period. In 1589, the first *yūkaku* (government-licensed plea-sure district) was established in Kyoto under Toyotomi Hideyoshi. In 1617, the Tokugawa shogunate granted permission to brothel owners in Edo (present-day Tokyo) to build what would become Japan's most famous *yūkaku*: the Yoshiwara district. As a rapidly developing castle town, Edo was filled with warriors and laborers and had a skewed sex ratio of more than two men for every woman at least until the start of the eighteenth century.[4] This disparity made the authorities favorably regard licensed prostitution as a convenient means for maintaining order by providing men with an outlet for their sexual desires.[5]

The operation of Yoshiwara and other *yūkaku* that followed, however, was contingent on brothel owners' enforcement of strict controls and oversight in the districts—commercial sex would be officially permitted so long as it was not excessive. Although commercial sex was regarded as necessary, the authorities also believed it needed to be watched closely to prevent it from generating other forms of social disorder. Both in the early modern period and in more recent times, commercial sex has been associated with forms of antisocial potential that include men's excessive indulgence (which could lead to the dissipation of a household's resources, the neglect of responsibilities, and damage to familial and other social relations); self-interested and finan-cially autonomous women; violent conflict; the harboring of criminals or en-emies of the state; and, more recently, delinquent adolescents and fears over the breakdown of parental authority.[6]

The solution arrived at to keep these forms of antisocial potential at bay was to spatially separate and structurally contain the *yūkaku*. Yoshiwara, for instance, was purposefully designated a space on the outskirts of Edo by the authorities. When urban growth reached the area around Yoshiwara, in 1656–57 the district was moved further away to an undesirable location in the vicinity of an execution grounds and an outcaste neighborhood (*buraku*).[7] Yoshiwara was surrounded by walls and a moat, had a single entrance—the great Yoshiwara gate (*Yoshiwara Ōmon*)—and was subject to strict entry rules, including a prohibition on weapons and surveillance of all who entered.[8] The residents of this walled-off district developed their own customs and prac-tices, which have been richly portrayed in Tokugawa-period literature, arts, and theater.[9]

Despite the central role that the *yūkaku* played in the state's regulation of commercial sex, however, containment was never as straightforward as

Tokugawa officials would have liked. As a lucrative business, prostitution almost immediately exceeded the legal bounds of the licensed quarters set by the shogunate. Early modern historian Amy Stanley has documented how Tokugawa officials recognized the efficacy of prostitution in developing prosperous local economies, filling administrative coffers, and—with changes in agricultural markets—providing the most desperate families with employment for their unmarried daughters.[10] As Stanley writes, for local authorities and entrepreneurs, prostitutes "aroused fantasies, not only of erotic fulfillment, but also of making money, reinvigorating neighborhoods, reviving failing domestic economies, or saving villages."[11] Thus, despite the existence of licensed prostitution quarters, the state's regulatory approach was actually "subject to constant renegotiation."[12] Although officials initially tried to ensure the monopoly of the *yūkaku* by punishing clandestine prostitution, from the eighteenth century on, magistrates allowed prostitution at teahouses close to temples and pilgrimage sites and at post station inns, and commercial sex gradually expanded from urban centers to provincial towns.[13]

With the vigorous turn to nation-building and modernization in the Meiji period (1868–1912), the state became concerned with regulating prostitutes in new ways. In the late nineteenth century, the Japanese state adopted European models of licensed prostitution, instituting a system of compulsory venereal disease examinations and granting local police new license in monitoring prostitutes and collecting revenues from brothels.[14] The expansion of the military in the late nineteenth and early twentieth centuries generated a parallel growth in licensed districts nationwide, and new concerns with hygiene and public health—especially as linked to the bodies of soldiers and sailors—reinforced medical scrutiny of prostitutes.[15] From the 1870s into the 1920s, adolescent girls and young women, coming from families in impoverished areas of Japan and known as *karayuki-san*, were sent abroad to overseas brothels, from which they sent valuable remittances.[16]

As has been well-documented, the Japanese military maintained so-called comfort stations (*ianjo*), or military brothels, across the Japanese Empire from 1933 to 1945 that involved the sexual slavery of women from a variety of nationalities. Although justifications for the establishment and operation of these brothels emphasized keeping social disorder at bay through preventing the rape of civilians in areas under Japanese military control, minimizing the spread of venereal diseases, and maintaining troop morale and discipline, rape and disease were widespread.[17] Within days of Japan's surrender on August 15, 1945, and in response to widespread rumors anticipating sexual violence by US occupation forces, the Home Ministry gave orders to the police to organize exclusive brothels for the occupying forces. On August 28, 1945, an association of businessmen inaugurated the Recreation and Amusement Association in Tokyo on the grounds of the imperial palace, declaring that the recruited women constituted a "breakwater to hold back the raging waves and defend and nurture the purity of our race"—that is, the "purity" of "ordinary" Japanese women.[18] High rates of venereal disease led the occupation forces to abolish licensed prostitution in 1946, although, recognizing the reality of destitute women (the so-called *panpan*) standing on the streets and soliciting members of the occupation forces, the Japanese government permitted prostitution to continue in designated areas[19] until the passage of an anti-prostitution law a decade later.[20]

The 1956 Prostitution Prevention Law (*Baishun Bōshi Hō*, fully enacted in 1958) prohibits prostitution but narrowly constitutes "sex" as penile-vaginal intercourse (*seikō suru koto*).[21] Not long after the passage of the anti-prostitution law, however, commercial sex reappeared at so-called Turkish baths (*toruko buro*; today, known as soaplands)—public baths with private rooms in which female attendants provided sexual services to male clients—and at strip theaters and nude studios.[22] In 1966, the authorities decreed that these businesses—which offered "acts resembling sexual intercourse" (*seikō ruiji kōi*) but not intercourse itself—would be incorporated into the postwar law overseeing all forms of potentially subversive entertainment: the Law Regulating Entertainment Businesses (*Fūzoku Eigyō Torishimari Hō*, abbreviated as *Fūeihō*; enacted in 1948).[23] Today, the *Fūeihō* regulates those businesses that have emerged from the three so-called traditional male pursuits of gambling, drinking, and purchasing sex (*utsu, nomu, kau*); this includes businesses as diverse as restaurants, bars, cabarets, host and hostess clubs, dance halls and night clubs, pachinko parlors, mahjong parlors, game arcades, horse races, and, with the creation of a separate category of businesses offering sexual services, soaplands, *fasshon herusu*, strip theaters, love hotels and rental rooms, adult shops, *deai kafe*, *deriheru*, telephone clubs, and phone sex hotlines.

Sociologist Nagai Yoshikazu has argued that the policy of "enclosure" (*kakoikomi*) famously exemplified by the *yūkaku* also characterizes the state's postwar approach to forms of entertainment and recreation as regulated by the *Fūeihō*.[24] These forms of recreation have not been seen to be harmful in and of themselves. Rather, Nagai argues, it is overdoing them or doing them under the wrong circumstances (which might allow things to get out of control) that has been seen to be the problem. Instead of forbidding something outright, the state has permitted these forms of pleasure and play (*asobi*) under circumscribed conditions, exerting its authority through setting the boundaries on how people can behave and enjoy themselves in commercial settings. According to Nagai, state policy has been to allow different forms of public pleasure but to set limitations on the age of entry, operating hours, and location, in addition to imposing numerous other conditions.[25] Notably, commercial sex is not singled out for special treatment under this law, although it is subject to slightly different kinds of regulations. So long as sexual services do not involve heterosexual intercourse, the criminologically relevant category for sexual commerce is "entertainment."

By and large, the relationship between the police and the sex industry today is not a hostile one. The police do not perceive the sex industry as intrinsically criminal or as necessitating moral reprobation—a point that the former police investigator Matsuki Takashi clearly conveys in his account detailing seventy years of accumulated observations and knowledge of commercial sex.[26] It has long been commonplace for sex industry management to be friendly (*nakayoshi*) with local police officers, creating a mutually beneficial—if unofficial—relationship based on informal information exchange. Moreover, in a context of widespread acceptance of the sex industry's existence, no tension is perceived between regulating the industry and making use of its services. Mr. Aoki, a police detective, grinned broadly as he told me that when he had been at the police academy two decades earlier, his instructors had recommended that all their pupils visit a soapland as paying customers "so that we would know what to do in a raid." As relayed to me by Aoki, the academy's faculty viewed personal indulgence of commercial sex as broadly in line with the goals of regulation and control. Aoki and his fellow detective Mr. Taniguchi told me openly about their own experiences purchasing sexual services. Although Aoki felt queasy about it and had been to the sex industry just twice while in the company of senior colleagues, Taniguchi had been a frequent customer up until his marriage.

That the sex industry is considered by the police to be just another type of entertainment business among many, one that has the potential to be problematic but is not assumed to be so a priori, takes material form in the occasional immediate proximity of neighborhood police posts to sex industry businesses (see Figure 1)—something that detectives Aoki and Taniguchi

FIGURE 1. A police post (the charcoal-colored building in the foreground) stands immediately in front of a soapland (the multistoried beige building in the center) in the Shibuya neighborhood of Tokyo, June 2011. The first floor of the building housing the soapland is home to an inexpensive Chinese restaurant. (Photo credit: Gabriele Koch)

jokingly suggested was convenient for officers finishing their shift. (In reality, Aoki confided, a police officer would only go to a sex industry business outside of his jurisdiction.) The sight of law enforcement and commercial sex operating side by side exemplifies the normalized status of an industry that is a relatively low priority in the eyes of the police.

Grayness

The sex industry's visible presence in entertainment areas across Japan might seem to suggest that it is completely legal. In reality, however, the industry's legal status is best characterized as ambiguous. A police handbook explains the authorities' position: "Although sex-related businesses risk violating the anti-prostitution law . . . , it is not the case that these businesses necessarily only conduct illegal acts and, considering the freedom to operate a business, we cannot just uniformly prohibit them. For this reason, we leave it to the Public Safety Commission to determine a business's circumstances and, if a business violates [any relevant laws], they will be subjected to the appropriate punishments."[27] Rather than refer to the sex industry as legal, the handbook, in circumlocutory fashion, only suggests that it is *not illegal* for sex industry businesses to operate so long as they do not violate any laws. Referring to the same handbook, the lawyer Tsunoda Yukiko similarly observes that the *Fūeihō* does not technically legalize businesses offering these services. However, "by making these types of services [the] target of business control, the [Law] essentially recognizes them as legally allowed business[es]."[28] In other words, the *Fūeihō* tacitly permits sex industry businesses by prescribing the conditions under which they can operate. If this sounds vague, that is, I argue, precisely the point.

According to the *Fūeihō*, amusement businesses involving drinking or gambling—everything from hostess clubs to mahjong parlors—operate on a permission-system basis (*kyokasei*). Owners of these businesses must submit their paperwork to the Public Safety Commission, consisting of senior police officials and high-status professionals, and wait for official permission to operate to be granted. The sex industry, on the other hand, is distinguished within the law by operating on the basis of a notification system (*todokedesei*). These businesses merely submit the necessary paperwork to the Safety Bureau of the local police station, thereby notifying the authorities that they will begin operating soon. Businesses such as soaplands or *deriheru* are thus subject to less stringent oversight than hostess clubs or mahjong parlors, comprising a hands-off approach that serves to keep the police a modest distance away from the sex industry. A National Police Agency (NPA) official from the division responsible for overseeing the entertainment industry explained to me that if the government placed the sex industry on the permission system, it would send the message that it was giving commercial sex a stamp of approval.[29] The official noted that while there had long been debates about the wholesomeness of the sex industry, generally the consensus leaned toward it being unwholesome (*fukenzen*). With the question of the morality of commercial sex seemingly ill-defined, the authorities are careful to avoid the appearance of endorsing the sex industry, preferring to convey the image that they are simply not standing in the way of an industry so long as it does not violate the law.

The paperwork for registering a sex industry business can easily be found on the website of the Tokyo Metropolitan Police (TMP).[30] On the registration form for a brick-and-mortar business, for instance, owners fill out basic information about themselves; list the name, location, and genre of their new business; and detail the building materials, the number of rooms, and the floor space measurements. A second document asks for specific information about the running of the business, including the hours of operation, advertising methods, how entry by individuals under the age of eighteen will be prevented, whether foreigners will be employed and in what capacity, and whether alcohol will be on offer.[31] Owners must also submit their lease contract, a floor plan, and their certificate of residence.[32] For those seeking additional guidance on the logistics of opening and running a business, regularly updated "how to" books could easily be found at bookstores during the time of my fieldwork.[33]

The contradiction between, on the one hand, acceptance of commercial sex and, on the other, the state's ambivalence about how to regulate it manifests in the common description of the contemporary sex industry as occupying a legal "gray" (gurē) area. In conversations, sex workers, sex industry staff, journalists, and police officers repeatedly referred to the industry as "gray," or, in some cases, as "vague, ambiguous" (aimai). Both terms invoke the liminal, neither-here-nor-there legal standing of the industry. To refer to something as gray means that it is ill defined and not easily categorizable. We can usefully theorize grayness as a way to think about legality and illegality in relation to state regulation of commercial sex. In Tokyo's sex industry, grayness signals the contradiction between what the authorities tacitly permit and what is officially allowed, between what those in the industry imagine is possible and the reality that the police can crack down at any moment.[34] It refers to the inherently insecure position that those working in the sex industry occupy within the state's strategy to traverse the competing imperatives of a discourse of necessity with oversight and control. Ultimately, it is the state that benefits most from imposing grayness on the sex industry. This strategic ambivalence points to both the centrality of sex in the wider Japanese economy and underscores the ways in which its importance—and the role of women's labor in it—is the source of some ongoing discomfort and uncertainty.

For example, dancers at Japanese strip theaters are occasionally arrested for kōzen waisetsuzai (the crime of public indecency). Plainclothes police officers in the audience need sit only a few minutes through a dancer's set for her to strike a revealing pose, especially during the short "open show" that many dancers include at the end of their set. After attending a performance with the *herusujō* (woman who works at a *fasshon herusu*) Rei, I asked her about the seeming clash between the law and the existence of strip theater. How could strip theater continue to exist in the face of a law that criminalized a central feature? Rei paused briefly, pursing her lips before nodding and responding, "This is very gray . . ." She explained that it would be all right if the dancer just happened to flash something. When I protested that dancers held their poses for several seconds, she shrugged: "Strip theater has a long history, since right after the war. The laws were created after strip was already around." Rei's observation that strip theater preceded the law suggested that it was unreasonable for the law to infringe on what was already an established form of entertainment. Whether her interpretation that longevity should trump the law would hold up is doubtful, but it exemplifies the desire for certainty in the face of a vague law and its seemingly random application. Dancers who are arrested for public indecency are considered unlucky for performing at the wrong place at the wrong time and there is a sense that there is no way to adequately protect oneself from the seemingly arbitrary enforcement of the law in which the police could turn up at any performance on any day and expect to find an illegal act occurring.

Effectively, the authorities can crack down at any time if they decide that a business is violating the law—although management might counter that there is no way for them to operate without doing so. In reality, the police typically investigate a business only if it is brazenly flouting the law or if they receive a complaint. Under normal circumstances, sending a message by shutting down one business is deemed sufficient, as the phrase *ichibatsu hyakkai* ("one punishment, one hundred warnings"), cited to me by a police officer to explain how a single police raid can reverberate through the industry, suggests. As the former reporter for the *Yomiuri Shimbun* newspaper, Jake Adelstein, writes, recalling what a vice detective in Kabukichō—Japan's most famous sex and entertainment district—told him in 1999, "As long as the [sex industry] shops don't go too far over the line, they can do whatever they want. Our job as vice cops isn't to put these places out of business, it's to keep them in line."[35] It is simplest for the police to raid a business based on a *Fūeihō* violation: for instance, if a business is operating outside of the permitted zoning or beyond the legally designated hours, hiring minors, or not registered with the authorities. For the police to make a case that a business is violating the anti-prostitution law is much more cumbersome, as this entails proving that it is store policy to offer intercourse, collecting customer testimony, or conducting a raid and catching customers and sex workers red-handed (*genkōhan*).

Grayness is thus efficacious for police regulation. The *imekura* where Sayaka had first begun working had been shut down suddenly by the police one day. The women working at this business never learned the precise violation responsible, but Sayaka thought it was irrelevant. Then, as now, she told me, "If the police want to raid a business they can do so for any number of reasons, so there's not really any point in looking for an explanation." To Sayaka, seeking reason in police enforcement of the law was wasted effort. Similarly, after a strip theater in Chiba, near Tokyo, was forced to close for several months during my fieldwork due to a violation, the customers I spoke to at the theater's reopening were cynical about police motives. As one told me, "The police know that anytime they go to a theater, they'll find something illegal going on . . ."

The grayness of the law means that police officers themselves occasionally need further information when faced with the realities of regulation. For instance, a police officer told me that because the law is so vague, reading legal decisions is often more instructive. By way of example, he posed a question: The *Fūeihō* prohibits businesses from renovating, but what constitutes a renovation? Does fixing the walls constitute a renovation? Surely not, he shrugged, suggesting that this would be an unreasonable interpretation. Due to the lack of clarity on this and other points, however, he acknowledged that an underground economy involving the yakuza (Japanese mafia groups) provides services such as covert remodeling.

From the standpoint of those working in the sex industry, the grayness of the law renders their position inherently insecure. Mr. Kaneko, a sex industry journalist who also worked part-time as staff at a sexual massage business, likened management's relationship with the law to trying to drive with a loose steering wheel. As he explained it to me, this simile underscores how managers and staff do their best to navigate safely within the bounds of the law, but ultimately have little control. At any moment, according to this simile, they might take an unexpected turn or slip into dangerous territory. Kaneko insisted that everyone wanted to follow the law, emphasizing that managers and staff were themselves hard-working men providing for their families and trying to do everything above board in order to make a living in what was, after all, not an illegal industry. Kaneko blamed the grayness of regulation for the insecurity he and his colleagues felt.

Mr. Iwamura, the former manager of a *fasshon herusu*, similarly portrayed himself as eager to stay on the right side of what he saw as arbitrary law enforcement. He described to me how he used to attend police information sessions so as to stay abreast of revisions to the *Fūeihō*. He and his peers had treated these sessions earnestly to look for guidance from the authorities. At these sessions, they were able to ask questions of the police but, he explained, they were always careful not to ask questions that were too detailed—one didn't want to give the police any reason to be curious about what one's business was up to. Even Iwamura's earnestness, however, did not seem to safeguard him. Two years after my meeting with Iwamura, I asked Shiori, who had been close to him when she had worked at his business, how he was doing. Her face clouded over. She hadn't heard from him in months and several attempts to contact him had been unsuccessful. To the best of her knowledge, Iwamura had been working as staff at an illegal maid *herusu* (a maid-themed *fasshon herusu*) in a residential area of central Tokyo. "He must have been arrested . . . ," she concluded, her voice trailing off.

Managers of sex industry businesses pay close attention to news of which businesses have been investigated and shut down by the police—and under which charges—to anticipate the direction in which regulation may be heading. Mostly, though, the state seems to favor oversight. When a new type of business first appears and becomes popular throughout the sex industry, the pattern of the authorities has been to recognize it by creating a new category in the *Fūeihō*, by the logic that the police can keep better tabs on businesses when they are legally registered and, in theory, at least, cooperating with the police. For instance, in January 2011, *deai kafe*, which had existed for some time prior and had been labeled as "hotspots" for under-aged prostitution by the media, were incorporated into the *Fūeihō* as a way of prohibiting the entry of minors. This tendency allows the state to impose conditions upon and oversee these businesses.

Cleanup

In April 2003, the conservative nationalist politician Ishihara Shintarō—widely known for his outspoken and often controversial views—won reelection to a second term as Tokyo's governor. Echoing the rhetoric of his colleagues in the Liberal Democratic Party about deteriorating public safety, Ishihara vowed to take a hardline approach to crime and quickly appointed the Hiroshima prefectural police chief, Takehana Yutaka, as one of several deputy governors. On August 1, Takehana launched the Tokyo Metropolitan Emergency Office for Public Safety to strengthen and coordinate crime prevention efforts between the police, the metropolitan government, and the public.[36] Within the year, Tokyo's anti-crime budget increased an incredible thirtyfold.[37]

Government authorities identified sex and entertainment districts as particular targets of the crime prevention campaign. It did not take much to convince the public as, by the early 2000s, many such districts were already associated with lawlessness and disorder.[38] The yakuza had long been known to have a hand in running sex and entertainment districts across the nation.[39] Kabukichō, in particular, was known as the site of turf battles among organized crime groups, including both the yakuza and Chinese gangs, and had been the scene of open gun fights.[40] These groups trafficked in illegal drugs and foreign migrant women, and extorted protection money from the many entertainment businesses operating with little or no regard for the law—hiring minors or foreigners, ignoring safety regulations, operating after hours or in the wrong areas or without bothering to register with the police, and committing tax evasion. Touts aggressively solicited male pedestrians for sex industry businesses, while public concern focused on the activities of adolescents loitering in sex and entertainment districts.[41] The Roppongi area was infamous for reports of drugging by Rohypnol and the presence of "rip-off" (bottakuri) bars, at which customers unknowingly amassed exorbitant bills. Sex and entertainment districts also featured conspicuous clusterings of foreigners—frequently associated with crime in the media—who often illegally staffed sex industry businesses. Deputy Governor Takehana himself referred to Kabukichō as "a dirty and unsafe area with a high concentration of sex industry businesses and lots of traffic by foreign mafia."[42] Convincing the public of the necessity of state intervention was therefore an easy sell.

In April 2004, one year after Ishihara's reelection, the TMP launched a "cleanup" campaign (jōka sakusen) of entertainment districts in the name of public safety. The TMP designated four major sex and entertainment districts in central Tokyo as targets: Kabukichō, Shibuya, Roppongi, and Ikebukuro. Taking a cue from the cleanup of New York City's Times Square in the 1990s, Tokyo police feverishly pursued businesses for all manner of infractions.

Within the first ten months of the campaign, 280 businesses—including illegal massage parlors, gambling dens, adult video stores, and sex industry businesses—were raided in Kabukichō alone, of which over 200 were shut down. Around 400 members of criminal gangs were arrested and 1,100 foreigners were either deported for illegal residence or otherwise prosecuted.[43] The TMP also expanded whom they would hold accountable for illegal businesses, going after landlords as well as management.[44] This campaign had effects outside of the capital almost immediately. The NPA, which paid close attention to the campaign's progress, held it up as a model and initiated similar operations nationwide, targeting eleven sex and entertainment districts in total across Japan.

Shock and a sense of crisis reverberated throughout Tokyo's sex and entertainment industry. Looking back at the mid-2000s, observers have noted how those in the industry had initially failed to grasp the serious intent behind the anti-crime campaign. Rather, they had interpreted the early efforts of the police as simply a matter of short-term zeal and had anticipated that they would soon pass. Matsuzawa Kureichi, a writer and frequent commentator on the sex industry, described the growing realization of those in the industry of the situation's gravity:

> At first, everyone including myself thought that the raids were just the usual thing and just for show. But it's the metropolitan government itself that's organizing things. . . . The TMP is taking the lead, so it's not the local district police who are doing things but police from other jurisdictions who are being brought in and they don't discriminate. They're being systematic. Gradually, people have realized that the police are serious and that Kabukichō is basically being destroyed. The manager of a *seikan herusu* who I'm close to told me, "I'm really nervous, but I'll do business as long as I can. We're actually doing really well since there are so few stores doing business." A few days later, the police raided his store. Just take a walk around Kabukichō at night and you'll see—one store after another is closed. For the customers, it's a "season of hell."[45]

Women whom I spoke with who had worked in the sex industry during the time of the cleanup told me of narrowly escaping police raids. Rei still expressed disbelief over her good fortune: within the span of one month, three of her workplaces were raided, but always on her day off. Foreign women in the sex industry—who were mostly working illegally—bore the brunt of the crackdown. Vanessa, an American woman who had worked as both a hostess and nude dancer in Roppongi, described to me how she had only just escaped the police by slipping out the back door of her club.

The deputy governor's Emergency Office for Public Safety expanded its campaign to the public. Taking advantage of disgruntlement toward minor but ubiquitous nuisances (such as the seemingly indiscriminate placement of advertisements for sex industry businesses), city authorities encouraged residents to form local anti-crime volunteer groups that would patrol neighborhoods, distribute information on "safe town" activities, notify the police of even minor infractions, and, in all ways, create a regular and imposing presence. Although an NPA official explained to me that residents themselves took the initiative to clean up their neighborhoods, the news archive clearly conveys that the Tokyo metropolitan government and TMP also actively fostered these groups. Tokyo became the first city in the nation to offer anti-crime leadership training for citizens. This training featured two months of lectures on creating crime-free environments, and included trips to local sex and entertainment districts in order to discuss problem points and possible solutions. Participants in these sessions received a diploma at the conclusion and the police designated them as local anti-crime leaders, providing them with both guidance and patrol clothing. In mid-2004, there were roughly five hundred such volunteer groups in the city; by the following year, there were two thousand.[46]

Local residents also mobilized to demonstrate against illegal sex industry businesses, in a more aggressive strategy meant to intimidate sex workers and their customers. Nami, who in the mid-2000s had been working in an Osaka neighborhood known for its illegal *manshon herusu* (a business in which *fasshon herusu* services are sold from an ordinary apartment), recounted her fear when protesters showed up one day outside the building where she was working. Each floor in every apartment building in this neighborhood housed one or two illegal businesses, she explained, "And I worked in the tallest building." The protesters appeared sometime between 7 and 9 P.M., the window when business usually began to pick up—a conscious effort to disrupt business. Nami was with a customer when the sounds of the protestors became audible. She told me about how the man froze up and how the atmosphere shifted: "No one enjoys themselves when there's a protest going on." Although she normally had a reliable stream of customers, no one else came that evening. Rather than go home herself, however, Nami waited until the last protesters had left. She told me that even though she didn't believe the protestors would call out to her if she left the building ("They know that would be going too far"), the thought of exposing herself to them left her deeply uncomfortable.

This grassroots activism illustrates how some urban residents rallied against what they perceived to be the excesses of the sex industry—its overly concentrated presence in certain neighborhoods; its proximity to residential areas and schools; advertisements placed in mailboxes, phone booths, and public toilets; and aggressive street solicitation by touts. Even so, it is notable that for all the considerable activity directed toward creating "wholesome" (*kenzen*) environments, grassroots agitation was focused only on *illegal* sex industry businesses. For example, placards placed around the entertainment district of Maebara in Okinawa Prefecture's Ginowan City by local politicians, women's group representatives, and members of the Parent Teacher Association declared only that the number of illegal sex industry businesses had been reduced to zero.[47] The cleanup campaign did not target commercial sex itself but only its excesses that went beyond the bounds of the law.

Over a decade later, the motives behind this unprecedented crackdown, which concluded in 2006, have remained far from clear for those most affected. The cleanup campaign was not a movement to criminalize the industry, a moral crusade to eliminate commercial sex, or an effort to combat forms of labor exploitation in the industry. Among my interlocutors, the most common explanations were that Governor Ishihara had wanted to clean up the city for an Olympic bid and/or to clear space for a casino in Kabukichō.[48] But it is noteworthy that not a single theory that I encountered entertained the thought that Ishihara might be anti–sex industry.[49] Although the intensity of the crackdown left sex industry operators reeling as they tried to negotiate the shifting terrain of what it meant to run a business and stay on the good side of the law, no one believed that the crackdown was based in a desire to eliminate the sex industry. Although some commentators have suggested we view the cleanup as part of a conservative nationalist effort to reassert state authority and discipline,[50] I suggest that we understand it also as the reflexive action of a long-standing state strategy to curtail and control commercial sex.[51] For many in the industry, however, the unexpected and seemingly inexplicable expansion of municipal, police, and grassroots anti-crime measures only exemplified their ambivalent status and insecurity—their grayness—vis-à-vis state authority.

From Brick-and-Mortar to Delivery

Even before the shock of the cleanup campaign, a transformation in the shape of commercial sex was underway in Tokyo and across Japan. From the early 2000s, a new type of business began to define the sex industry, as it shifted overwhelmingly from a brick-and-mortar model (*tenpogata*) to a "delivery" (escort) model (*mutenpogata*, literally "nonstore model"). Police statistics on the numbers of registered sex industry businesses nationwide dramatically illustrate this shift. First incorporated into the *Fūeihō* in 1999, *deriheru* outnumbered brick-and-mortar businesses from the start. By 2000, more than twice as many *deriheru* existed and by 2005, *deriheru* outnumbered physical storefronts ninefold. Although the number of *deriheru* plunged in 2006, during the crackdown (as did, to a smaller degree, the number of registered store-based businesses—although many more were simply unregistered with the police and thus not reflected in these statistics), today they again outnumber storefronts ninefold (see Figure 2).[52] Commercial sex in Tokyo and elsewhere across Japan is no longer primarily centered in physical locations with a visible, public presence, but broadly dispersed off premises to the love hotels, rental rooms, and private homes where sex workers meet their customers.[53] This upheaval of sexual commerce has led to a remaking of city microeconomies and presented challenges for regulation.

Every year, the number of brick-and-mortar sex industry businesses in operation nationwide decreases slightly, and with my every visit to Tokyo there are a handful less storefronts visible. Zoning regulations are behind this gradual disappearance. A 1984 revision to the *Fūeihō* granted prefectural and metropolitan governments the authority to stipulate prohibited areas of operation for sex industry businesses—beyond the 200-meter-radius prohibition from schools, libraries, and public buildings already decreed in 1964. Following the mid-2000s cleanup campaign, the authorities have pursued stricter enforcement of municipal zoning regulations such that, in metropolitan Tokyo today new soaplands and *fasshon herusu* may be established only in the several-block area in the northeastern part of the city that comprises the former Yoshiwara district, although *deai kissa*, adult shops, and strip theaters can be built in any business district, while love hotels and rental rooms can be opened in limited areas close to Kabukichō, Yoshiwara, and Ikebukuro.[54] Those brick-and-mortar businesses still operating are those whose establishment prior to the zoning regulations grants them *kitokuken* (vested

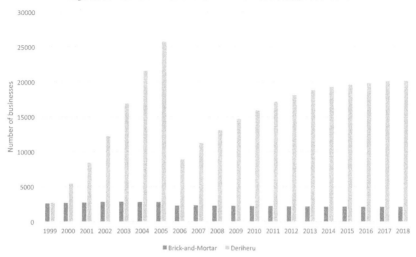

FIGURE 2. The relative number of brick-and-mortar sex industry businesses and *deriheru* businesses registered with the police from 1999 to 2018. Source: Keisatsuchō 2004; 2009: 20–21; 2014: 20–21; 2019: 10. (Credit: Gabriele Koch)

rights). Although there is some ambiguity around how these rights may be assessed (for example, whether a corporate entity may register as the owner), the regulations portend the eventual disappearance of the brick-and-mortar sex industry.

When a popular and long-established business is forced to shut down upon the retirement or death of the owner, it can create a depressing situation for industry insiders and customers mourning the disappearance of a beloved venue.[55] This was something that I witnessed firsthand in October 2010, when I attended the closing day of a famous Nagoya strip theater. The owner, knowing that his retirement would shut the theater down and feeling obligated to a loyal customer base, had long delayed this life event. Although there would have been no shortage of willing candidates to succeed him, the law prevented the business's continuation. But after around forty years at the theater, he had decided to finally retire. In my conversations with dancers and fans, they praised the theater for its size, beautiful layout, and spectacular lighting. Throughout the day, from the first show (at noon) until the grand finale (at midnight), I observed the gradual heightening of emotions at the packed theater. Upset fans spoke wistfully of their memories of the theater and shared with me how they saw the law as having unfairly cornered the theater into closing.

The aftermath of the cleanup campaign has demonstrated the reliance of some local economies on the brick-and-mortar instantiation of commercial sex. Brick-and-mortar businesses draw customers to a neighborhood, where they may enjoy not just commercial sex, but also stop by local bars and restaurants and make use of hotel and taxi services as well as other forms of entertainment. The disappearance of these businesses underscored their important role in the local economy. Within central Tokyo, the premium real estate value of the neighborhoods targeted by the crackdown generally led to rapid redevelopment. In Roppongi, for example, which had long had a reputation as a sleazy nightclub district rife with scams and other crime, developers lost no time in remaking the neighborhood with luxury condominiums, high-rise office buildings, upscale malls, and glitzy art museums.[56] But in sex industry districts in Tokyo's vast suburbs and in surrounding towns, the absence of brick-and-mortar businesses was more keenly felt. In some neighborhoods, so many businesses were shuttered that they came to be described as "ghost towns"—once bustling centers now emptied of people and business.[57]

This became a predicament for municipal planners and local entrepreneurs confronted with the problem of how to re-envision and revitalize neighborhoods long associated with commercial sex. The neighborhood around Nishi Kawaguchi Station in Saitama Prefecture, part of a commuter town just outside Tokyo, is one such ghost town and exemplifies some of these problems. Prior to the prefectural police's launch of a cleanup campaign in 2005, the Nishi Kawaguchi sex industry had been known for a wide range of sex industry businesses: pink salons, *imekura*, *herusu*, soaplands, and massage parlors. The neighborhood was even implicated in a slang term—*NKryū* ("NK style")—adopted by sex industry businesses around the country to signal the availability of the illegal act of intercourse.[58] As in nearby Tokyo, in order to prevent the type of cat-and-mouse game that often marked raids—in which a business would shut down only to reopen shortly thereafter under a new name—the police began arresting landlords on charges of aiding and abetting crime, even appearing at local real estate brokers' meetings to call attention to the policy.[59]

By late 2007, the local sex industry had been devastated. Over two hundred businesses had been shut down. Moreover, the collateral damage of the raids soon became apparent as neighborhood drinking holes, snack clubs, and other businesses left their leases.[60] In the 200-meter radius of the train station alone, there were roughly two hundred vacancies across ninety buildings.[61] A neighborhood revitalization committee launched a campaign to rebrand the area as a destination for hearty and affordable fare such as ramen noodles, curry rice, and Chinese dumplings.[62] But the images associated with this area have lingered on, preventing an influx of "ordinary" businesses. Although the sex industry had once been immediately apparent from the train station's exit, when I visited the area in 2011, my companion and I had to inquire at the local police outpost for directions to the now anemic district. The signage of many multitenant buildings in prime real estate was completely blank, evidence of the struggle to reestablish the local economy even several years on. We saw a series of colorful shutters painted by local middle school students as part of an effort by the local chamber of commerce to beautify the streets, turning the depressing shuttered storefronts into something more cheerful looking.[63] Brightly colored flags hung from many of the electricity posts and pictured a smiling cartoon sunflower with the words, "I shop in my town, in Kawaguchi." But the small streets were mostly empty that afternoon.

Mr. Hatoyama, the director of the Kabukichō Shopping Center Promotion Union, an association of property owners in Tokyo's most well-known sex and entertainment district, was frank about his conviction that commercial sex is good for the neighborhood and a key element that distinguishes it from its competitors. Hatoyama described how commercial sex facilitates the circulation of money across the neighborhood: customers visit sex industry businesses and hostess clubs. Those sex workers and hostesses then visit host clubs after work. And those hosts spend their money at local arcades and amusement centers. If commercial sex were all there were to a neighborhood, Hatoyama explained, that would be problematic. Kabukichō, however, he said proudly, had long been a "comprehensive amusement town," with many types of businesses operating side by side. Commercial sex—or, what he called "ejaculation businesses" (nukikei)—was an essential part of this, without which, he said dismissively, the neighborhood would be reduced to "being a Disneyland."

Women's sexual labor is vital to Hatoyama's imagining of what makes economic life possible in an entertainment district. In a diversified neighborhood bustling with local visitors and tourists from across Japan and overseas alike, commercial sex is understood as an important component in fulfilling customer desires and in allowing money to flow from one business to the next. In sex industry districts that had been devastated by the crackdowns, however, it became clear that the local economy had perhaps been overly reliant on this labor. These economies not only relied on women's sexual labor, they seemed to depend upon it.

Today, commercial sex remains a part of economic life in Tokyo, albeit in changed form, as "delivery" businesses dominate the market. An NPA official listed to me the advantages of running a *deriheru* as a business operator might see them: first, because there is no physical storefront, *deriheru* are less likely to attract the attention of the police. The official quickly added that these businesses cannot avoid police oversight entirely: "They still need to advertise, and whatever customers can find, the police can find, too." Second, *deriheru* require less capital to open. At a minimum, all one needs is an office, a telephone, and a website. In contrast to brick-and-mortar businesses, *deriheru* save money on rent, utilities, and cleaning fees—although they must invest significantly more in advertising. Third, unless they have a reception counter for customers, *deriheru* offices are not subject to zoning. And, fourth on the police official's list, while brick-and-mortar businesses can only operate from 6 A.M. until midnight, *deriheru* can operate twenty-four hours a day.

With stricter police enforcement of *Fūeihō* regulations, opening a *deriheru* is not only an appealing option for many business operators but often the only option available that is above the law. In other words, the police and municipal administrators have essentially pushed the industry toward a *deriheru* model. Among sex workers, this transformation is commonly described as a movement underground (*andāguraundoka*; *chika ni moguru*), to underscore how things are not necessarily being done legally as businesses escape the more intense glare of police oversight. Without a doubt, this shift has had serious and often harmful effects on the individuals selling their sexual labor—as I discuss in Chapter 6.

Conclusion

The last two decades have witnessed a transformation in the shape of commercial sex in urban Japan. Although strategies for regulating the sex industry have historically focused on permitting—albeit carefully containing and overseeing—forms of sexual commerce, today the overwhelming dominance of *deriheru* businesses has largely moved the sex industry out of public sight in Tokyo and elsewhere across Japan. Observant eyes can still single out seemingly incongruous couples entering or exiting a love hotel together, but the legibility of commercial sex in public space in the material form of storefronts, store signs and flyers, and aggressive touts has given way to businesses with a mostly virtual, Internet-based presence. As in other contexts, neoliberalism has shifted "sex in public" into the private spaces of hotels, rental rooms, and homes.[64] In these sites, customers have the convenience of having sex workers "delivered" (as the name *deriheru* explicitly suggests) to them.

Grappling with a sense of loss, some longtime observers have produced nostalgic accounts of the many famous sex industry districts that have disappeared as a result of police crackdowns, lovingly depicting neighborhoods that formerly were replete with visible markers of the sexual economy.[65] Others, including business operators and veteran sex workers, occasionally describe contemporary sex and entertainment districts as "boring," diminished versions of their former states. And, as I have described, municipal planners and entrepreneurs have, in some cases, struggled to revitalize their neighborhoods as the crackdowns have made their reliance on commercial sex manifest.

Commercial sex exists in a gray space in contemporary Japan—not legal, strictly speaking, but not illegal either. Who does the "grayness" of the state's regulatory approach serve? Neither the anti-prostitution law nor the *Fūeihō* address male customers, who thus remain largely unaffected by regulation, except in the options for consumption it makes possible. Meanwhile, the managers of sex industry businesses are left guessing to some extent over the conditions under which they can actually operate—as Kaneko suggested with his simile of driving with a loose steering wheel. Grayness is most efficacious for the authorities themselves, who can crack down whenever they perceive the industry as flouting the law or whenever it is politically convenient.

Certainly, it is not sex workers themselves who benefit from the grayness of regulation. For women who work in the sex industry, the shift to "delivery" businesses, for example, has precipitated a change in the conditions under which they labor. When sex workers are dispatched to spaces where they are separated from management and on their own with customers, the risks that they face increase. The grayness of the sex industry does not serve sex workers but only makes their insecurity more apparent.[66]

What is striking about the discourse of necessity that drives regulatory approaches to the sex industry in Japan is how sex workers themselves barely figure. Rather, this discourse centers on the importance of providing men with a means to sexual gratification as a way of maintaining order. The focus on male needs obscures and only ever leaves implicit how the women who provide these services are central to the functioning of the economy. Regulatory discourse generally takes up the subject of the providers of sexual services only if they are minors or foreigners—in which case they are perceived to be a social problem—and not if they are the mainly adult Japanese women working in the sex industry. The regulation of the sex industry keeps the role of sex workers themselves hidden, if implicit, reflecting ambivalence about the economic importance of women's participation in stigmatized labor. It is to the women providing this labor, and to their place in the gendered economy, that I turn to next.

2 First-Timers Welcome!

"I WANTED TO WORK somewhere where I didn't have to go in more than two, three times a week," Megumi explained. "Where I didn't have to ride the train every day and where I could take the day off on short notice without inconveniencing anyone if I woke up feeling unwell. I was thinking about what kind of work would fit these conditions and that's when the sex industry occurred to me."

Megumi was a twenty-nine-year-old employee at a *deriheru* in central Tokyo. We were having dinner at an inexpensive family restaurant not far from her apartment and she was telling me about how she had found employment that offered such enviable conditions—unimaginable in most Japanese workplaces—while still being financially viable. She looked chic in a smart gray silk blouse and matching skirt. One of the first things that struck me about Megumi was how much she laughed: she laughed all of the time, even after making matter-of-fact statements. This affect, which she had cultivated in her work, gave a charming effect. Weeks later, I learned that her maternal grandmother had been a geisha. Charming and entertaining ran in her family.

Megumi had begun her working life in unimpeachable respectability as a public servant. Her parents had divorced when she was seventeen, after a childhood in southern Kagoshima Prefecture in which her father's perennial absence had been counterbalanced by the material effects of the significant gambling debt he had landed his family in. Megumi and her mother decided to make a dramatic change in their lives by moving to Tokyo after Megumi's high school graduation. Megumi wasn't interested in going to college but just wanted to start working right away to support this new life with her mother. Without any leads on where she could find work in the capital, she sat the civil service exam. To her surprise, she passed. Public sector jobs are highly respected in Japan for their association with serving the greater good. Although the pay is modest (and one's behavior is often subject to scrutiny), being a public servant is perceived as a decent job with a secure future.

Megumi's health took a downward turn during her four years working at a municipal office. No medical cause was ever determined but she suggested that her body did not want to cooperate with the (male-gendered) workplace culture of long hours with overtime and peer oversight. "I worked so hard that I hurt my health. I'm not sure exactly how. But suddenly I just felt really bad all the time." No treatment seemed to make a difference. As her absences from work accumulated, the feeling of being a burden on her colleagues became intense. Eventually, she just quit. Megumi began part-time work but found it hard to make ends meet. This was when she decided she would enter the sex industry.

By the time we met, five years later, Megumi had worked in just about every sector of the legal sex industry except for soaplands, which she found too physically laborious. She estimated that, all told, she had worked at about twenty different businesses—some for just a daylong trial and others for months at a time. As with many of the women I spoke to, Megumi emphasized how little she had known about sex, sex work, or the sex industry before joining: "It was a totally unknown world to me, I knew *nothing*." Her very first store was a *fasshon herusu*. She quit after just one week when the manager propositioned her. Despite feeling discouraged by what she bluntly called sexual harassment, she immediately began looking for another workplace.

But although Megumi did well at the work and had an impressive base of regular customers, she was disappointed in her economic fortunes. The market rate for commercial sex had been going down. She explained:

I entered this industry because people were saying that the recession would only get worse. So, I've never experienced a good economy. If you ask an *onēsan* [literally, "older sister," woman with more experience] who's been around for a while, she could tell you how things have gone downhill. In the past [until the mid-2000s], it used to be that once you decided you were going to work in the sex industry and gathered all of your courage and took the plunge, that just about anyone could achieve whatever their financial goal was. That was one of the really great things about this work. That's not true anymore today. No matter how much you try, you'll earn about the same amount as a salaryman.

Megumi's conviction that there would always be a market for sex, no matter the state of the economy, sat uncomfortably with the diminished potential for earning well in the industry. Was commercial sex not worth as much as it had been a few years prior? Although Megumi had achieved white-collar male wages, she felt unlucky to have entered the industry at a time of increased competition and depreciating rates.

Megumi indicated that high earnings should be the trade-off for doing stigmatizing work. The isolation she often felt in carefully managing what others knew of her work had worn on her. Her boyfriend was a former customer. She was relieved not to have to worry about hiding the work from him but believed that "most men don't want their girlfriends to be sex workers," and she was not planning for a long-term future together. Her mother, whom she lived with, did not know about her work. Megumi had briefly worked at a twenty-four-hour call center once and had led her mother to believe that she had been working there the past five years. The hourly wage for the night shift was higher so that was a reasonable account for her late-night absences. "But," she said, her voice trailing, "we never really talk about work." It was an uncomfortable topic for her. It was easier to avoid the subject than to lie to her mother outright. "It's so hard to live without being able to tell anyone what you're doing. It doesn't have to be everyone. It would be enough for me if just a few people knew. Continuing on with this work without being able to talk to people about it is so hard for me. It's a very lonely existence for a young woman."

Despite these disappointments and her loneliness, Megumi had no plans yet for a future outside of the sex industry. She had picked up several side commitments over the years. For the past two years, she had been commissioned to write serial fiction in a monthly column for a free sex industry employment magazine. Once a week, she wrote an erotic column for a men's sports paper— one of the papers infamous for the salarymen who read it on trains, openly displaying pornographic images for all to see. She had also recently begun working at a phone repair shop. After five years of working only in the sex industry, "Suddenly, I felt like doing some normal work on the side." She wanted to experience a "normal" workplace where she could relate to customers in a different sort of way.

. . .

The story of Megumi, a young woman who leaves her stable and respectable public sector job to wind up in sex work, offers us a way to think about the diversity of who is in Tokyo's cisheteronormative sex industry and what attracts them. Studies of sex work generally explain women's participation in this work in terms of a lack of viable labor market alternatives or the allure of an informal economy. Similarly, representations of sex work in US popular media often suggest that women only enter the industry due to desperation, coercion, or addiction and trauma. In contrast, Elizabeth Bernstein has described the postindustrial shifts that have made sex work appealing to a subset of privileged American women in the San Francisco Bay Area, leading her to ask the provocative question, "Can sex work be a middle-class profession?"[1] In Japan, representations of female sex work frame women's entry in terms of either poverty or crass materialism. But Megumi's story highlights the connections between a gendered economy and sex work in a way that productively moves it away from such simple narratives. While there is no doubt that there are women who are heavily in debt or living under or near the poverty line in the Japanese sex industry, there are also many others who lead relatively comfortable and privileged lives.[2] Megumi and many others who staff the sex industry *do* have other options. How, then, can we make sense of their entry into this stigmatized work? And, once we set aside the assumption that women's entry into sex work need be exceptional in some way, what can we learn about both the work and the terms of a gendered economy?

This chapter explores how the place of female sex work in the gendered economy in Japan shapes women's entry into the sex industry. Sex work is generally lucrative work that offers a high return on time. As Megumi's ruminations suggest, these highly remunerative earnings are made possible by the reality of the stigma associated with the work. But explanations based solely on a financial rationale miss much of what sex workers themselves describe as appealing about the work. In a context of women's limited access to the professional economy, sex workers foreground the forms of autonomy and flexibility offered by sex industry work and contrast it favorably with the conditions of "ordinary" employment. Many of the same conditions that women may find attractive about the work, however, reflect the marginalization of sex work from the dominant norms that structure the male-gendered economy. Examining this contradiction exposes how women in the sex industry imagine what "work" can and should be.

"A World That Was Irrelevant to Me"

"Before I entered the sex industry myself, I had never really spent any time thinking about it," Sachiko told me when I asked her about her impressions of the industry prior to working there. "If I did, it was only to think that it was a world that was irrelevant to me." We had met at frenetic Shinjuku Station and had walked a few minutes from there to a quiet basement café popular among middle-aged men. One block away was the upscale shopping district of Shinjuku San-Chōme, bustling even on this weekday afternoon. Two blocks away in a different direction was the sex and entertainment district of Kabukichō. In Shinjuku, as in other neighborhoods throughout the city, spaces of white-collar work and feminized consumption border and occasionally spill over into the sex industry. But Sachiko, a college graduate who had entered sex work in her early twenties, had paid the gaudy storefronts of brick-and-mortar sex industry businesses no heed until she herself began working in one of them. The sentiment she expressed was generally true for all the women I spoke with, whether they had experience in the sex industry or not. Although the dense imbrication of businesses of all kinds means that venues where commercial sex is sold are inseparable from other aspects of day-to-day urban life, Sachiko and others had seen (or see) the sex industry as a realm of social life without meaning to them. As Shiori, a veteran sex worker, explained, "The sex industry has always been there since we were children. But 'ordinary women' don't see it as concerning them and so they don't pay any attention to it." The basic necessity of the industry's existence is accepted and taken for granted, with the sensory experience of viewing and passing by seemingly failing to register women's attention.

In fact, many women express a complete lack of interest about the workings of the industry. It is a topic outside of the realm of acceptable female curiosity, as if knowing too much—or, indeed, anything at all—might be read as evidence of personal experience.[3] The overwhelming reactions of "ordinary" women in their twenties or thirties with whom I brought up my research were blank faces and/or apathy. The conversation would temporarily grind to a halt before they changed the subject. It was an improper subject of interest and conversation for respectable women. No questions were asked. No small talk was exchanged. The former *deriherujō* Hiromi nodded vigorously as I told her about these reactions. She had had similar experiences. Proud of her work, Hiromi was eager to "come out" to a few select friends and had been disappointed and hurt when their response had been to shut down. Although she had always shared details of her life with these friends, they didn't comment or ask her any questions. "I really had the feeling they didn't have any interest at all," she said, describing the telling silences they imposed on the subject. The almost unanimous lack of interest among what was otherwise a diverse group of women suggests that the topic itself was off-putting.

Despite the visible, public presence of the sex industry and the assertiveness with which messages about the availability of commercial sex circulate, many Japanese women have little or no accurate knowledge of the industry. When Shiori decided to begin working at an *imekura* at age twenty-two, she thought she would enter "a room full of desperate women crying in a corner." Influenced by negative media representations, she imagined that the sex industry was staffed by gloomy women who were there because they had no other choice. On her first day of work, she threw up midway through the threesome she had been assigned to so that she could learn by following the lead of an *onēsan*. On this occasion, Shiori's embodied experience confronted her fears of the work in violent fashion. She went home but returned to work the next day and over more than ten years in the industry never had any further problems. Years later, she treated this account of her first day as a comical example of the misconceptions she had started with. Many other sex workers I spoke with similarly described thinking the sex industry would be frightening or dark, possibly even dangerous. The former *hoteherujō* (woman who works at a *hoteheru*) Ayano said, "All I really knew beforehand was that the way the world sees me would change after I entered sex work. I thought [the sex industry] would be a terrible place, but once I started working, I calmed down as I realized that there wasn't really anything unusual about it"—a statement that I understood as a realization that the sex industry is an ordinary place made up of ordinary people. Hiromi, on the other hand, thought that sex workers were either "gal"-types (*gyaru*, a term for women with dark suntans and dyed blonde hair often associated with delinquent behavior), women with heavy debts, or women who were working to support their unemployed boyfriend. She assumed that the customers "would all be weird and unpopular guys or old men."

Sex Industry Employment Magazines

When Yumi, a petite and soft-spoken woman from the Kyoto suburbs, was looking for a new career at age thirty, she collected all the employment magazines she could find. Since finishing junior college and dropping out of a technical program in computer graphics, she had worked in beauty salons for eight years doing oil massage and aromatherapy. She had begun to feel burned out from the work, especially after having been propositioned by an older male customer who had wanted her to become his mistress and had gone so far as to bring up the subject of an "allowance." Yumi didn't like the idea of living off of someone whom she was not married to and had rejected the proposition. But she did determine that it was time to try something different.

Yumi described to me how she had carefully looked through each of the employment "free papers" she had picked up around town. She had already told me that her longtime passion was stage acting and that in her free time she enjoyed going to drag shows. She liked how the performers transformed their personas and bodies for an audience. Laughing and gesturing wildly with her hands, she described her fascination with the camp outfits of drag queens, including what she referred to as the incredible breasts that they made for themselves. Putting her hands to her own breasts in mock self-assessment, she shook her head and told me with a laugh that hers, unfortunately, were just ordinary. Talking excitedly and gesturing for emphasis, Yumi expressed her astonishment when, flipping through one of the magazines, she had come across a wanted ad for dominatrices at an *SM kurabu*. "Huh? What is this?!" she cried, dramatizing how she had looked at the magazine cover in shock and realized only then that it must be a magazine specializing in sex industry work. Until that moment, this had been unapparent to her. But now that it was in her hands, she was surprised to find that she wasn't particularly bothered by it. After a moment, she flipped back to the ad that had caught her attention. With her interests in performance, Yumi found the idea of S&M work appealing. Without thinking about it too much, she arranged an interview and was hired.

It may seem surprising—unlikely even—that Yumi would have been unaware that she was browsing through a sex industry employment magazine. How could she not have known? And how would she have acquired it? These questions, however, belie a set of assumptions about how the sex industry recruits. Just as the legal sex industry operates openly in Japan, so it also recruits

FIGURE 3. A billboard located prominently across from a train platform at busy Shibuya Station, Tokyo, July 2011. In this advertisement for "Vanilla," an employment website for the sex industry, the "cute" graphics highlight innocence, naiveté, and access to a consumer lifestyle. The text reads, in part, "Get information on high-paying work!! I want to earn more! I really love money! Access us now and get information by searching 'vanilla' and 'wanted ads.'" (Photo credit: Gabriele Koch)

openly, with magazines and other media that highlight the attractiveness of sex work circulating throughout public space such that they easily land in the hands of women for whom the thought of sex work may be furthest from their minds. In Tokyo and other cities, recruiting for the sex industry is normalized and media that portray short-term sex industry labor as a viable source of fast cash or casual income are often prominently placed (see Figure 3). Sex industry employment magazines (*kōshūnyū kyūjin jōhōshi*) and their associated Internet portals are a pervasive conduit of this message. These magazines are region-specific monthly free papers that advertise "high-paying work" (a euphemism) for women. They are marketing devices for an industry with high turnover. Although some of the magazines may include a handful of advertisements for jobs outside of the sex industry (mostly hostessing work), most focus exclusively on sex industry advertisements. During the time of my fieldwork, I counted at least half a dozen such magazines in the greater Tokyo area alone, of which *Momoco* and *LunLun Work* were the most visible.[4]

These magazines circulate in commercial neighborhoods with high foot traffic, but are especially prominent in shopping areas popular with young women. At busy intersections, such as Shibuya Crossing, or locations outside of train stations, such as Shinjuku Station's East Exit, female pedestrians of all ages may be handed the magazines.[5] The individuals passing out these magazines are part-time workers hired by a distribution company to hand out a range of advertising products, including pocket tissue packs with advertisements slipped into the plastic covers, handheld fans, and various product samples. As with these other items, the magazines are often accepted unthinkingly by pedestrians as they move through a busy crowd only to have a young man or woman thrust a hand in front of them. The item is usually only examined once already in hand, and, wanted or not, tucked into a bag for dealing with (and perhaps perusing) later, due to the scarcity of trash cans in public spaces. Publishing companies might also pay local businesses (such as mom and pop groceries) a small fee to display a free paper stand in front of their storefront. Billboards and trucks also advertise these employment media. One night I saw an ad truck for the magazine *Momoco*—with the catchphrase "the bible for girls" (*onna no ko no baiburu*)—circling the upscale department stores and boutiques of Tokyo's Shinjuku San-Chōme neighborhood. A recent news item reporting on complaints about ad trucks notes how a Tokyo mother was bewildered when her six-year-old belted out the musical ditty of a sex industry employment magazine blasted on speakers by one such truck ("Vanilla, vanilla, vanilla, job offers!"), demonstrating how effectively these media may transmit their messages.[6] Nothing reflects the profound normalization of the sex industry more than the fact that the industry openly recruits at all days and times in prominent locations that are associated with normative Japanese youth and femininity.

Yumi had been unable to register the nature of the magazine she was browsing as a sex industry recruitment paper because of the very *ordinariness* of it. The magazines are discreet, designed precisely to be inviting to women without any knowledge of the industry. Their design does not make them stand out obviously from other free papers. Many of the magazines have bright, glossy covers with a smiling cover girl wearing the latest fashions. The opening pages of several of the more prominent magazines take their cue from features found in ordinary women's magazines, such as close-ups on fashion and makeup trends ("Learn how to do AKB48's[7] natural look!"), popular entertainment reviews, and romance and dating tips, all color-printed on relatively high-quality paper. Some magazines offer giveaways of brand-name goods: prizes for the fastest respondents in one magazine included two Louis Vuitton purses (valued at ¥95,550 and ¥75,600, respectively) and a Coach wallet (¥34,800). The magazines emphasize consumption, free time, and a disposable income. Their purpose is to draw women in through normative messages of respectable femininity and consumption. As Yumi's experience exemplifies, except for references to "high-paying work," there is often no obvious sign that these are sex industry magazines until one is already browsing the advertisements.

The magazines highlight the possibility of earning considerable money with relatively little effort. They contain subtle yet powerful messages about the convenience, easiness, and attractiveness of sex industry work and suggest that there is nothing out of the ordinary about either the work itself or the women doing it. The cover of one issue of *LunLun Work*, for example, squeezes in as much text as possible to make its pitch to readers.[8] Large headlines urge the reader to "Debut into high-paying work!!" while assuring them that "First-timers and those without experience can relax." Smaller boxes and bubbles explain that the work is untaxing, "small" part-time work for those over eighteen and note the availability of a guaranteed minimum salary for newcomers, transportation funds, and the option of participating in a one-day trial. One line directly under the magazine title assures the reader: "You will definitely find something! [We have] 106 ads for workplaces that will suit you!" Anticipating the concerns of slightly older readers, a small pink box assures readers that there are also thirty-nine listings for businesses that hire women in their thirties and forties. This is not too late to "debut," the cover informs the reader, adding that having children is no problem and that women need not worry about their identities getting out.[9]

Other standard features of the opening pages of these magazines include a close-up profile of the cover girl. A brief interview typically includes questions such as, "Were you nervous the first time?" (typical answer: "Yes, but the staff was really supportive, so I was able to relax"). Another common feature referred to by one magazine as the "wallet check" does important rhetorical work by featuring short profiles of several women and inquiring into the content of their wallets and their spending habits. Twenty-nine-year-old Seira, for example, averages ¥1,000,000 per month working four to five days per week at a *fasshon herusu*. She reports spending ¥100,000 on rent, ¥50,000 on food, ¥100,000 on clothing, ¥60,000 on makeup, and ¥120,000 on going out every month, and is able to save ¥400,000.[10] Profiled in a different magazine, nineteen-year-old Yū made ¥60,000 in one day by working at an *onakura* from 1 P.M. until 9 P.M. and taking five customers. She is saving money for college tuition and reports: "Most of the women at my business had no experience when they started. You don't need to be perfect when you begin, so long as you can convey your kindness and effort to the customer. You can talk to the staff about anything you don't know or any concerns you have."[11]

Every magazine has a "work guide" that functions to explain the basic categories of sex industry labor—although in ways that Sachiko mused were exceedingly "polite." Invariably, these guides adopt what Sabine Frühstück refers to as the "strategic use of cuteness," using cartoon figures representing women in different types of work to make the work legible as something appealing and approachable—something that ordinary women need not be wary of trying.[12] The cartoon figures have oversized heads with disproportionally large dark ovals as eyes, and pose in an iconic costume. For instance, the figure representing soaplands has just a towel wrapped around her and smiles coquettishly. Their facial expressions and gestures suggest the work is light-hearted and fun, based as they are on a visual repertoire of cute graphics familiar to readers to convey images of innocence and wholesomeness. One work guide, which was in a magazine for sale for ¥200 at a bookstore, plots out four elements of the work—potential earnings, the intensity of the sexual service involved, the extent of conversation required, and the performative degree—with mathematical precision on a graph, making the work legible in terms of different aspects. Soaplands, for instance, register as full 10s on earnings and sexual service but only as a 6 on conversation and an 8 on performance, while *pinku saron* register as a 2 on performance, a 3 on conversation, a 4 on sexual service, and a 6 on earnings.[13] Importantly, however, there is little concrete information given. What Sachiko referred to as "polite" is a euphemism for "vague." Sex is not directly alluded to. At most, it is only vaguely gestured at. Finally, the advertisements themselves offer little information and are full of "cute" imagery, such as teddy bears and puppies, which bears little connection to the work.

These magazines are mostly oriented toward first-timers or relative new-comers to the industry. Women with more experience criticize them as misleading at best and full of untruths at worst. Megumi told me flatly, "Everything is a lie except for the phone number." Experienced sex workers know how to read between the lines to winnow out claims in the advertisements that are exaggerated (such as the average daily earnings) or simply untrue ("You can work within your own comfort zone"—as Megumi put it, "They don't know what my comfort zone is, how could that be true?"). Megumi and other experienced sex workers use the magazines to keep tabs on which businesses are hiring. For accurate information, they rely on information-sharing with peers and online discussion boards for sex workers. Several sex workers explained that the best way to learn about a business is either to speak directly to the manager or to search for its customer website and see for themselves how the store "concept" and standard services are described.

These magazines (and their online portals) are a gateway for many women who are interested in sex industry work but do not know where to start. Unlike "ordinary" job seekers, women looking for information on the sex industry are unable to consult openly with family members, friends, or guidance counselors in finding a suitable workplace. Unless an individual already has a close friend or acquaintance in the industry who is "out" to them about their work, they will be on their own. Sex industry employment magazines are thus important for providing basic information and serving as a navigational tool for first-timers. These magazines are of course not the only way in which women are recruited to the sex industry. Although they are now prohibited, even today, on the streets of Tokyo one can see "scouts" at work. These are young men who chat up women on the street, hoping to catch their attention through their often ostentatious and self-consciously fashionable style and entice them into high-paying work. But the free employment magazines played some role in helping each of the women in my study to select a workplace, whether it was their first or their tenth.

Autonomy and Flexibility

Against the backdrop of a limited female labor market, the sex industry represents a lucrative economic opportunity for many women. In general, sex work is high-paying work that offers a high return value on time. In fact, many of my interlocutors insisted that it offered the *highest* return value on time for

women, especially those without privileged class backgrounds, university degrees, or professional training. A woman working in the sex industry can earn
a substantial sum of money in a relatively short period of time. As sex workers pocket their earnings on the same day, it can be particularly attractive to
individuals in need of immediate money in hand.

Average earnings for sex workers vary drastically as they depend on numerous factors, including a woman's age (or, more accurately, how young she
can appear), her level of experience and skill, the number of regular customers
she has, how many days and hours per week she works, whether she is willing
to appear in advertising, her willingness to offer nonstandard services, the
type of establishment and whether it is high-end or low-end, and the reputation of the business. It is thus difficult to generalize about sex workers' earnings. Among the women I met, some made around ¥50,000–70,000 per day
but most seemed to average approximately ¥20,000–30,000 per day of work,
although this was also subject to change as a woman aged. Other data suggests that the youngest women in the sex industry (aged 18–22) earn an average of about ¥51,200 per day, while women in their mid- to late twenties and
early thirties average between ¥38,400 and ¥46,500, and women in their mid-
thirties earn an average of ¥30,450 per day;[14] another survey suggests the average
store-based *herusu* worker in Tokyo, Saitama, and Sapporo earns approximately ¥341,000 per month (compared to the national average of ¥248,000
per month for women in their early thirties).[15] Importantly, there is no hourly
wage in the sex industry—sex work is not waged work but work paid for services rendered—so a woman must have customers to earn money. Although a
few sex industry businesses offer their workers a minimal guaranteed amount
(*gyara*) for showing up, at most businesses, if a sex worker has no customers,
she will make no money that day.

The earnings possible in the sex industry are particularly attractive in
comparison to the wages of part-time work, which many women considering
sex work view as their alternative. As of October 2011, the average national
(hourly) minimum wage was ¥737. The minimum wage was highest in Tokyo
at ¥837, with neighboring Kanagawa Prefecture just behind at ¥836. Osaka's
minimum wage was ¥786. There was—and continues to be—a significant
disparity between average wages in metropolitan centers such as these and
economically depressed rural prefectures, many of which did not exceed the
¥700 mark.[16] As of October 2016, the national average had increased to ¥823.
Tokyo's minimum wage was again highest at ¥932, while in Kanagawa and

Osaka it stood at ¥930 and ¥883, respectively. Miyazaki and Okinawa had the lowest wages at ¥714.[17] Although these figures represent an all-around increase, youth labor activists have pointed out that these wages are still hopelessly inadequate given the costs of daily life in Japan. A commentator for the *Mainichi Shimbun* newspaper noted that a yearly income of ¥3 million is considered the minimum threshold (for a man) for marriage, but that even in Tokyo, working 1,800 hours a year at minimum wage would amount to only ¥1.67 million.[18]

Against the backdrop of such relatively low earnings for part-time work, the cash in hand that a sex worker gets at the end of her shift is a powerful material incentive. Yamada Shiori, a student working her way through college, was astonished on her first day at a *deriheru* when she received ¥30,000 for three hours of work. It took her a month to make the same amount working her ¥900/hour job at a restaurant, to which she rushed every evening after her classes were over. The stark difference in exchange value for her labor made the decision easy for her. Yamada immediately began working three to four days per week. No longer shut out from the pricey social activities of her friends and able to take advantage of her college's study abroad program to the United States, the rhythm of and sense of possibility in her daily life transformed itself dramatically.[19]

Explanations that base women's participation in commercial sex solely on a financial rationale, however, miss much of what sex workers themselves describe as appealing about the work. There is more to what draws women to— and keeps them in—the sex industry than just "the simple calculus of return on investment."[20] Many women find sex work attractive out of a desire for a particular kind of autonomy. These women foreground the forms of personal and economic freedom, possibility, and flexibility offered by sex industry labor. Foremost, sex industry work allows women great freedom to set their own schedule and to easily take days off.[21] Depending on a woman's financial needs and responsibilities, she need not go to work very often if she finds her earnings sufficient for her living standard and can pursue other activities in the remaining days of the week. Sex work offers the possibility of filling one's days with things other than work.

This relative freedom from work was important to all of the women I spoke with. As with Megumi, whose health had taken an inexplicable downward turn at the municipal office where she had worked for four years, several women told me that they were unable to discipline their bodies to the conditions of "normal" workplaces, with their regular hours (and overtime hours), hierarchical relations, excessive expectations of dedication to the company, and little flexibility. Sayaka told me, "At a regular workplace, you can't really take time off when you feel like it. You only get the weekends. Regular employees really have it tough. But I want to be able to have my own time. Mentally, working at a normal workplace doesn't sound good to me, and I don't want my boss to be mad at me either. Working normally would be impossible for me." Sayaka suggested that there was something exploitative about normal workplaces. Similarly, Shiori often asked me with an air of puzzlement, "How do people stand doing boring work day in and day out?" Shiori had worked in the sex industry on and off for the greater part of twelve years. During that time, she had briefly returned to ordinary work several times but quickly found that she had become averse to the predictable, menial, and low-status nature of female office work. Through her work at an *imekura*, *SM kurabu*, and *fasshon herusu*, she told me, "Every day I come home with interesting stories to tell my roommates." Shiori seemed to flourish in the unpredictability of her work and praised it precisely for its inversion of dominant qualities of ordinary work. Sayaka, Shiori, and others I spoke to were women who rejected the (male-)gendered and generational association between one's sense of social identity and one's workplace.[22] They saw themselves as having autonomy in sex work and, implicitly, asserted a critique of what they saw as the exploitation and monotony of dominant work structures.

The lucrative potential and flexible conditions of sex industry work can make it especially attractive to single mothers (most of whom are divorced), who receive little welfare assistance from the state.[23] Although there is no data on the number of single mothers in the sex industry, anecdotal and other evidence suggests the figures are relatively high. The *Tōkyō Shimbun* newspaper, for example, has reported that two-thirds of the parents sending their children to one twenty-four-hour day care in the Kabukichō sex and entertainment district are sex workers.[24] Aimi is a single mother originally from the regional city of Tottori. At age twenty-eight, with a four-year-old to raise and concerned about money, she left her job as an office lady and began working in the sex industry. "I had begun volunteering at an HIV/AIDS hotline after a friend of mine got HIV. Once a week, always when I was on my shift, a sex worker would call in and talk to me about her work. She was always very respectful to me and spoke as if there were a great social distance between us—as if she were a bad person and I was graciously listening to her problems.

But I didn't think that way at all. It got me thinking. At that time, I really needed money and I wanted a job where I could be there when my daughter came home from school, without being pressured to work overtime. If I didn't think sex work was bad, then why had I never considered it before?"

Foremost on Aimi's mind was shielding her daughter from the consequences if her identity were outed. "Being exposed was my biggest fear," she told me. In order to give herself additional assurance against being outed in case she ran into an acquaintance at work, Aimi had purposefully chosen an *SM kurabu*. "With S&M, the customer is [considered] a pervert, so they would want to hide that they were at such a club. So, even if I met an acquaintance, they wouldn't say anything. It's in their interests to keep it a secret, so I thought that I would be okay, too." Like many single mothers, Aimi chose to work only during the unpopular daytime hours while her daughter was at school. Aimi spent five years in S&M before moving on to a soapland for another five. She quit when her daughter was fourteen and Aimi felt that she had saved up enough money. But as a single parent who had received little support from the state, sex work had played an important role in how she had been able to raise her daughter. Aimi felt that the work had given her the autonomy to raise her child on her own as a single mother, without being reliant on anyone else.

Finally, the lucrative nature of sex work allows women to expand their sense of possibility and participate in activities that otherwise would be inaccessible to them.[25] Many of my interlocutors had traveled abroad extensively through their sex industry earnings, taking extended vacations or participating in formal language or study abroad programs. Hiromi had worked at a *deriheru* until age twenty-five and then spent a year in Ireland studying English and living off of her substantial savings. Yumi used her sex industry earnings to subsidize her passion for theater, which on its own would not have been financially viable. Those from regional towns or the countryside were able to fashion cosmopolitan and urban identities for themselves, while women from less privileged class backgrounds were able to experience upward mobility.[26] Their earnings allowed them to sustain particular lifestyles. All the women in my study were able to participate in shopping, leisure, or social activities that previously had been closed to them. They enjoyed the ability to be generous and not having to worry about money while still being independent of their parents or a husband. Their sense of themselves and of what they could accomplish changed. They moved into their own rental apartments for the first time and could assist family members with financial concerns. The *deribari esute* (callout sexual massage) therapist Shizuku emphasized how she made a point to maximize the forms of happiness made possible by sex industry work, just as she might make the most of those available to a housewife or an office lady if she were in those positions.[27] These included taking time off whenever she felt like it and using her earnings to travel all over the world on her own. She had also chosen to focus on self-development and exploration and pursued the processual "path" of numerous arts like flower arrangement, the tea ceremony, and calligraphy.[28]

Although sex work is the principal occupation for some women, for many others it is only one of multiple part-time income-earning activities or a side job that supplements more socially acceptable work that they can include on their résumés.[29] Some women enter sex work immediately following high school (or when they turn eighteen if they had dropped out of high school), while others begin working during college or afterward. Most women who enter at a young age have done at least some other part-time work before entering. Other women enter after they have already been in the labor market for several years and begin doing sex work as a side job that they may turn into their main income-earning activity or after quitting a full-time job and wondering where to turn next. Many women have some kind of debt that motivates their entry, whether it is their own or that of a family member or lover.

In contemporary Japan, it is still noteworthy to be financially self-sufficient as a woman without relying on either a husband or one's natal family (including living at home). The young women working in the sex industry whom I spoke with desired to be relatively autonomous and to participate in the economy as they pleased. For them, sex work was by no means considered to be a terrible occupation and, instead, was understood as having many elements that distinguish it positively from other "women's work." These women often speak at great length and with pride about the autonomy it offers—an autonomy that sets them apart within the female labor market.

Work Sense

The social marginalization of sex work keeps remuneration high and produces working conditions distinct from those of many Japanese workplaces. But many of the same aspects that sex workers find appealing about their work also reflect back to them their insecure place in the economy. Despite widespread notions in Japan of the social necessity of the sex industry, the basic conditions of this industry underscore that sex workers are not formally recognized as laborers in an "ordinary" category of work and that they are outside of the structures of the formal economy. Legally, sex workers are not employees and they are not paid wages. Rather, they are independent contractors who are given a place to legally work and are paid only based on the time they spend with a customer. Women in the sex industry receive roughly half of the earnings that they bring in and are paid daily in cash.[30] In contrast, male management and staff members are considered regular employees and have their wages deposited to their bank accounts. Although most sex workers will earn at least double what the average office lady makes, the average manager will earn roughly the same wage as a typical salary-man.[31] Moreover, sex workers do not pay taxes on their earnings. Sex industry businesses neither withhold taxes nor provide women a written record of their annual earnings. Although many sex workers are pleasantly surprised to learn that they do not need to file taxes and can simply report that they are unemployed, this has important implications for their social adulthood and citizenship. Without documented evidence of their earnings, women working in the sex industry experience obstacles to securing loans, signing up for a credit card, and enrolling their children in particular schools. All major purchases must be made in cash, which can turn an unwanted gaze on oneself.[32]

Attempting to bridge this gap between their own work and forms of labor associated with the valorized and protected areas of the economy that are implicitly gendered male, some women in the sex industry self-consciously apply dominant norms of work to their everyday lives. For instance, Sachiko, a former *fasshon herusu* worker who had married and was working part-time caring for children with disabilities when we met, complained to me about the work ethic of her onetime colleagues: "I want the girls who work in the sex industry to approach the work a little more as work."

"What do you mean? Do you mean in terms of their interactions with customers?"

"No, I mean in terms of their entire work attitude." She laughed. "I'm really talking about a basic level of things here, like showing up on time. I'd like them to see it *as* work. Right now many girls have an attitude of, 'We're just here [for the day] to earn some money.' [That attitude] has nothing to do with age."

Sachiko's complaint about her former coworkers expressed frustration with how their attitude seemingly justified the informal status of sex industry work. In her eyes, these women's lax and casual attitude expressed a troubling lack of recognition that they were workers with skill who put effort into their encounters with customers and deserved respect. Sachiko described to me how she had been able to do the work for eight years precisely because she had treated it like any other job: keeping a regular schedule, coming in on time, showing deference to her boss, and giving her best effort with every customer. Making the work more "work-like" and doing it "properly" (tekitō) had made it something she could stick with, whereas she felt that if she had disregarded these norms she would have quickly lost motivation. Sachiko told me that she had socialized only with those women at her former workplaces who had shared a similar outlook that she felt evinced a more serious sense of purpose. Elsewhere in my fieldwork, I encountered other sentiments that echoed the premise of Sachiko's complaint. Shiori, for example, explained to me that her former managers had regarded single mothers and women who confessed to having credit card debt favorably in job interviews because they presumed that such women had a concrete goal that would drive them to work hard. As relayed to me by Shiori, this anecdote suggests that these managers assumed a different type of attitude and work ethic on the part of the average job applicant looking to support herself.

Kathi Weeks has pointed to the hegemony of an ideology of work ethic as virtue in the United States, asking why this hegemony is so rarely challenged.[33] Although reflecting a very different context, it is noteworthy that Sachiko applied conventional expectations and values around what "work" is supposed to be like to a form of labor that many women choose *specifically because of* the relative autonomy and flexibility it grants in contrast to what they see as the often harsh and disciplinary nature of "ordinary" work. Sachiko herself had internalized a particular notion of how productive labor is constituted and made sense of her own participation in the gendered economy through the dominant norms associated with it, even as she also rejected other conditions of such labor and had herself never participated in full-time work. Although Sachiko's resentment of how her coworkers' attitudes seemingly undermine the status of sex work as work is understandable in its desire to convey the value and dignity of sex work, it also reflects a contradiction of working in the sex industry: many aspects of the work that are appealing to sex workers derive from its informal status, but this informal status also has other consequences that they find distinctly problematic, as I will discuss at length in Chapter 6.[34] Following Weeks, in some ways, sex workers' critique of what they refer to as "ordinary" (*futsū no*) work envisions an alternate way of imagining what a fulfilling and meaningful relationship with work might look like—one that involves flexibility and autonomy, and the ability to determine one's own schedule and how much or how hard one works. At the same time, this relationship to work, which the most fortunate women in the sex industry can embody, at least for a period in their youth, is only made possible by conditions deriving from the differentiation—and, ultimately, marginalization—of sex industry work from dominant norms that structure the male-gendered economy.

Other women voiced their concerns over how participation in sex work might distort their ability to habituate themselves to conventional work values or dispositions in the future, after they had moved on from sex work. In addition to work attitude, these concerns centered, in particular, around one's sense for money (*kinsen kankaku*). The former *deriherujō* Hiromi, who had moved to Tokyo after graduating from college in rural Shimane Prefecture, was concerned with what might become of her values around work and money, and also keenly aware of the problems that a blank résumé might pose for her in the future:

> If I had been doing nothing but working in the sex industry, there'd be an empty space on my résumé and I knew that I would always be asked in interviews about what I had been doing during those years. Of course you can't put sex work on your résumé. I also didn't want to lose my sense for money or my work ethic. [Sex work] isn't easy work but in one hour you can earn an incredible amount of money. So, during the day I always did regular part-time work. I worked at a coffee shop and at a restaurant in my neighborhood. Then in the evening, I'd work at a *deriheru*. It'd be hard for me to have that kind of a schedule now, but I did it for a few years. I'd get home in the early hours of the morning and sleep until noon, then go to one of my part-time jobs. I'd go back home and eat dinner and then go to my sex industry job.

Hiromi had regarded sex work as only ever a temporary occupation and had been concerned over how it might distort her grip on normative values around money and work. To avoid this, she purposefully participated in part-time work at minimum wage on the side.

Yumi, the former massage therapist who had stumbled upon sex industry employment magazines by accident, blamed her younger sister's inability to participate in "normal" work on her too-early career in sex work. After five years of working in the sex industry, Yumi had moved back to the Kyoto suburbs following a breast cancer diagnosis. She lived with her younger sister a short distance from their parents' home and both of them worked at their father's company doing clerical and administrative work. Yumi's younger sister, it turned out, had also once worked in the sex industry, many years ago, when she was around fifteen or sixteen and still in high school. Although it was illegal for minors to work in the sex industry then as well as now, prior to the mid-2000s, few businesses had bothered to check identity cards. Yumi had only learned about her sister's past a few years ago, by chance. Although it was unclear how the knowledge that her sister had worked in the sex industry had affected her own decision to enter, Yumi clearly thought it was not a good idea for someone so young to work there: "At that age, you haven't entered society yet. It affects your set of values around money and men. When you do enter society, you don't have the right work attitude. My sister has never been able to get used to normal work. She just doesn't get the notion that you might have to adjust to work in stages. She's never really been able to do it." Yumi treated her sister's first experiences with work as indelible and judged that her time in sex work would forever affect her work capability. She and her sister, two former sex workers, now both worked in their father's company, each seeking solace—but for different reasons—in a family enterprise.

Yumi and Hiromi both demonstrate concern over how sex work might affect one's values. Its potential for substantial remuneration is viewed as something that has to be carefully balanced with a pragmatic attitude, lest one's values and expectations be set off-kilter. Behind such concerns, we can read another example of how female sex work embodies the gendering of the economy. Women who engage in sex work typically have the most freedom in their twenties and thirties, when they have little experience but their youth and beauty (these are of course seen as linked) are highly valued. This stands in contrast to the male-gendered "professional" economy, in which it is seniority and experience that produce value. The concerns of women working in the sex industry around the distortion of their values speaks to their fears that this will be the best it ever gets because they are destined for tedious low-pay work or for marriage (or both). Sex workers assume that the work will only ever be temporary and thus one must not get habituated to its conditions because they will not last. In other words, this has to do with the futures that sex workers can imagine for themselves.

An Economic Barometer

Although it is widely assumed in Japan that there will always be a market for sex—regardless of recession, national disaster, or other calamity—this market, it is clear, is itself subject to broader political-economic trends. Nakamura Atsuhiko, a nonfiction writer who has prolifically covered the mainstream sex industry, argues that, in the face of slow economic growth punctuated by periodic recession since the early 1990s, many women in the Japanese sex industry today entered just to make ends meet financially. In one recent book, Nakamura's coauthor, Teshigawara Mamoru, a sixteen-year veteran of sex industry management, describes how his many years of interviewing job applicants has made him keenly aware of the extent of female poverty in Japan and of the difficulty of supporting oneself on a typical woman's salary in an urban center. Pointing to government data showing that the number of unmarried women in their late twenties tripled from 1973 to 2010, Nakamura and Teshigawara underscore that with the decline of marriage rates nationally, young women now have to be self-sufficient in an economy with few high status or high-paying positions for women.[35] However, they question how well any woman not from a privileged background—especially one without a university degree or specialized skills—can get by without being married or living with her parents.[36] According to them, the sex industry has thus become a means for many women just to make do—and not merely a place of last resort, as the media often portrays. In another recent book, Nakamura focuses entirely on the phenomenon of university students paying their tuition through sex work, highlighting both how falling national household incomes have strained the ability of families to pay for their children's education and the effects of debt from a predatory student loan system.[37]

What is most striking about Nakamura's economic analysis, however, is his forceful argument that the sex industry itself is a stratified, unequal society. Painting a bleak picture of an industry in which the entrance of college students and other "high spec" women pushes others to lower rungs of the industry, Nakamura and Teshigawara point to the disparities—sometimes more akin to a wide gulf—between the industry's highest earners, those who earn a decent amount, and those who merely scrape by.[38] They note that, contrary to stereotypes and media portrayals of the sex industry, many more women interview for sex industry positions than will be taken on and bluntly observe that in the context of an oversupply and stiff competition, "Women who can't make money [in the sex industry] won't make money."[39] Even as the sex industry is often portrayed as a safety net, Nakamura positions it instead as a barometer of the national economy's failure to address the needs of young women.

In contrast to Nakamura's bleak view, others from within the industry have more sanguine perspectives on the average woman's prospects in sex work. When I asked the veteran sex worker Sayaka about the majority of sex workers—those who will never become the Number One (or, highest-earning sex worker) at their business and who don't make a small fortune every month but who nevertheless have their own modest base of repeat customers—she drew a comparison to the marriage market: "In general, most women are able to earn money. It's just like with marriage. Most people get married, don't they? Even if they're overweight or plain-looking, they'll still marry. It's the same in the sex industry. If you find just a few customers who come to see you each week, you'll make money." Sayaka believed that most women get by on sex work, even if they are not considered to be exceptional in some way. "The ones who don't earn are those in whom it's obvious that they don't want to be there. But if you put in some effort and show attention and care to the customers, you'll do alright." Sayaka did not discount stratification and differential success in the sex industry, but her longtime observations nevertheless led her to believe that most women manage to make a decent living—or, at the very least, earn more than they would elsewhere.

In contrast, Sora, a *nyū hāfu* ("new half," transgender woman) in her thirties who worked in the sex industry at the same time that she was active in anti-prostitution causes, spoke bitterly about how it was "Lies, lies, lies!" that the sex industry is a source of fast cash. She explained that she thought young women fell for a fantasy of "easy money" (*abukuzeni*); once they realized that they would not actually make as much as they expected, Sora continued, they were already settled in the work and usually just decided to stay in sex work. Sora told me that she herself was only working in the sex industry because discrimination against *nyū hāfu* left few workplaces open to her and she needed funds for hormone treatment. Sora regarded her participation in sex work as degrading but, given her social marginalization, also spoke of it as seemingly inevitable.

These conflicting viewpoints about the financial viability of sex work reflect individuals' own experiences and vantage points as well as different women's imagining of economic possibility. Chie, a woman who had worked in several different sectors of both the legal and illegal sex industry, likewise offered a cynical perspective. Chie repeatedly characterized Japan as *rorikon* ("Lolita complex," favoring young girls) to indicate the dwindling returns that she had experienced in the sex industry as she aged. Originally from Kyoto, Chie had moved to Tokyo to attend college and began working at a *kyabakura* to support herself. By age twenty-six, she felt as if she had aged out of hostessing and was being pressure to leave. Chie had a friend who was working at a *hoteheru* (a callout business at which a woman meets a customer at a love hotel or rental room) and earning well, so Chie decided to enter the sex industry. Over seven years, she had worked at numerous businesses. Now, at thirty-three, she felt that she was still doing better than she would outside of the industry but acknowledged, "I have a lot of free time when I'm at work," indicating that she was not attracting customers. "In the ten days that I've worked this month, I've only made ¥200,000 in total. One day, I didn't make anything."

Chie felt her options dwindling. At the same time, however, she had not given much thought to a future outside of the sex industry. When I asked her about what she wanted to do after leaving the industry, she said, "There isn't really anything in particular. I haven't really thought about it." Was she saving money? "Saving? Mmm . . . I'm not earning that much right now but I can still make do." When did she think she would leave the industry? "I'll quit when I think I can't make it at any store anymore. But I don't feel that that time has come yet. I've had a lot of free time at work lately, but I think I'll still be doing this for a while, especially since the economy doesn't seem to be getting any better. Once, a few years ago, I quit the sex industry for a little bit. But I had a hard time and ended up coming back. Because I was already around thirty, I felt like I didn't have that many choices in front of me."

Chie echoed the general agreement among women in the sex industry whom I spoke with that in the past (loosely defined), the economic situation in the sex industry had been better and everyone had generally earned well. But, a combination of an oversupply of sex workers and intense competition among businesses due to the recession had pushed down the market rate for standard services and depreciated earnings. To stay competitive, some businesses were relying on offering "harder" (for example, nonstandard) services. Chie observed: "These days it's hard to earn well in the sex industry. Only a small number of women really do well anymore. There are too many women working, there's too much supply. The women who will always do well will still earn, but it used to be that any girl would do well. Now it's not enough to just be cute. Especially with the effects of the [March 11, 2011] disaster. Even the most popular businesses aren't getting enough customers. It's not going to get better." In this context, Chie was both keenly aware of her limited options but also reluctant to leave sex work, convinced that it still offered her higher earnings and more security than her alternatives in part-time work.

Finally, the effects of slow growth and the recession on the sex industry can also be viewed in the emergence of "bargain rate" (*gekiyasu*) businesses. The success of the "39 Group" *deriheru* chain, for instance, has concerned some observers and sex workers as it offers rock bottom prices: ¥3900 for thirty minutes. The sex worker receives ¥2500 of this amount and another ¥2000 if she is designated by the customer. This has reportedly led to women competing aggressively for designations by offering (illegal) intercourse and/ or anal sex without a condom and suspicions that the management is actively encouraging this.[40] The overwhelming dominance of *deriheru* businesses, discussed in Chapter 1, is itself also an effect of recession and poses new risks for sex workers who must now work without staff nearby to assist them in case of a troublesome customer.

Conclusion

In this chapter, I have shown how some of the contradictions that shape sex work in Japan lead to the presence of a diverse group of women in the sex industry. In contrast to popular associations of sex workers with desperation or, conversely, materialism, my fieldwork suggests that many sex workers are young women—including, among others, some from middle-class and college-educated backgrounds—who find the financial opportunity, autonomy, and flexibility of sex industry labor appealing in contrast to more dominant forms of feminized employment. For a time, this work can offer the options and comfort of a middle-class lifestyle without dependence on one's family or having to rely on marriage as an economic strategy. Moreover, it can expand individual women's sense of possibility in their lives, as sex work provides them with the time and financial wherewithal to engage in hobbies or travel, pursue a qualification, spend time with family members or friends, participate in a consumer lifestyle, or raise a child on their own. But many of these same women are also keenly aware that, financially, their time in the sex industry might represent the peak of their economic fortunes, as they imagine futures of low-status and low-pay—albeit respectable—feminized work.

Many women in the sex industry reject negative characterizations of their work and suggest that it is, in fact, "ordinary" employment that is exploitative. This critique presents us with an opportunity to consider the structure and conditions of work in normative Japanese workplaces. In particular, it highlights the male-gendered nature of the formal economy, in that the long hours and expectations of overtime, excessive commitment, and hierarchical relations that define it implicitly rest on a gendered division of labor in which a wife's care for the household frees her husband to devote himself to his work. The women whom I spoke with were happy to escape—for a time—the need to discipline themselves to some of the normative values of Japanese workplaces, and their critique suggests desires for other ways of imagining a relation to work more generally.[41]

Over time, the exigencies of women's changing life circumstances necessitate, in different ways, that they leave sex work, whether this is due to the achievement of a short-term goal (like paying off one's college tuition or a debt), getting married, a child reaching primary school age, the availability of a viable alternative employment option, the feeling of diminishing returns in the sex industry, or an increasing frustration with work that one cannot be open about. Although few of the women in my study who had left the industry expressed a desire to return to sex work, they largely did not regret their participation in it and valued what it had allowed them to do.

Sex workers benefit from the marginalization of the sex industry in some ways—in the form of higher wages, flexible conditions of work, and relative freedom from rules or hierarchy—but they are at the same time profoundly affected by the forms of insecurity, stigma, and risk this marginalization produces. Sex workers are deeply aware that their work is not considered to be respectable and is generally regarded as shameful and low-status. How do women in the sex industry resolve the moral conflicts generated by the tension between what is appealing about the work and the stigma it produces? In the next chapter, I turn to how sex workers navigate the often contradictory social expectations of them.

3   Stigma and the Moral Economy

A MAP TOWARD THE BACK of an issue of the sex industry employment magazine *Hanamaru Work* depicts the larger Tokyo metropolitan area and the commuter towns of three neighboring prefectures as a web of interconnected train and subway hubs. The two-page spread is a workplace navigator designed to help readers select a suitable working neighborhood. A comment at the top of the page advises readers, "If your workplace is too close to home, you might have the unpleasant experience of running into an acquaintance. But if it's too far away, you could lose your motivation to go to work. . . . A good rule of thumb is to aim for an hour-long commute each way."[1] The graphic highlights nine areas with sizable sex industries and provides short descriptions of their local color, clientele demographics, and shopping and entertainment options. The Ueno area, for example, is described as the doorway to the northern Kantō region. Commuter trains carrying tired workers back to Saitama, Chiba, and Ibaraki Prefectures run until late at night, meaning a sex worker might have clients through the early hours of the morning. Shibuya, on the other hand, is described as a center for "gal"-style fashion and a bustling shopping district where one can observe the newest trends and easily find reasonably priced places to go out and enjoy oneself.

This workplace navigator depicts one of the first ways in which women contemplating sex industry work must learn to keep aspects of their life hidden from their social circle. Even in the seemingly boundless anonymity afforded by Tokyo's dense urban expanse, sex workers are always cognizant of the possibility that they might run into an acquaintance. Concerns about one's identity getting out—and the devastating social fallout presumed to follow—are ever present. The map thus exemplifies one method through which sex workers think about how to effectively separate their working lives from their "real," socially legitimate identities. For example, Sachiko, a native Tokyoite, chose a sex industry district in neighboring Yokohama because she imagined it as outside of the limits of her social network. "My friends don't go there," she told me, shrugging. Yamada Shiori did the reverse: a college student from Kanagawa Prefecture whose university was in Yokohama, she chose to work at a *deriheru* in Shibuya, a little over an hour away by train.[2]

This chapter asks how sex workers manage a problem central to their work: it is both uniquely lucrative *and* stigmatizing, simultaneously opening up personal and financial possibilities at the same time that it is unmentionable. The vast majority of women working in the sex industry are not out about their work to even those closest to them. In Kaname Yukiko and Mizushima Nozomi's study of 126 sex workers, for instance, 93 percent of respondents had not spoken to their family about their work, while 57 percent had not spoken to their lover/romantic partner about it.[3] The stigma of working in an illicit industry that runs contrary to normative notions of feminine respectability is always on women's minds as they maneuver the moral conflicts that accompany their entry into and departure from (or not) the sex industry. This chapter argues that the sexual economy is always also a moral economy and that how women represent or talk about their work is shaped by moral ideologies of whom or what women's labor should be for.[4]

Day and Night Faces

Stigma toward women in the sex industry stems from widely held notions that, for women, sex should be reserved for monogamous "private" relations, not commercial ones. A woman's sexuality should not be too available but should be circumscribed by intimate, ideally domestic, relationships. Megumi, the former civil servant turned *deriherujō*, explained to me the double standard by which women are only ever expected to have sex for love:

> The existence of women in the sex industry threatens the value system and sense of ethics that many people construct for themselves. There are lots of people who wonder how a woman can have sex with someone she doesn't love.

They understand—well, kind of—that some women might be direct about wanting to have sex, but to do it for money is something that people don't really accept. If you have sex [as a woman], the reason has to be for love. Of course, it's different for men. People excuse promiscuous male sex by saying, "Men can't help it, they have a 'natural instinct' (*honnō*) for sex . . ."

In contrast to widespread tolerance of male sexual indulgence, women's sexuality is expected to be contained within particular kinds of relationships.[5]

This ethic that underlies stigma around women's sexuality produces other types of discriminatory claims about sex workers. For instance, I occasionally heard or read about sex workers being accused of being "freeloaders" who don't pay taxes and thus don't contribute to society, or as women who break the law. More common is the perception that sex workers are motivated by purely materialistic goals—especially the acquisition of brand-name goods—and would do anything for money. Other claims are that sex workers carry diseases. Or, as Shiori put it, that they are "using the body that their parents gave them" in an immoral way—a claim that signals particular ideas about how social relations are inscribed onto women's bodies, circumscribing how they should or should not be used.

The potential consequences of having one's work in the sex industry revealed include rejection by family members, friends, and lovers, harassment and social isolation, and risks to one's marriage prospects and future (or concurrent) employment. Even a rumor can be devastating, and sex workers may take care to keep their neighbors from picking up on their working hours. The need for concealment continues throughout a woman's post–sex work life.[6] The former dominatrix Suzuki Minako recounts how the man she was in a serious relationship with threatened her after she told him about her past, wanting to share this aspect of her life with him. Although he initially claimed not to be bothered by it, when Suzuki later told him she was pregnant, she was dumbfounded when he suggested it was another man's child and accused her of using this tactic to demand money from men. After Suzuki retorted that a DNA test would prove the child's paternity and that a court would force him to recognize the child, her lover threatened to tell her employer about her former work. Like many sex workers, Suzuki hadn't done any "normal" work during her ten years in the sex industry. When she applied for nursing positions, she had filled in the gaps on her blank résumé by fabricating some part-time jobs. She would certainly be fired for misrepresentation. Even if she weren't, she dreaded the rumors that would circulate and what her boss and coworkers—individuals who trusted her—would think. Her lover even demanded she get an abortion. Suzuki credits only the intervention of a friend in preventing her from meekly submitting to the man's demands.[7]

A news story picked up by numerous national print and television outlets in May 2013 about an Osaka public school teacher who, it had been discovered, was working in the sex industry, further illustrates the fallout, judgment, and lack of sympathy that can attend a woman's being outed. The Osaka Board of Education had received an anonymous notification that a twenty-nine-year-old high school teacher was working at a *hoteheru* after school hours and on her days off. When confronted, the teacher confessed to having shopping debts and student loans. She explained that she had chosen work in the sex industry because of its flexibility and had hoped to pay off her debts as quickly as possible. Over the course of six months, she had made ¥1.6 million. Unfortunately for her, several media outlets pointed out that the teacher had put very little of her earnings toward clearing her debts. Although the teacher had clearly violated local regulations prohibiting public servants from engaging in part-time employment, the administrative and media response had little to do with this infraction and everything to do with the work she had chosen. The Board of Education declared that she had betrayed the trust of students, parents, and Osaka residents by engaging in this "extremely inappropriate" work and imposed a hefty suspension. Media coverage coolly reported on a teacher whose actions were deemed unsuitable: the implied excessive materialism, debts, irresponsibility, violations of work restrictions, and, underpinning it all, her work in an illicit and disreputable industry. Following a semipublic shaming, the woman resigned, deciding that she had no future in this school district.[8]

Thus, women working in the sex industry always have to be aware of what information might get out and proactively protect themselves from leaks or exposure. Erving Goffman famously observed that individuals whose stigma is not immediately perceivable must carefully manage information about themselves: "It is not that [the discreditable individual] must face prejudice against himself, but rather that he must face unwitting acceptance of himself by individuals who are prejudiced against persons of the kind he can be revealed to be."[9] In the context of the sex industry, women's passing is often characterized as a type of duplicity referred to as having "day and night faces" (*hiru to yoru no kao*), which captures the sense of presenting different selves to the world and destabilizes the authenticity of those selves.[10] Sex workers become used to ironing out the incongruities presented by this. When Shiori invited me to a new year's celebration with friends from her time studying computer graphics, she explained to me that she divided her social network into two groups: friends with whom she felt that she could talk about her work and those with whom she could not. Shiori felt able to share freely with just a handful of individuals and these friends were not in that group. It was at times like these, she told me, when her working life rubbed up against her "real" life, that the sex industry was "tiresome." The constant management of information could be exhausting. Shiori decided that she would introduce me as a friend of her fiancé, who was North American. This would deflect the potentially uncomfortable fact of my research away from her. Over dinner, Shiori and her friends spoke about everything but work. They believed her to be working in a hostess club and even that was hard to talk about. On the other hand, however, the *sōpujō* (woman who works at a *sōpurando*) Risa had wanted her parents and sister to know about her work and had told them (as I will discuss shortly). Once, while having dinner with me, Risa took a phone call from her mother and discussed whether her cold-like symptoms might be indicative of a sexually transmitted infection. But even Risa spoke only about the effects of the work (for example, getting a cold)—a subject that her mother could show concern for—and not about its contents.

This stigma creates anxiety, fear, stress, and above all a sense of isolation among sex workers. As the "chat lady" Akira mournfully notes, "Even telling close family and friends is scary. If you let down your guard and talk to them about your work, you never know if it might come out at some point. It's profoundly isolating."[11] Beyond their discomfort with lying to loved ones, sex workers must hide aspects of their everyday life from their intimate social circles; they cannot truly be known by them. For many women in the sex industry, it is a relief to find people with whom they can talk relatively openly without worrying about censoring themselves or concealing aspects of their daily lives. Although many choose not to socialize at work, preferring to keep to themselves, others may form close friendships with coworkers or with the male staff.[12] Similarly, sex workers may also become frequent customers at host clubs, due to the affinity they may find with male hosts as sharing a common experience in *yoru no sekai* ("the night world"). As with their own customers, sex workers can find solace in someone whose relationship with them is mediated by money and who has a general familiarity with and lack of judgment toward their work.[13]

For instance, Shiori had had numerous roommates who were also coworkers. She was able to talk freely with them about her daily experiences without worrying about managing information. She was able to make fun of customers and let off steam. When Shiori and Erina were living together, I visited them at their apartment one evening. After dinner, they egged each other on to recount their favorite stories of unusual customers for my benefit. Erina told us about a customer who had asked her to join him in dramatically reenacting a well-known double suicide by seppuku, or ritual disembowelment. The three of us bowled over with peels of laughter as Erina knelt on Shiori's bed and rehashed her performance with a flourish, including her futile efforts to keep from breaking character after she hurt herself jabbing the plastic blade into her abdomen. Shiori went into detail about a customer who had tried for years to persuade her to let him watch her defecate, a desire that—she explained at length—she sympathetically attributed to a childhood playground trauma that had developed into a fixation. And then there was the customer who had shown up one day dressed as a woman—down to having borrowed his wife's lingerie. These stories of customer encounters—of historical reenactments, scatophilia, and cross-dressing—were shared and reworked at home with a sympathetic audience. Workplace problems, troubles, and bafflements that might have otherwise become isolating experiences were topics of shared discussion and contemplation. For women who had relationships like this, they were a source of release. The camaraderie they shared helped them through the lonelier experiences of sex work.

On a day-to-day basis, sex workers fabricate a separate working identity through a number of means. At the simplest level, all sex workers create stage names (*genjina*) for themselves and may have several over their sex industry career. They are known strictly by these names at work.[14] The identity associated with this stage name can be more or less extensive. For example, sex workers who write blogs or use social media write under their pseudonym and can, occasionally, become quite well known, leading to a sizable dual social life. Not only one's name but one's age and appearance are malleable. Women typically give a fake age in their store profile (always younger) and, given the risks that online advertising presents for women trying to maintain anonymity, many women change their appearance in their website profile photos using Photoshop. When a sex worker advocate posted before and after shots of herself on social media to demonstrate the dramatic effects of photo editing, she looked unrecognizable. Her cheeks were slimmer and her face smaller, while her eyes were larger and rounder. This technique, however, makes it possible for women to access more lucrative opportunities by advertising themselves without compromising their private identities. Their manipulated faces become masks for their real selves. Other women choose to obscure their faces altogether in store advertising using either "mosaics" (purposeful graininess) or their hands.

Some women register more than one mobile phone and separate these into work and private, a way of managing one's contacts in both realms without fear of accidental cross-contamination. Finally, there are also "alibi companies" (*aribai gaisha*) that form another measure of protection from being outed. As the name suggests, these are businesses that profit from creating the illusion that their client leads a particular kind of life. The *deriherujō* Chie paid ¥5000 per month to such a company for its services. For example, she listed the alibi company—which had a generic-sounding name that made it seem like a temp agency—as her employer on her apartment rental contract. If the real estate agent called the number she had listed and asked to speak to her, a receptionist would politely tell them that she was not available but would return their call when she returned, and then pass the message on. The alibi company was a practical work-around to particular everyday quandaries for women like Chie.

"Amateurs"

In 1995, the journal *Bessatsu Takarajima* characterized the present as the "era of amateur prostitution" (*shirōto ga baishun suru jidai*). What distinguished commercial sex in Japan, the editors wrote, was that the individuals involved were not "professionals," but rather housewives, high school and college students, and office ladies. Amateurs (*shirōto*), in a word. These women were entering the sex industry "of their own will," by which the editors meant for reasons other than poverty—the only frame through which many commentators, then as now, have been able to understand engagement in sex work.[15] The special journal issue was a call to rethink basic assumptions around commercial sex in the face of this qualitative shift signaled by women's seemingly casual entry into sex work.

This same term *shirōto* was central to how the women in my study thought about themselves. In fact, it is a term that was so implicit to their self-identification that it typically only came up as an aside when they were commenting on the nature of the industry in the abstract. It was directly in line with their presentation of themselves as completely ordinary women, no different from their friends or acquaintances, who just happened to be engaging in sex work at the moment. Their usage of this term bears little relationship to the length of time a woman has been engaged in sex work or to whether it is her primary income-earning activity or not. Identifying as *shirōto* is a way for sex workers to deal with the moral conflicts of being involved in this work.

First, *shirōto* mitigates stigma by drawing boundaries between oneself and a stigmatized identity. *Shirōto* stands in contrast to *puro* (professional), which is a label that sex workers tend to disassociate themselves from. The women I met would have been taken aback if I had addressed them as professionals, which indicates the deeper degree of stigma of a woman who not only is doing what is understood to be shameful work but who has developed expertise in it. In fact, much of how the sex industry operates seems to underscore that women are *not* experts (or, for that matter, even employees). In an important sense, this self-descriptor reflects the casual labor structure of commercial sex and the reality that women who enter often have little or no knowledge about what to expect until they actually begin working, as there are few reliable means to acquire information beforehand. At most, businesses offer a short orientation and the majority of sex workers are essentially left to their own initiative in learning to engage with customers and in developing a facility with the affective and erotic elements of the work.[16] In our conversations, my interlocutors often emphasized to me how little they had known—about sex, the sex industry, or sex work—before they entered.[17] Any skills or technique they had acquired they had done so through trial and error, information-sharing with others, or their own research. Thus, it is not surprising that sex workers think of themselves as relying on their own intuition and wits to get by, and on their own sense of what feminized care entails, rather than seeing themselves as professionals.

Second, the language of *shirōto* underscores sex workers' limited temporal commitment to their work. Sex workers' attitude toward their work, that is, is typically characterized by a sense of temporariness. Even if, in reality, a woman has no plans for leaving the industry, she will typically speak about the work as if it were something that she might leave at any time. In this sense, the language of *shirōto* is also very much about feminine respectability. It is important to individual women that they can imagine themselves as getting out at any time and of not feeling anchored to the work.

Although *shirōto* is usually translated into English as "amateur," it diverges in important ways from, say, American cultural understandings of amateurism. In American usage, "amateur" refers, somewhat contradictorily, to both those with a passion—but little experience in or skill for—a subject and those who pursue a subject outside of professional institutional frameworks.[18] Although *shirōto* may similarly refer to someone without professional affiliation, training, knowledge, or experience, it can also designate individuals who are highly experienced or trained. The theater scholar Maki Isaka Morinaga has described how the theater practitioner Osanai Kaoru, upon launching the *shingeki* ("New Theater") genre in the early twentieth century, which was intended to mark a break from the "old" Kabuki theater, nevertheless recruited established kabuki actors who continued their craft on the side for his productions. Morinaga interprets Osanai's slogan, "We will turn professional actors into amateurs," as meaning that only outsiders to the genre who did not seek financial support from it could fully manifest the docility and artistic capability necessary for this theater.[19]

This cultural politics of someone with experience nevertheless being able to manifest the authenticity of an amateur forms another aspect of the multivalent term *shirōto*—and, as we will see in Chapter 4, an important aspect of sex workers' healing labor. Practically, *shirōto* qualities are desirable for how they produce economic value. The sex industry places a premium on youth, innocence, and a sense of "freshness" (*seiketsukan*). The commonplace assumption is that customers prefer a sex worker who may be fumbling and occasionally awkward or clumsy, and who appears to not have a lot of experience but seems to show genuine and sincere feelings. As Sayaka told me, "Customers want *shirōto*. They all prefer someone who seems more like a lover or girlfriend, not someone who's operating as if out of a manual. Someone who feels authentic."[20] She explained that *shirōto* could refer both to women who had recently begun working and women who already had a few years under their belt—those who, strictly speaking, were more *shirōto*-like (*shirōtoppoi*) than *shirōto*. The critical point was to not come off as a professional, which has the implication of a woman who is working mechanically, not authentically. Young women's ability to convey a sense of "freshness" means that they are typically able to earn well with relatively little effort. It is as a woman grows older that it becomes more important for her to cultivate the skill necessary to be successful at the work, as I will discuss in the next chapter. The work itself is shaped by notions that one is supposedly better at it if one does not really know what one is doing—or, more precisely, if one can *appear* to not know what one is doing.

Teshigawara Mamoru, the sixteen-year veteran of sex industry management introduced in the previous chapter, indicates the aesthetic associated with amateurism when he explains what customers at his escort businesses typically ask for: "When customers call to make an appointment, they usually ask, 'Do you have any amateurish women?' They say things like, 'Someone prim and proper,' or 'Someone with black [that is, undyed] hair,' or 'Someone inexperienced,' or, even, 'I don't like pro[fessional]s.' What they hope for most is to have sex with an unsophisticated beauty with little sex industry experience, with whom they can have an experience as close to 'love' as possible."[21] These features, which signal different aspects of normative feminine respectability, are associated in the clients' imagination with qualities belonging to someone whom they would not expect to be in the sex industry.

This emphasis on youth and inexperience is also reflected in the way that women in the sex industry are commonly spoken of. Among sex workers, management, customers, and even police officers and bureaucrats, women working in the sex industry are referred to as *onna no ko*. The term is a generic expression for "girls" when used to refer to female children and adolescents, but becomes a diminutive expression when applied to adult women, as *onna no ko* literally means "woman child." In the context of the sex industry, the term has a double valence. On the one hand, it connotes social immaturity and trivializes these women, signifying that they are not full, responsible, and contributing members of society; that they have not taken the expected route to female social adulthood—namely, marriage and motherhood. On the other hand, because youth—or its appearance—is a profitable selling point among sex workers, who often go to great lengths to appear younger than they are (especially when they are "past their prime"), the term is embraced and ubiquitously used. Ironically, women in the sex industry thus replicate a linguistic practice that implies that they are not fully mature actors. Youth is a selling point; maturity is not.

The question of who is an amateur becomes murkier when one considers individuals who engage in monetized "one-night stands" (*warikiri*) that they arrange via "encounter-type" (*deaikei*) websites or "encounter cafés" (*deai kafe, deai kissa*). The latter have been regulated by the police as a genre of sex industry business since January 2011, in order to prohibit minors from entering. Ogiue Chiki, who conducted interviews with 100 women who use these venues to find paying partners for sex, reports that around half had either previously worked in the sex industry or were currently working there.[22] *Deai* venues allow women to negotiate terms for themselves and are attractive to sex workers who are not getting many customers at work. For example, Chie, the woman who had used the alibi company to rent an apartment, was frustrated with her recent glut of free time at work and wanted to seek out new opportunities. "If I can earn at a *deaikei* business, I'll do that, too. Anything that happens would be my own responsibility. But if I can make money there, I have no problem with it, even though it's not a [sex industry] business," she told me. Sayaka had offered to show Chie the ropes and I watched them get ready to go to a *deai kissa* as we spoke.

But there are also "ordinary" women at these venues who, as Shiori described, "cannot cross the line" to working in the sex industry, even if the transaction they are engaging in is also mediated by money and, typically, involves intercourse (which sex work legally does not). These include many single mothers and other women struggling to make ends meet.[23] Some of these individuals cannot get over the stigma of working in the sex industry and do not want that label. They do not want to be defined by what they are doing, or to even see it as work. The women who engage in this type of informal prostitution are also amateurs but with no institutional support whatsoever. Although they are able to negotiate all terms themselves and to refuse men, there is a significant risk and danger insofar as *deai* businesses take no responsibility for what happens off premises between those who use these venues to arrange assignations.[24] In February 2011, for example, I joined a sex worker advocate at the sentencing of a man convicted of murdering a woman he had met at a *deai kafe*. At the trial, he had confessed to murdering the woman after she (allegedly) threatened to accuse him of sexually assaulting her after he (allegedly) caught her stealing some money from his wallet.

When Chie commented that she would have to take all responsibility for anything that happened with a customer, she meant that any problems that followed from an assignation would be entirely her own issue to deal with. She would not be able to seek recourse with the business. In contrast, a woman working at a sex industry business receives the benefits of relatively greater safety and predictability (for example, standardized services and prices). These provide her with greater assurance over what she is doing and what she can expect as an outcome, but they also come with the label "sex industry woman" (*fūzokujō*).

A Willing Daughter

It is not just women's engagement in sex work itself but also *the implications* of this work that are stigmatized—as we saw with the media shaming of the Osaka public school teacher above. Given widespread beliefs that it is immoral for women to participate in this work, some women explain their presence in the sex industry by casting their accounts in terms of the base assumption that a woman's entry into it should always be unwilling. "Of course," Tomoko, a sex workers' rights advocate, told me, explaining to me what she knew about the treatment of sex workers during police raids on illegal businesses, "it's best if women themselves say to the police that they're victims. I've heard lots of people say that."[25] She explained how the manager of an illegal business whom she knew through her advocacy work had expressed this attitude in warning women working at his business about the contingency of a raid. She raised her voice, mimicking the lines the manager had suggested the women repeat in the event that the police showed up: "I didn't want to work in the sex industry, but I didn't have a choice. It's so horrible, I want to get out of here as quickly as possible." That was what he had told sex workers to say to the police, she told me, her voice returning back to its normal pitch. She continued to impersonate him:

> If the police come and try to arrest you, say it like that. You can't just tell people that you're working because you like it or because you voluntarily chose to do it. If you say that to the police, they'll look down on you and treat you like an accomplice.[26] Saying you're a victim is just easier for the other person to understand. If someone asks you why you're in the sex industry and you say, "I wanted to do it and decided to give it a try," no one will understand you. But if you say, "I didn't have a choice, I had to do it for the money, I had to do it to help my family," then people will feel for you and tell you they admire your strength.

Tomoko's commentary illuminates the parameters of what constitutes a socially acceptable account for a woman's participation in sex work. Through drawing on the anecdote of her manager acquaintance, Tomoko suggested that expressing anything short of poverty or selfless sacrifice would bring scorn and suspicion down on oneself.[27] Women in the sex industry cannot present their entry into sex work in terms of supporting or enriching themselves. Dominant discourses around sex in Japan maintain that women are supposed to feel *teikō* (resistance or an aversion) to commercial sex. *Teikō* here refers to an internalized moral sense that mediates one's actions. But many women do not feel this *teikō*. Even if they would prefer to do another kind of work, they do not mind sex work or find it a terrible occupation. To avoid the harsh glare of social judgment, however, they can perform *teikō* through framing their narratives in terms of unwilling participation and self-sacrifice.

The account given to me by one sex worker presents an especially striking example of this. Risa, a twenty-eight-year-old *sōpujō*, made an impression on me almost as soon as I met her when she declared—nonchalantly, as if it were nothing out of the ordinary—that she felt as if her parents had sold her into the sex industry. And not just into any sex industry, but Yoshiwara, the nation's oldest and most famous sex industry district. With a history spanning four centuries of operation, the word *Yoshiwara* is synonymous with commercial sex.[28] Moreover, when Risa referred to herself as having been sold, she used the historical term for sale into debt bondage (*miuri*; literally, "body selling") that recalls a history of women's obligations to the household economy, suggesting that she was not unlike those daughters from the Edo period (1603–1868) and later who had submitted to indentured prostitution for the sake of a cash advance that could ensure their impoverished family's economic survival.[29] Dumbstruck by Risa's casually uttered but explosive comment, I immediately asked her what she meant.

Over milkshakes at a family restaurant in Ikebukuro, northern Tokyo, Risa explained to another soapland worker and me how she had decided to enter the sex industry to support her sister Haruka. Risa's paternal grandfather had been a doctor. Although her father had tried to follow in his footsteps, he had been deeply ashamed by his failure to do so and had pressured Haruka instead. After Haruka failed the national medical exam for the second time, Risa decided to support her financially to enable Haruka to devote herself entirely to her studies. Risa herself had attended a well-known private university in Tokyo—a considerable distinction for a young woman from the rural northeast—but had only worked part-time jobs since graduating. At the time, she was employed as a hotel receptionist. "Everyone knows that the fastest way for a woman to earn money is at a soapland," Risa told us. In an exception to the rule of women being disinclined to tell their family about their work in the sex industry, Risa told her parents of her intention. If she was going to do it, she wanted their recognition. Her mother protested but accepted her daughter's resolve. Her father, although refusing to discuss the matter, did not forbid her.

"The work is so difficult and I've suffered a lot," Risa said. "But Haruka was finally able to pass her exams." Thanks to Risa's sacrifice, Haruka was now a physician at a hospital in nearby Ibaraki Prefecture. To my surprise, however, Risa denied being particularly close to Haruka, who was only remunerating her with a minimal stipend. They did not see one another very often, either. Moreover, instead of leaving the sex industry once her stated goal had been achieved, Risa was still working and had no plans to stop. In fact, she had switched workplaces twice recently in search of higher earnings, moving first to a soapland in Kawasaki and then to one in the northern suburbs of Tokyo.

Risa's account of her entry into sex work puzzled me for a long time. It seemed full of what appeared, at first, to be contradictions. Convinced that I had gotten some element wrong—Risa's ambivalence, her relationship with her sister, her parents' involvement—I asked Risa about her entry again the next time we met. She reiterated every element, neither embellishing nor leaving anything out. Risa characterized her entrance into the sex industry as an act of care for her sister and family, including herself within a valorized genealogy of filial daughters sacrificing themselves for the collective good. This stark articulation of her motive in terms of filial devotion and sacrifice seemed anachronistic and incommensurate with her middle-class background and private university education. Her friend and coworker, however, apparently having heard Risa's explanation several times before, nodded along without comment. On one level, the historical comparison was absurd. Risa's parents had not signed over her labor to a soapland in return for a cash advance and one less mouth to feed. On another level, however, Risa clearly found that this historical idiom evoked something of her own experience.

Several months later, I was still puzzling over Risa's Edo period-inspired account of filial sacrifice. Over lunch one day, I shared what I knew about Risa with Sayaka, a veteran sex worker with a vast information network inside the sex industry. I expected Sayaka to find Risa's story noteworthy as well. Instead, she listened without expression while eating and when I had finished gave a bored, "Oh?" With a bit of prodding, Sayaka told me that she had heard stories like this before. She found the story unexceptional and said that she knew many Risas.

Sayaka, however, cast doubt on what Risa's possible motivations could be. If Risa was like other women she had met, Sayaka told me, there was another layer to her narrative. Sayaka did not doubt that Risa loved her family and had wanted to help her sister. But she was skeptical whether supporting Haruka had been Risa's sole motivation. She questioned me: Risa had gone to a well-ranked university, right? And had only been working part-time jobs since graduation? Sayaka suspected that Risa, like many women she knew, did not have any particular work ambitions or aspirations. She had probably never been encouraged to think seriously about a career and just assumed that she would work for a bit before getting married and becoming a housewife. It was likely that she wanted to make enough money (more than she could as a part-time hotel receptionist) to live comfortably on her own, be able to purchase nice things occasionally, and travel. But, Sayaka continued, Risa was also eager to lend meaning to her labor. Although many women would not consider sex industry work, Risa obviously felt that she would not mind it; she did not feel *teikō* toward it. But she was also aware that she would be judged for this lack of aversion. Using her earnings from the work to support her family would make it meaningful to her. She would be doing work that would allow her to be financially self-sufficient but also participating fully in gendered expectations of familial care. Presenting self-sacrifice for her family as her primary motive, Sayaka concluded, would elicit admiration and respect, lending dignity to her work, as well as transform Risa's own subjective attitude toward and experience of her work.

As these overlapping anecdotes from Tomoko, Risa, and Sayaka illustrate, women who enter the sex industry have to carefully navigate their presentation of their motives. A mitigating factor, today, as in the past, is a woman's expression of self-sacrifice for the family. This aligns with widespread ideas about the centrality of care in defining moral femininity in Japan.[30] Presenting the motive for their labor as directed toward the family and not the self would, in other words, exonerate them in the court of public opinion and offer them the positive identity of being exemplary daughters, mothers, and siblings. As Tomoko's commentary suggests, this is not just a narrative that sex workers give to confidants but also the one they present in legal and juridical spaces.

To be clear, I am not claiming that sex workers opportunistically legitimate their work by saying they want to support their families while their "real" motive is to enrich themselves. Rather, my claim is that, as in any work, motive is complex and always already shaped by broader gendered and moral ideologies around the purposes of economic activity. According to Sayaka, Risa imagined her participation in sex work through the central model for feminine moral personhood—care—even as it also allowed her to support herself. It is worth asking, why are poverty and self-sacrifice acceptable reasons through which sex workers can articulate their motives, while simply wanting to lead a decent, comfortable, and self-sufficient life are not? Are women expected to express unwillingness toward economic independence? Women such as Risa both want to support themselves and endow meaning to their work through assisting their families. But these narratives also reveal a deep ambivalence about what it means to support yourself and to have more than you need in a context of women's labor market exclusion—and to do so by breaking norms of acceptable female behavior. Women in the sex industry reinscribe themselves into norms of feminine respectability by foregrounding their contributions to their family, even if these are true alongside other motives. At the same time, the rhetoric of reluctant acceptance for the sake of the family obscures the reality that there are sex workers like Risa who are middle-class and college-educated who find the financial opportunity and flexibility of this industry more appealing than other forms of feminized labor. These women, I propose, express the ambivalence of their desires for economic self-sufficiency through narrating the dependence of others on them.

Transitioning Out (or Not)

Women's fortunes typically shift downward over their time in the sex industry. In an industry that places a premium on youth, "freshness," and the appearance of inexperience, this trend is inevitable. Although for some women it will be a gradual shift, for others it happens more rapidly. A *nanbā wan* ("Number One"; the woman designated as the highest-earning employee at a business) will see her earnings decrease as she ages, and women who once always earned a decent living might only scrape by a few years later. This downward trend can involve movement across or within genres of the sex industry, from high-end to low-end businesses and from less to more stigmatized forms of work. With this inevitability in mind, women in the sex industry themselves express limits on how long it is appropriate to stay in this work. From the perspective of those doing it, sex work is configured as work that is meant to be short-term. In this last section, I examine a cautionary tale that expresses how sex workers perceive the risks of overstaying in this industry—of having it slip from temporary into long-term work. This allows us to see how ethical agency and self-care among sex workers are configured as the ability to not become reliant upon or complacent about the work.

One of the first things I learned about Shiori was how much pride she had in her work and in being recognized for her skill. The first time I met her, just outside Ebisu Station, in central Tokyo, Shiori told me that she had arranged for us to meet there because she wanted to show me something. We had walked about five minutes when she suddenly stopped and pointed: "Look over there. It's me." Not knowing what to expect, I was surprised when I saw a banner with a larger-than-life image of a slightly younger-looking Shiori. It was hanging from the storefront of an expensive *fasshon herusu* business with a long-established reputation for excellent service. Shiori had once been the "Number One" there and had been asked to, literally, put her face on the store. Even though she had moved on to another business four years ago, it was still her image that greeted customers and pedestrians. In contrast to how anti-prostitution advocates (in Japan and elsewhere) often speak about sex work as inherently debasing to the self, it was clear that the work had given Shiori a tremendous amount of self-confidence. Shiori would become one of my most enthusiastic interlocutors. She often told me about how much she enjoyed her work, especially when she was working as a dominatrix (*joōsama*). She was an autodidact who took pleasure in learning about the industry and talking to others in *kono gyōkai* ("this industry"), often remarking with a sense of wonder when we encountered a case of only one or two degrees of separation that "this industry really is small!"

A native Tokyoite, Shiori had graduated from a women's college with a degree in computer graphics. She had worked briefly as a programmer but had been frustrated with the low salary. When she learned, at age twenty-two, that her boyfriend—several years her senior—was actually married, she experienced the subsequent feelings of betrayal as a life-changing event. Motivated by her anger, she decided to begin working at an *imekura* in order to "do to men what they did to me"—a vague assertion that I understood as referring to a deliberate flouting of the conventional sexual norms for women in favor of an assertive sexual freedom.[31] There was a material basis to her motivations as well. She had accumulated some credit card debt and knew that the sex industry would provide her with an efficient means of paying it back. It was Shiori who had harbored the image of sex industry businesses as "full of desperate women crying in a corner." After being cheated on, however, she didn't care anymore.

When Shiori and I first met, she had already been in the industry for over ten years. By the time she finally left for good, it would be twelve years. During that time, she had briefly returned to "ordinary" work a few times, but quickly found that she had become intolerant of the predictable and menial nature of female office work. Moreover, she had become accustomed to a degree of everyday extravagance afforded her by her sex industry earnings. "When you get used to going everywhere by taxi, it's hard to go back to commuting by train and subway," she told me. Still flush with the successes of her twenties, she found sex work more attractive than her alternatives.

Although it was not clear to me yet at the time, Shiori's decisions were a sign of her decreasing options now that she was in her early thirties. At thirty-three, she began commuting to a *fasshon herusu* in Ibaraki Prefecture. This is referred to colloquially within the industry as "migrant work" (*dekasegi*), underscoring how it is about seeking better opportunities elsewhere. In regional sex industry districts, a woman who is considered past her prime in the city can recoup some of what she is no longer able to earn there. A driver would pick Shiori up after midnight and take her to her workplace in the middle of the night. Shiori would travel in her pajamas with a duffel bag of belongings and doze in the car during the ninety-minute drive. She would work three days straight before returning, again ferried back to Tokyo in the dead of night, her wallet fattened with cash in the meantime. Shiori maintained her positive attitude and was usually full of light-hearted banter when she returned to the city. After one work trip, she joked about how a local farmer who was her customer had just brought her some radishes as a gift. Shiori found it charming but also helplessly provincial. But these working circumstances were a sign of her declining fortunes in the industry. In her twenties, she would never have considered leaving Tokyo to work in a regional sex industry. She often complained to me of the tedium of working three days straight and that her cell phone did not get reception at work—a tangible sign to her of her peripheralization.

Shiori finally quit the sex industry for good in early 2011 shortly before she got married.[32] Her fiancé was a North American man who had known for years about her work. In his eyes, it made his girlfriend even more alluring. But during their engagement, he encouraged her to leave the industry. Shiori had been thinking about "washing her feet" (*ashi o arau*) of sex work for some time. She hadn't been able to make up her mind but now she let her fiancé's concerns force her decision. Shiori decided she would quit shortly after the

New Year holiday, which is a profitable time for the sex industry. This is especially true in rural areas as urban residents often return to their familial homes at this time. Shiori anticipated ending her career on a spectacular note: her retirement and the holiday would bring all her regulars in. That first week of the year, her fiancé sent me a promotion her store had made for her: "Our super popular Hana-chan is graduating!! Jan 13–15 is your last chance!!"[33] When I saw Shiori and her fiancé in Tokyo on January 16, the day after her "graduation," they were both in high spirits. Shiori had made ¥800,000 in the few days she had worked since the start of the new year—a tremendous amount. On her last day of work, five customers had booked extended appointments that covered the whole day. It was the successful final day that she and her manager had hoped for.

After the exhilaration of her final days wore off, Shiori's new reality set in. She began a job as a clerk at a shipping warehouse. Before long, she began to speak wistfully about her old work. It wasn't just the adjustment to lower (but predictable) earnings—although there was that, too. She was not accustomed to working full time and ordinary hours. She complained that her three-hour round-trip commute ate up her free time. Moreover, the work was monotonous and she chafed at its low status, contrasting it unfavorably to the creative freedom she had had previously. Before two years had passed, Shiori had had enough and went to Thailand for several weeks to become certified as a massage therapist. A former roommate of hers—also a former sex worker—was opening a massage business and had invited Shiori to work for her. In fact, all of the employees at this business were former sex workers. Although it was not a sex industry business, it marketed itself as offering "sexy massage" and had a mostly male clientele, indicating the sex industry's often porous borders.

The next time I saw Shiori, in the fall of 2016, she had just had a baby. She had quit her friend's massage business and begun working as an office lady again. Her boss had been supportive of her pregnancy and had encouraged her to take advantage of the company's parental leave policy to take a full year off from work with partial pay. When I saw her, she was already talking excitedly about her plans for returning to work, still at least another half year away. Something had evidently changed from her older attitude toward "boring" office work. Moreover, she felt that it was important to set a good example for her daughter as a working mother. Shiori and her husband, who was also a contract-based worker, were making do but struggling for a degree of financial stability. Maybe Shiori was not as confident about her long-term prospects as she made out and felt insecure or self-conscious about her past decisions. I began to think this might be the case after reflecting on her stories about her ex-roommate and friend, Erina. Although Shiori and Erina were good friends and, until recently, had been coworkers in the sex industry, privately Shiori spoke about Erina as a cautionary tale. She clearly thought that Erina had made some bad decisions with her career; in Shiori's eyes, it was clear that Erina had overstayed her time in the industry.

Erina had grown up in a rural area of Tochigi Prefecture, about three hours north of Tokyo. Her parents divorced when she was young and had split their children up between them. Erina had ended up with her father who had largely neglected her, while her mother remarried and started another family. Without much of a home life, Erina had dropped out of high school and, even today, had trouble reading newspapers due to her inadequate knowledge of Chinese characters. Eager to leave home, Erina had moved to Tokyo at age twenty-two after working a few dead-end jobs around home. Without a high school diploma, Erina's prospects were not much better in Tokyo. Moreover, she had no savings and needed money immediately to cover her living expenses. Not unlike other young women who move to Tokyo without a preexisting support network—especially those not from privileged class backgrounds—Erina looked to the sex industry. Before long, she began working at a *fasshon herusu*.

Erina had done well her first few years. She was young, attractive, and popular and had made a lot of money even without working that much. Her mid-twenties were filled with shopping and travel and going out with her friends. She spent her earnings freely but also managed to save quite a bit. She and Shiori met and became friends at the well-known *fasshon herusu* featuring Shiori on the banner. As Shiori told it to me, however, around this time, Erina let her comfortable life go to her head. She "became lazy" and stopped coming in to work as often. The future was a topic she always waved off. A few years later, Shiori and Erina were again coworkers, this time at the *fasshon herusu* in Ibaraki. But Erina's employment at the Ibaraki *herusu* was abruptly cut short when the March 11, 2011, earthquake caused significant damage to the local infrastructure. Many of the businesses in the district closed for repairs. Temporarily out of work while her manager decided whether to invest in reconstruction, Erina found work at a soapland in Kawasaki, just outside Tokyo.

When a sex worker moves down the hierarchy of businesses in a stratified industry, the downward trend is typically irreversible. Shiori saw this happening to Erina. In Shiori's eyes, Erina was rapidly falling down the sex industry hierarchy, from where it would be nearly impossible to climb back up again. The soapland at which Erina had found work was a cheap business where she would not earn much. The rate for an hour of physically laborious service was only ¥8,000.[34] Soaplands are widely known to offer intercourse as a standard service and thus constitute a more stigmatized genre of sex work. Moreover, this soapland did not permit condom use. To compare, at the *fasshon herusu* in Ebisu where Erina and Shiori had once worked, clients paid ¥36,000 for a sixty-minute session involving oral sex and/or a hand job. On top of the decreased earnings, Shiori was concerned that Erina would soon have to start offering services that others were unwilling to do to stay afloat financially. Within the sex industry, the abbreviation NG ("no good") refers to services beyond the standard service "menu" that an individual sex worker has decided in advance that she will not offer. The management registers these preferences such that they can direct a customer desiring a specific service to a woman willing to provide it. As a sex worker ages, however, her limitations may become negotiable. Shiori was concerned that Erina would soon agree to services outside of her comfort zone in order to attract customers.

Alternatively, Shiori explained, Erina would have to begin "store hopping" as a financial strategy. Typically, when a sex industry business receives a new customer who does not know which sex worker to designate, the staff recommend either a popular worker with many repeat customers, whom they know will offer a satisfactory service, or a woman whom they have just taken on in order to help her build a customer base. But this goodwill only lasts so long. Once a woman has demonstrated that she cannot attract repeat business, the staff will only send her undesignated customers in the absence of other options. In Shiori's words, Erina was such a *yobigun*, a sort of "reserve" that the store could rely on as a last resort but who would never be their first choice. Women who were unsuccessful at attracting a regular clientele could store hop. If a woman switches workplaces frequently enough, she can make up for not having a base of regulars by surviving off of those customers the store sends her way. This is a precarious strategy, however, that is only available for so long—it is not effective in the long term.

Shiori was uncharacteristically harsh in speaking about her friend. According to her, it was clear by that point that Erina did not have a good attitude for the work and had not bothered to cultivate the skills necessary to do it well. Instead, Erina had been relying on her youth. But, Shiori pointed out, she was losing her good looks and had put on weight. Moreover, she now had credit card debt that needed to be paid off. Erina was not one of those who, as Shiori described it, pushed themselves hard to achieve a particular goal or who could make their way on their own. In contrast to this, Erina seemed to live as if she would be working in the sex industry forever. And Shiori seemed to think that might be the case. "She's not even any good at housekeeping!" she exclaimed with exasperation, suggesting that Erina would not even be able to marry her way out of the industry, obliquely referring to the reality that marriage is always an economic strategy available to single women in Japan. The implication was that Erina could only get out of the sex industry by outside intervention. At the time, Shiori was trying to set her friend up with an acquaintance also from Tochigi who was looking to marry. A few months later, when I asked Erina how she had gotten along with Shiori's acquaintance, she shook her head. It had not worked out.

Aside from Shiori's harsh judgment of her friend—which, I surmise, reflected her own insecurities, at least in part—tragically, Erina exemplified the decreasing opportunity of sex workers as they age. In 2013, Erina managed to pay off her debts and quit the sex industry. Unable to afford Tokyo rents any longer, she returned to Tochigi to live with her father and sought work at the local unemployment office. Her blank résumé, however, was a problem. It had been ten years since Erina had done "normal" work. With no explanation of what she had been doing in the intervening years or skills that she could freely talk about, she was not an attractive prospective employee. Unable to find anything beyond temporary work, she had returned to the sex industry after a few months. Shiori worriedly told me that Erina was not doing well. "All her friends in the sex industry are telling her to get out now and do something else, but she doesn't have the courage anymore," she said. Even though Erina was dreadfully unhappy, the anxieties she felt around leaving the relative stability of soapland work, despite its undesirability and unattractiveness, were too powerful. "She's never been the type of person to make her own path," Shiori diagnosed, and now she believed that Erina was unable to imagine another life for herself.

Erina's downward trajectory reflects how, after a certain point, some women working in the sex industry find it difficult to imagine themselves doing another form of work. These are women who wonder what else they can do besides sex work.[35] Shiori, too, had for a long time been unwilling to make the transition. Similar to Risa (according to Sayaka), neither of them had particular work aspirations, only ever hazy ideas of what else they might do. There are many sex workers who delay making plans outside of the industry. Eventually, this shuts out other options. The exclusions that women, especially, face in the labor market discourage them from thinking about themselves as laborers, precluding active strategizing and planning for the future. Undoubtedly, there is also a class element involved, although Risa herself came from a middle-class and private university background. As with other Japanese women, many sex workers put aside planning ahead under the assumption that they would get married soon, allowing that expectation to solve the question of their future finances. Marriage continues to figure in Japan as an idealized solution to the reality of low-paid women's work, even as many young women today delay marriage. Tomoko, the sex workers' rights advocate, pointed out to me that many of the sex workers she meets dream of becoming full-time housewives and assuming a place on the other side of the sexual economy that they are in. Of course, overstaying in the sex industry can also jeopardize one's marriageability.

Shiori's telling of Erina's story reflects the type of cautionary tale that sex workers circulate. It wasn't that Shiori felt sorry for Erina because she thought that sex work was debasing or shameful. Rather, her pity for Erina hinged on her increasingly limited options. Erina's trajectory was problematic to Shiori because it had no clear direction except down, and it threatened to damage her employment and marriage chances. Sex work, the consensus seemed to be, is good work so long as one does not become complacent about it. It is work that is meant to be temporary. One is not supposed to allow oneself to become bereft of all other options and unable to leave, as Erina seemingly had. In other words, this is about ethical agency: Erina's problem, in Shiori's eyes, was a lack of self-knowledge that had prevented her from taking proper care of herself and leaving the industry at an opportune moment. Erina was not successfully managing her way through this stigmatized work.

Within the sex industry, it is not uncommon to hear a woman spoken of—or for a woman to speak about herself—as "flowing into the sex industry" (fūzoku ni nagareru). The language of "falling"—or "dropping" or "sinking," as in the statement fūzokujō ga dondon ochite iku ("sex workers fall rapidly")—is also common. Both in its first- and third-person usages, this language frames entry into this industry in terms of passivity and, even, inevitability.[36] The use of the nonagentive intransitive form suggests that a woman has been swept up in forces beyond her control and landed in sex work. It contrasts to the use of the agentive transitive form (for example, *fūzoku ni hairu*, "to enter the sex industry"), which denotes action and intention.[37] I often heard this language invoked to signal a form of self-evident transition: for instance, a *kyabakura* hostess told me that more than a few of her peers who had aged out of the hostessing scene had "flowed" into the sex industry, transitioning as if by natural force from a slightly morally compromising industry to an illicit one. Similarly, I often heard gossip about former peers who had "flowed" downstream into a less desirable rung of the sex industry.[38]

It is interesting that this nonagentive language is used to describe women entering a stigmatized but highly lucrative industry. That women's agency in entering the sex industry is downplayed makes sense when we consider that the wages are attractive but that it is also work that is not considered respectable. There is a parallel here to how Risa described herself in the passive sense of "being sold" by her parents, indicating that it was not her choice but that she only allowed it to happen—even as self-sacrifice could also be viewed as a manifestation of the ultimate agency. And indeed, in written narratives, women in the sex industry often matter-of-factly state that they "flowed" into the sex industry, without explaining the course of events that led up to this. Through such language, women can avoid taking personal responsibility for their presence in the sex industry.[39] Moreover, the language resonates in a second sense as well: it indicates the path a woman in the sex industry *is not supposed to take*. Erina could easily have been spoken of in this language (and perhaps she was). It then refers to the unhappy reality that many women who enter the sex industry for its economic opportunity seem unable to extricate themselves from it happily. Erina's misstep, in other words, was having let herself float along in the current until she had gone too far downstream to safely evacuate. Concerningly, this nonagentive intransitive language becomes a way of endowing labor market realities with a sense of inevitability or even futility.

"Flowing" captures the sense of passivity through which women's participation in commercial sex is often imagined and articulated. Using a very different metaphor, however, we can also usefully think about the seeming difficulty of Shiori, Erina, and others in extracting themselves from the sex industry in terms of what Kimberly Walters has called the "stickiness" of sex work.[40] As Walters demonstrates through focusing on the intersubstantial aspects of the practice of commercial sex foregrounded by Telugu-speaking sex workers in South India, sex workers understand themselves as being changed through their work. From this perspective, the pleasures associated with the work affect their inner dispositions and "transform them both in mind and in form," thereby tying women to the work.[41] Although Japan is not a context understood in terms of intersubstantial relations with persons and things, many sex workers are similarly changed by their access to the everyday conveniences and opportunities made possible by the work, which "simultaneously tie sex workers to the world of sex work while making other modes of work appear increasingly unappealing."[42] What Walters refers to as the "decency of the life that they can purchase" can make women in the sex industry complacent.[43]

Conclusion

For women working in the sex industry, their very engagement in this work presents a moral problem—one which threatens the perception of them by others as "good" and "respectable" members of society, and which may haunt them long after they leave the work. Sex workers are always aware of the necessity of managing what others know—if anything—about their work. They are careful to create and maintain a separation between their "day and night faces," even as a sense of duplicity, being on one's guard, and feelings of isolation may wear heavily on them. Sex workers may feel great pride in their work and recognize its social value, but they must also take care to hide what they are doing. The temporal commitment of sex workers is limited, as they disassociate themselves from their work and imagine themselves as being able to quit at any time—regardless of the length of time an individual might ultimately spend in the sex industry.[44] The moral urgency of keeping sex work a temporary occupation is grounded both in labor market realities and in the conviction that one cannot end up in an industry that necessitates concealing aspects of oneself from family, friends, and acquaintances. And yet, for some women, like Shiori and Erina, their successes in sex work at the peak of their youth can make other employment seem unattractive until, eventually, they may lose confidence in pursuing other employment opportunities.

At stake in the conflicts faced by sex workers is the question not only of their own morality (as perceived by themselves as well as by others) but of the morality of women's economic self-sufficiency more generally—of whether, in other words, the types of autonomy and remuneration that women can enjoy through sex work are considered to be ethical. Regardless of how appealing women may find aspects of sex work, normative values of feminine respectability demand that their labor be narrated not in terms of their own needs, but in terms of sacrifices and contributions to their family. By using a language of unwillingness and reluctant acceptance, women working in Tokyo's sex industry deny that their participation in sex work could be a source of personal fulfillment or a sense of identity, or even of some productive good, and inscribe it within gendered and moral ideologies of whom and what women's labor should be for. Risa's account of feeling as if her parents had sold her into commercial sex reflects a deep ambivalence about wanting to support an independent and comfortable lifestyle, not feeling aversion to sex work, and awareness of the negative social valuation of women in the sex industry. In a national context in which the media generally vilifies young women as the cause of demographic problems—in particular, for supposedly rejecting marriage and childbearing—it does not seem far-fetched to assert that financially autonomous young women whose labor is not directed toward the household are perceived as threatening.

Ultimately, women in the sex industry see themselves as no different from other, "ordinary," women and identify themselves as *shirōto*. To refer to oneself as *shirōto* in the context of commercial sex is to underscore one's innocence, naiveté, and, above all, authenticity, and to deny one's skill and experience. Although this works to mitigate stigma, it also produces economic and social value and is understood as more effectively serving the needs of the customer. Sex workers' self-presentation as *shirōto* is key to the reparative, feminized care that they offer to their customers and articulate as *iyashi* (healing). This healing labor is a central illustration of the contradictions that define female sex work in Japan and manifests the simultaneous importance and marginality of the women who labor in the sex industry.

4 Healing Customers

ONE EVENING IN LATE NOVEMBER 2011, a taxi driver taking the *sōpujō* Risa and me to a nearby train station in northeast-central Tokyo gave us his unsolicited opinion about the sex industry's existence. Risa and I had spent the evening touring the Yoshiwara sex industry district, and we struck up a conversation with the taxi driver, a sexagenarian native to the area. We had been talking about recent changes to the district's physical landscape when he suddenly seemed to want to make sure that I—his young, female, and visibly foreign customer—understood the significance of the sex industry's existence. "Japanese men," he told us, as Risa nodded along, "work so hard that they just don't have the time to spend on seducing a woman. It's easier to just pay a woman to be healed (*iyasareru*) by her instead of investing a lot of time and money in a relationship."

The taxi driver was conjuring up normative images of men laboring under an excessive work ethic. Whether he was speaking from personal experience or from his observations of the countless male customers who had climbed into his cab (perhaps heading toward or leaving Yoshiwara), he was suggesting that being a productive worker is incompatible with having romantic relationships. Male workers did not have the time for emotional investment, yet there was something they apparently needed to be successful: *iyashi* (healing) from sex workers.

A few weeks earlier, Shiori had offhandedly told me something similar about the men she encountered in her work: "Most customers are sincere and completely ordinary individuals. They put all their effort into their work and when the exhaustion and stress become too much, once in a while they go to the sex industry and refresh themselves. I've often had customers show up exhausted who left saying, 'Thank you so much. I'm really glad I came. Now I'm ready to face anything again.'" In our conversations, Shiori had often mentioned *iyashi*. Now, in referring to exhausted customers coming to the sex industry to "refresh themselves," she was suggesting—as the taxi driver had—that her customers came for a "healing" that replenished their productive capacities as laborers.

During my fieldwork, I became accustomed to such references to healing in the sex industry. The sex workers I spent time with foregrounded healing—whether as *iyashi* (healing) or *iyasu/iyasareru* (to heal / to be healed)—as the central service of their industry. But healing *from* what? And *for* what?

In this chapter, I explore how sex workers themselves understand the services that they offer to their customers. Women working in the contemporary Japanese sex industry value their care—or *iyashi*—for what they see as its contributions to the well-being and productivity of male white-collar workers. I call this *healing labor*, for how sex workers view the reparative aspects of their care as necessary for the successful functioning of the male-gendered economy. This healing labor is a form of women's reproductive labor and a central illustration of the contradictions of Japanese sex work. Through revealing how sex workers view their encounters with customers as socially and economically essential at the same time that the value of their labor rests on its marginalization—that is, on its concealment within performances of naturalized femininity—healing labor helps us to see how the gendering of the economy is constantly reconstituted.

Scholars of sex work have shown how the precise forms of care, concern, attraction, romance, or love that sex workers may perform for customers emanate from particular political-economic moments.[1] As Elizabeth Bernstein has argued, "bounded authenticity" may best capture the nature of postindustrial commercial sex, wherein sex workers offer their customers "authentic emotional and physical connection" but maintain boundaries so as to keep this intimacy firmly in the marketplace.[2] The emotional labor of sex workers, Bernstein suggests, lies in producing intimacy that customers experience not only as authentic but also as equal—or even preferable—to that found in "private" relationships.[3] Women in the Japanese sex industry likewise implicate aspects of their "real" selves in their work, in ways that make the work personally meaningful and endow it with a sense of value and distinction. Similarly, there is something specific about the postbubble economy in Japan that has paved the way for the emergence of healing labor. This healing is a response to what sex workers assume to be the needs of male workers at a moment of ongoing, widespread concern about Japan's economic health and the structure of male labor. Intimacy in the Japanese sex industry relies on both normative, middle-class family tropes of nurturing and on relations that are only possible outside of households and domestic units. This is particularly apparent in how *iyashi* commingles maternal care with sexual gratification and the sensation of "being a man." The touch, attentiveness, intuition, indulgence, and maternally inflected erotic care of *iyashi* produce feelings in customers that sex workers understand as allowing them to relax and, ultimately, to work again, renewing and enabling their productivity. This healing labor reinscribes gendered hierarchies of the value of labor—ideas of whose work really counts—thereby demonstrating how intimate encounters in the sex industry cannot be separated from the gendered nature of conceptions of "the economy."

The Emergence of *Iyashi* Discourse

To consider what forces are supposedly exhausting Japanese men, I return now to what the taxi driver and sex worker from the introduction collectively asserted: that men are excessively productive workers who periodically go to the sex industry to "refresh" themselves. Both speakers were referring to the dominant gender ideal of postwar masculinity: the "salaryman," a middle-class white-collar corporate or government worker.[4] Credited with producing the postwar economic "miracle," this figure—whose hegemonic place in the national imagination stands in contrast to the reality that "in practice, they were never as ubiquitous as the symbol suggested"[5]—has long been defined by excessive work and devotion to his employer, an entity whose corporate paternalism deeply remaps the lines between public and private, work and play, in employees' lives.[6]

Recent political-economic and social precarity has recast this gender ideal as a source of tremendous social anxiety. Since Japan's asset bubble burst in 1990, the national economy has suffered more than two decades of slow growth punctuated by periodic recessions. Neoliberal reforms implemented by Prime Minister Koizumi Jun'ichirō in the mid-2000s and large-scale economic restructuring have refashioned the dominant postwar employment system, whose hallmark had been (male) lifetime employment and seniority-based wages.[7] Workers of all statuses now experience more instability and risk. To lower costs, companies have slashed full-time entry level positions for university graduates. Nonelite young men who previously had been guaranteed stable employment upon graduating high school now face the emergence of multiple tracks within companies and the rise of temporary work.[8] Similarly, job security is no longer assured for middle-aged and older male employees, and although seniority remains important in determining promotion and compensation, performance factors have become more significant.[9] Most striking, however, has been the rise of nonregular (meaning part-time or temporary) employment as a permanent sector of the male labor market: about 20 percent of male workers are now nonregular.[10] The rise of male economic precarity has prompted national political and media attention to growing inequality and male poverty, including anxieties about the end of the "mass middle class."[11]

The postwar male breadwinner ideology has eroded hand in hand with decreasing rates of marriage and childbirth among the younger generations, calling into question the nuclear family's continued dominance.[12] The unpaid reproductive labor of the housewife, in particular, which has long subsidized male labor, is no longer available for many men in their twenties and thirties, as women delay—or put aside entirely—marriage and childbirth. This altered picture of male economic stability has led to simmering anxieties about Japan becoming a "sexless" society, as media commentators view men who are not competitive economically as losing out in the marriage market as well.[13] These men are widely expected (by those in the media and elsewhere) to seek sexual partners in the sex industry instead.

Since the late 1990s, salarymen have become the cultural representatives of both depression and suicide in the popular imagination as depression has become a more culturally salient category and diagnoses of it have skyrocketed.[14] It turns out that salarymen's "self-sacrificing devotion, discipline, and sense of responsibility," vaunted as their normative values, have made them not just ideal workers but also the most likely candidates for excessive fatigue, alienation, and workplace-induced stress.[15] This is especially so as the strains of a long-term economic recession have reconfigured which workers are valuable assets.

Against this backdrop of economic and social dislocation, a generalized and multivalent discourse has emerged around the concept of *iyashi*. *Iyashi* first became a focus of popular attention in the mid-1990s, amid a growing adoption of psychiatric categories of mental illness and increased concern with forms of "existential alienation, loneliness, and loss of meaning" in the face of both national affluence and economic restructuring.[16] Its prominence as a discourse only increased in the 2000s, as Japanese commentators coined the term *muen shakai* (a society without connections) to characterize the moment of insecurity and alienation that captured the nation.[17] The term recalls "the multiple forms of nightmarish dispossession and injury that our age entails," as Andrea Muehlebach notes in summing up recent ethnographic attention to precarity.[18]

The continued discursive salience of *iyashi* in postbubble Japan reveals a widespread sense of incompleteness, stress, and trauma that existing social relations have left unaddressed. Alongside these influences, *iyashi* also refers to the need for relief from the unhealthy or antisocial buildup of exhaustion, tension, or negative feelings. More concretely, *iyashi* (along with related terms) has been used as an umbrella term for a diverse set of activities and services aimed at helping those affected by the March 11, 2011, earthquake, tsunami, and nuclear disaster to overcome tragedy and trauma, especially through methods that physically or mentally displace people from their everyday circumstances. The use of *iyashi* by counselors and therapists coexists with statements by figures such as the president of the Japanese Olympic Committee, who announced in 2012 that securing the 2020 Olympic bid for Tokyo would "heal" the nation.[19] The writer Ono Ikkō has documented how, in the postdisaster areas of northeastern Japan, the healing labors of sex workers were in great demand among those who had lost family members, their home, and/ or their source of livelihood—sometimes all three. Chako, a *deriherujō* in her late twenties, described the changes that had come over her customers in devastated Ishinomaki: "My customers have become gentler since the disaster. Before, most of them would be burning with desire, but now everyone is so gentle it's as if they have no energy. I also get the feeling that in these terrible circumstances, for many of my customers, meeting me is probably the only enjoyable time they have."[20]

Iyashi, then, is less about healing in a medical sense and more about "something that is soothing, is comfortable, or brings one heavenly feelings," thus spanning a broad range of mental, emotional, and psychological meanings.[21] Perhaps unsurprisingly, a consumer market quickly developed around proliferating discourses of *iyashi*. Today, it has an expansive use as a marketing term and all manner of products and services are advertised as "healing type," including vacations, music, aromatherapy packages, yoga courses, food, and collections of puppy or kitten photographs.[22] Even personalities—such as those of actors or musicians—can be signified in this way. The market for *iyashi* falls along gendered lines, with products and services aimed at women centering on health and beauty, while for male consumers *iyashi* typically implies sexual services.[23]

In the sex industry, this generalized discourse around *iyashi* is modified in deeply gendered ways. Here, *iyashi* figures as a pivotal discourse in relation to which sex workers conceive of and articulate both the nature of the intimacy they provide and its importance.[24] Although there are historical continuities running through the affective, emotional, and intimate dimensions of sex work and other forms of commodified erotic intimacy in Japan, *iyashi* is peculiar to the postbubble economy sex industry. For instance, the elite hostesses whom Anne Allison worked with in Tokyo during the bubble economy did not use *iyashi* as an operative term and Allison did not mention it in her ethnography.[25] Rather, it is under conditions of increased concern with an imperiled masculinity that *iyashi* has become a key term within the sex industry.[26] The sex workers I spoke with echoed one another in commenting that although sexual gratification was ostensibly what was on offer in the sex industry, *iyashi*—the "natural" product of the encounter between female sex worker and male customer—was what they understood as the central service.[27]

Producing *Iyashi*

In September 2011, I participated in a training session for new employees of a sexual massage (*kaishun massāji*) business at the invitation of Mika, the session's instructor.[28] For me, this was an occasion to observe sex workers articulating and reflecting on the technique and meaning of their work in a non–sex work environment. At the time of the training session, Mika was twenty-eight and had already worked in the sex industry for twelve years, having furtively (and illegally) started during high school. Since then, Mika has worked in almost every sector of the sex industry and been the "Number One" numerous times. Being ambitious as well as entrepreneurial, Mika had started a successful side career as a sex industry instructor and consultant three years earlier. Businesses interested in increasing their clientele and reputation hire her to train employees in everything from technique to conversational skills to creating an appropriate ambiance for customers. These sessions are also available for purchase on DVD.

Mika is friendly and outgoing, with a charm capturing one of the qualities most highly valued among unmarried women in the Japanese sex/gender system: being *akarui*, or bright and cheerful with a consistently positive outlook. She also manifests the highly developed interpersonal skills that seem to be shared, without fail, by successful sex workers: conversational dexterity, a memory for small details, and a seemingly effortless ability to personalize relationships. Speaking with Mika, one feels what Sayaka summarized as the essence of what all customers yearn for: "the sense that the other person really understands you and that your individual existence matters to them." As in other healing contexts, these healers perceive things that others cannot—or, at least, do not.

When I exited the ticket gate at Gotanda Station, central Tokyo, early in the afternoon on the designated day, Mika was there waiting for me, smiling broadly. A few minutes later, the training session's live model showed up: a man in his late twenties named Mr. Mori, dressed casually in jeans and a T-shirt.[29] Although he did not volunteer any personal information, Mr. Mori's availability in the middle of the afternoon suggested that he, like many of his generation, was a nonregular worker.[30] He had participated in Mika's demonstrations several times before as a way to earn extra income. The three of us left the station on foot. In keeping with the general proximity of sex industry businesses to central commuter hubs and entertainment districts, our destination was only a two-minute walk from the station. Twenty meters down a side street off the main avenue, we turned into the entrance of a multistory building housing several sex industry businesses.

The training session took place in a former Internet café being converted into the office of an escort sexual massage business. There, eight spectators, including myself, sat on the floor around a massage bed in the center of the room. As Mika changed into a "sexy nurse" tunic with hearts on the sleeves and bust—visually exemplifying gendered care—a staff member distributed clipboards, notepaper, and pencils for us to take notes with. Over the next two hours, Mika and Mr. Mori demonstrated to us an ideal encounter between sex worker and customer. The spectators watched closely throughout the session, nodding attentively as Mika spoke and, in some cases, taking detailed notes. One woman sat at the edge of the massage bed to observe Mika's movements at close proximity. Two others captured her routine in pencil sketches, taking assiduous note of the order and pacing, stroke movement, the ideal amount of pressure, and Mika's suggestions for conversational points.

What can be described as making a customer "feel like a man" was made manifest through the collapsing of the roles of child and lover in the customer. Mika narrated as she performed on Mr. Mori, often pausing to comment on her actions. She explained to us that the reigning metaphor for the encounter between sex worker and customer should be a maternal one. Assuming a maternal stance allowed sex workers to create the circumstances in which a customer could momentarily suspend his responsibilities and obligations, replacing them with a desire to be indulged and to act selfishly. For example, Mika told us that women should speak to their customers as mothers to their children. If men were going to the sex industry to seek *iyashi* from work and responsibilities, then doing things "like a mother" (*okāsan no yō ni*) was the ideal position from which to praise them and acknowledge their efforts. Similarly, when Mika demonstrated how to carefully dry a man off following the shower that preceded the massage, she suddenly enveloped Mr. Mori's head in the towel and vigorously rubbed his cheeks, mimicking a familiar childhood gesture. In a high-pitched voice she exclaimed, "That felt good, didn't it!" This explicit infantilization served to highlight that these white-collar salarymen could allow themselves to be passively guided by the sex worker.

In articulating this interpersonal dynamic, Mika was borrowing, in part, from highly influential Japanese psychoanalytic discourses. The formulation of a performance of a mother-child relationship expresses a model of social relations developed by the psychiatrist Doi Takeo in the early 1970s.[31] Doi's widely popularized theory holds that *amae*, or the desire to be passively dependent on a benign caregiver, governs all Japanese social relations, including those between mothers and children, wives and husbands, and companies and their employees.[32] Thus, when Mika told us that the customer desired to play *amaechan* (spoiled child), she was drawing on the expectation that (male) selfish behavior would be indulged by an unconditionally nurturing and warm caregiver, and that this indulgence would endow the customer with a deep sense of psychological well-being and security.[33]

Framing the sex worker's care as maternal also allowed Mika to foreground the customer's laboring status, enabling the man to recognize himself as a white-collar worker through the sex worker's expression of intimate concern. This was evident during various subtle physical and verbal references. For example, later during the massage, as Mika was rubbing Mr. Mori's shoulders, she told us to express concern, saying, "Your shoulders are too stiff. You're working too hard again, aren't you!" It was not expected that the customer would respond to this with anything other than perhaps a grunt. In making such a comment, Mika acknowledged both the man's efforts as a productive and capable worker and the importance of this work in her resigned reference to the habitual state of the man's exhaustion—he was working too hard *again*. His hard work was corporeally manifest to her in his tight shoulders and his weary body, in his passivity and desire to simply let himself be taken care of.

At different points in the session, Mika also deployed the intimacy of a girlfriend. Mika advised her audience to begin the massage by "showing love to the customer's back" (*senaka ni ai o miseru*). As Mr. Mori lay prostrate on the bed, she lay on top of him and rubbed her hands, breasts, and legs all over his body, periodically entwining her legs with his and resting her head on the center of his back. These actions, Mika explained, would produce a sense of well-being and calm. From time to time, she would nuzzle his ears with the tip of her nose and lips and make kissing noises, which she described as "drawing forth a lovey-dovey feeling" (*raburabukan o hikidasu*).

Although Mika highlighted the importance of maternal intimacy in producing *iyashi*, the forms of eroticized flirtation, arousal, and indulgence that constitute this "healing" depart in many ways from the types of intimate and personal relations linked to households and domestic units, such as mother-child or even wife-husband relations. The difference here is that the relationship between sex worker and customer is *not* a durable one saddled with implicit obligations and future expectations. The exchange of money frees the customer of these obligations. Instead, these are relatively anonymous relationships that are made to appear highly personalized. Rather than another mother or wife, what customers desire is someone skilled at making them "feel like a man," including carrying the service through to (male) orgasm.

Following the initial warm-up, the greater part of the massage focused on the man's prostate, perineum, testes, and penis. Mika explained how each of these was the site of important acupuncture points. Properly activated, these would rejuvenate the customer's vitality, making him feel young again—"healing" in this sexual massage had a literally reparative aspect.[34] After an hour, the massage concluded with Mika providing Mr. Mori a hand job as she leaned forward into his chest and purred into his ears. The customer's orgasm, however, should not mark the close of the service, Mika cautioned sternly, saying that the customer would feel an acute sense of loneliness if the woman moved away immediately following an intense physical and emotional experience. They should stay together for a few moments and then the massage should properly end with the customer's head in the sex worker's lap as she rubbed his temples and shoulders and gently stretched him.

Mika had a twofold understanding of *iyashi* in relation to male laboring bodies. First, *iyashi* involves an acknowledgment of the efforts, burden, and hard work shouldered by the individual. She explained to us that to succeed, men must steel themselves, subordinating their needs and desires to put all their energy toward a larger goal. "Lots of individuals," Mika told us, "at their companies and in their families depend on them to do this, but no one ever thanks them. That's what being a man means, after all." Mika and the other sex workers I spoke with imagine *iyashi* as both an acknowledgment and a momentary suspension of customers' responsibilities and obligations. In other words, *iyashi* is understood, in part, as a form of deep psychological or mental relief.

Although Mika thought that this first understanding of *iyashi* was primary and the most important, a second conceptualization acknowledged a carnal aspect. Mika dramatically explained male sexuality as following a wavelike trajectory, wherein male workers are asked to "endure, endure, endure, and then phewww! They can release." Rather than explaining this aspect of male sexuality in biochemical terms, however, as she had earlier when discussing what happens in the brain during an orgasm, she reiterated her earlier description of pushing oneself for the sake of a larger goal. Her description of male orgasm, in fact, imagined it as an act of social reproduction necessary for the continued existence of the company, the family, and, even, society at large.

Postwar Japanese corporate settings have long relied on commodified erotic intimacy to motivate or reward male productivity (for example, through company-organized international sex tourism in the 1970s), but *iyashi* presents an important departure. As Anne Allison has illustrated, Japanese corporations during the 1980s bubble economy devoted significant time and money to male after-hours "play" in Tokyo's high-class hostess clubs as a way of reinforcing social attachments within and between companies. The hostesses' feminized and often highly sexualized conversations flattered male egos, catalyzing a corporate masculine bonding that produced committed workers for Japanese companies.[35] Crucially, in the recession and restructuring of the mid-2000s, corporations scaled back their funds for hostessing and sexual entertainment. Although the Ministry of Finance in 2013 adjusted its tax policy such that 50 percent of selected entertainment expenses would be tax-deductible for large companies, this has not included expenses for sexual services.[36] In this era of flexible spending, individual men must now take on their own commodified erotic intimacy without explicit company sanction or financial support. As companies have reconfigured which workers are essential, their workers have become responsible for their own healing, even as this is still understood as ultimately directed toward the company's benefit.

Attendant with the changing political economy of both corporate entertaining and labor relations, it is the *reparative* dimension of *iyashi* as manifest in the reenactment of a relationship of care and indulgence—and even infantilization—that is characteristic of the new era of social and economic precarity. At the same time, even without overt corporate financial sanctioning, patronizing the sex industry still figures within the realm of corporate leisure. Visits to sex industry businesses are still often a social event facilitated by relations between coworkers, often senior and junior colleagues. According to the women I spoke with, many of their customers have regularly scheduled visits, suggesting that using these businesses is less a leisure activity than part of a health maintenance regime. Furthermore, deal making still occurs around the parameters of a night of corporate entertaining, of which a visit to a sex industry business may still be one component. In Mika's description (echoed by other sex workers), the sex industry has now taken over the integral function of caring for exhausted workers.

Cultivating Attentive Empathy

The qualities that make sex workers' healing labor effective rest precisely on the downplaying of it as labor—that is, as work that is productive of capital. Generating affect in this context rests on establishing intimacy. This, in turn, rests on the assumption that sex workers' performance emerges not from the pursuit of wages but from a basic kindness that is naturalized as female. Through their reiterative performances of normative femininity, especially maternal intimacy, women in the Japanese sex industry naturalize *iyashi* as deriving from the very "essence" of being a woman.[37] As with other forms of affective labor and care work, however, the supposedly effortless femininity seen to produce *iyashi* is grounded in deliberate and often exhausting labor. In this section, I look at the work that women do behind the scenes in order to cultivate their skill.

Despite claims by Japanese commentators (on Internet discussion boards and elsewhere) that sex work is "easy for women," most of the women I spoke with vehemently rejected the idea that "anyone" can do it. Such misconceptions infuriated Aimi, the single mother who had worked in the industry until her late thirties whom we met in Chapter 2. Seated in a crowded Starbucks with the next patrons only half a meter away, she exclaimed angrily, indifferent to her surroundings, "I think every woman should really have to do an interview [at a sex industry business] once in their life. That way they'd understand that you could be the cutest girl in the world and still fail your interview!" Like Aimi, other sex workers bristle at people who fail to appreciate the skill and effort their work demands, and who instead attribute a sex worker's success to factors such as personal attractiveness. Mika impatiently brushed such stereotypes aside with uncharacteristic brusqueness: "Any woman can just spread her legs and say, 'Come on!' but that's not what we're selling in the sex industry." That this is not what is expected of sex workers is further reflected in the disparaging sex industry term *maguro onna*—literally, a "tuna woman." The term evokes the heavy immobility of a dead tuna to refer to women who are passive in sex. Moreover, the number of women in the industry who "cannot sell" (*urenai*) also suggests that there is much more to the interaction than the passive receipt of the customer's actions. Women without technique, empathy, or interpersonal skills, my interlocutors told me, cannot attract a regular clientele, and those who do not think beyond their own needs cannot offer *iyashi*.

Successful sex workers, I was unanimously told, are those who are—through effort and cultivation—able to embody customers' desires. This requires significant self-awareness and dedication, work that is accomplished individually through the woman's own initiative. In fact, the sexual massage training session that I attended was something of a novelty. Across the industry, substantive training for new employees rarely extends beyond a short orientation and a brief run-through of the standard service "menu" with a staff member. Women working in the sex industry are, in other words, left almost entirely to their own devices in cultivating erotic technique, interpersonal skills, and industry savvy, and in finding legal and sexual health information. Job training is thus incumbent on women's individual initiative and takes numerous forms. Mika, for instance, uses her free time to immerse herself in music, movies, and manga comics popular among men. This gives her a repertoire that she can draw on to converse with customers and produce a sense of connectedness. More critically, she is always on the lookout for models that she can emulate in embodying an "ideal" feminine figure to her customers, and she scrutinizes women who, she is told, possess strong erotic energy.

Attentive care in the sex industry comprises the numerous "subtle and mundane acts of care" that make up care work generally[38]—for instance, warming up the shower beforehand, carefully deflecting shower spray from the nape of the customer's neck, kneeling in front of the customer while taking off his shoes, and suggestively grazing a customer's knees with one's breasts while undoing his belt. Sex workers' care also involves a deeper approach to attentiveness itself, which is a central component of hospitality and sociality in Japan generally and a key aspect of intimate labor elsewhere.[39] Attentiveness is especially associated with service work, in which workers are expected to think on behalf of the customer, anticipating, for example, when customers will want their sheets turned down, ice or alcohol added to their drink, or a lighter for a cigarette. When prompted, Mika easily rattled off five different forms of attentive empathy that she employs in her work. Drawing on overlapping (and perhaps at times conflicting) notions of the body, its feelings, and its capacities, they included *mekubari, kikubari, kokorokubari, kizukai,* and *kokorozukai.* Although the first three compound words can cumulatively be glossed as variants of "to be considerate" or "to take care of," the first parts of the compounds refer to the *kubari* (distribution) of senses originating in different parts of the body: *me* (eye), *ki* (vital energy in the body), and *kokoro* ("heart-mind," understood as being "the locus of feelings, consciousness, and authenticity").[40] Similarly, *kizukai* and *kokorozukai* refer to an earnest concern or solicitude mobilized through the use of one's *ki* or *kokoro.* For sex workers like Mika, these embodied forms of attentiveness are understood as assisting them in knowing how to care for customers.

When producing *iyashi,* sex workers do not rely on attentiveness alone. Equally important is a form of cultivated deep association or empathy that recalls Viviana Zelizer's definition of intimacy as interactions that depend on "knowledge and attention that are not widely available to third parties."[41] Shiori summed up this necessity with a piece of wisdom passed down to her by an *onēsan* ("older sister") at her first workplace: *Kiku jyanakute, kanjiru* ("Don't ask, feel"). The exhortation to "feel" expresses the need to build a deep association with each customer that is both intuited and based on experience. In doing this, sex workers construct male workers as individual selves who need to be—and can be—intimately understood. This contrasts considerably with how workers are treated in the male-gendered corporate or bureau-cratic workplace, where their needs are wholly subsumed under those of the company.

A story about another Number One told to me by Sayaka illustrates this.[42] The highest-earning woman at a store where she had previously worked was much older than the other employees. Although she was not stylish or attrac-tive and had never appeared in any of the business's advertising, she always put in more effort than anyone else, Sayaka said.

> She would write notes about each customer so she could remember details, like what they had spoken about. She would bring new socks as presents to her bachelor customers and would always remember birthdays. When she was with a customer, you could hear her moaning from across the store. Because she put in more effort than anyone else, the customers took a liking to her and would become her regulars. I always thought it was strange that she did so well since she was a single mother and could only work in the early afternoon [an unpopular time]. When I think about it now, though, I see that it's *because* she had had various life experiences—like raising a child—that she really un-derstood what hardship was and what it meant to do this work well.

Sayaka's statement that the woman "understood what hardship was" suggests that this older employee had a heightened capacity to genuinely empathize with others and to offer them understanding and acknowledgment. This ca-pacity, coupled with the woman's ability to personalize each encounter, gener-ated an attentive empathy that set her apart from her peers as an exemplary sex worker.

For the former *herusujō* Eiko, in contrast, this attentive empathy mani-fested as self-effacement. In order to focus only on the needs of the customer, Eiko imagined herself as a type of blank slate:

> Whenever I was at work, I only thought of the customer. That was so that I wouldn't dash his dreams or hopes. There was no me. But that's sex industry work. . . . The work is about understanding the other person. When you adapt yourself to your companion it goes on and on forever, because you're doing what he wants. The sex industry is the ultimate customer service. When you undress and have sex it's a world of [the customer's] real feelings.[43]

Eiko's comments convey the notion that, through healing labor, a sex worker can momentarily glimpse an individual's "real feelings" while remaining tightly in control of her own emotions, implicitly suggesting that healing is a means of accessing what is imagined as the authentic and sincere inner self of another person.

Similarly, Saki, a soapland worker with a qualification in communication psychology, used her training to great effect: "[Since my training,] I don't find any customers unpleasant anymore. If a customer is irritable, I know that it's because something happened at work or in their private life. And I know that they want to get rid of their stress so I think of how I can heal them and direct myself toward that."[44] Saki led seminars for less experienced sex workers, in which she highlighted how the work is about becoming the type of person who looks for—and can find—another person's good points. Eager to improve her customer skills, she visited top restaurants and hotels in her free time in order to experience good customer service for herself and to understand her own expectations when she paid a particular amount.[45]

In contrast to the appearance of an intensely personalized service associated with mainstream sex industry businesses, the thirty-three-year-old sex worker Chie told me about how she had approached her work a few years earlier at a *chon no ma* in the Tobita Shinchi neighborhood of Osaka. *Chon no ma* constitute a sector of the illegal sex industry. Behind small shopfronts masquerading as bars or restaurants, sex workers (including foreigners) offer (illegal) penile-vaginal intercourse.[46] Chie summed up the abbreviated nature of the service she had offered: "It's a short-time service. When the man has finished [that is, ejaculated], he leaves. We fuck and then we're done. He showers and then it's, 'Okay, bye bye!' Once he comes [*haku*, meaning "to throw up or emit"], that's the end."

Chie described to me how she had depersonalized her customers during the three months she had worked at the *chon no ma*. Her goal had been to get as many men in and out as possible. "Every business is a bit different, but at my place every customer got forty minutes total. Twenty minutes were taken up by showering, so the play time was just another twenty minutes. I'd get ¥5000 for that. You might be thinking, 'Huh? That's not a lot of money . . .' but if you take eight customers, you make ¥40,000. It was tiring but I made good money."

Chie used colorful language to describe the mechanical rhythm with which she had taken her customers: *ponpon*, an onomatopoeic word equivalent to the English "bam, bam, bam," as in, "I took customers *ponpon* one after another to maximize my earnings." And *chokochoko* (moving continuously), which has a motorized sound to it, like a machine slowly puttering forward toward its goal. And *kaiten suru*, which refers to things that rotate, like sushi conveyor belts or a revolving door of men. Chie did not mention the physical or emotional labor involved, but foregrounded only her drive to achieve a particular financial goal every day. "I didn't see each customer as an individual. I just saw them as a body that needed to ejaculate and that I'd get ¥5000 if I [made that happen]. It was all about racking up customers. It was totally different from a business like a soapland, where you spend a long time with each customer and the service is really personalized and polite." Chie's blunt manner of speaking about the work came off as almost crass in contrast to the conversations I had with other women, who often spoke about sex in roundabout or delicate ways, such as only obliquely referring to body parts.

And yet, as Chie was relaying this to me matter-of-factly, she added that the customers would still thank her when they left, saying, "Thank you. I'm ready to work hard again tomorrow," sounding not unlike the customers described by Mika and others who were subject to much more extensive services and caring labors.[47] Even without the provision of an intensive attentive empathy, the expressions of gratitude by her customers indicate that the outcome of Chie's service was also reparative. Chie was also offering her customers a form of healing labor, albeit of a qualitatively different degree, adapted to the shorter and less expensive *chon no ma* services that are often associated with a more blue-collar clientele.

The relative lack of knowledge that most women who enter the sex industry have when they first begin working makes many insecure about whether they can do well in the industry if they are not normatively beautiful or feminine. Although they initially believe that such factors will determine their success, they gradually learn that, while not unimportant, they are outweighed by other factors. As Sayaka commented: "In general, most customers have pretty low specs [specifications]. It's not the cutest or the most beautiful woman that they want but someone ordinary who can make them feel good. Someone with whom they can relax. And they don't want to go through a lot of different women but will stick with someone they like."

In the previous chapter, I discussed how sex workers self-identify as *shirōto* ("amateurs") and the economic value that follows as customers place a premium on youth, naiveté, and a "sense of freshness." Here, we can see further the economic and social value of *shirōto* (and its multivalent nature) as women in the sex industry talk about the importance of authenticity in providing healing labor. Megumi, the former civil servant turned *deriherujō*, explained this necessity, echoing Sayaka's comments on beauty:

> It's not usually the most beautiful girl who becomes the Number One. I've been the Number One any number of times so I know that's true because there have always been women who were way more beautiful than me. It's enough to be just a little bit pretty. To get a customer to visit you for a second time, it's not your outward appearance that's most important. That's something I learned along the way. Good technique is important, too, but that's not enough [on its own] either. . . . Men have a lot of pride. They like women who are beautiful and they like women who are kind-hearted. But the one that they like the most is the one who seems to really like *them*. It's the girl that makes them think, "Actually . . . could it be that she genuinely likes me?"—that's the girl that they open themselves up to.

As Megumi imagined it, her customers desired the sense that the woman who was with them would like them outside of the transactional space as well, and that there was a sincere sentiment in her attitude toward them.

As the discourse of *iyashi* suggests, in this context to appear genuine or authentic means to perform that you have no skill.[48] It is women's ability to appear as if they do not know what they are doing that is valuable. A sex worker's success rests in appealing to the customer on the basis of her girlish or young womanly charm (*onna no ko rashisa o apīru suru*). This does not necessitate beauty or sophisticated technique so much as the ability to create an atmosphere in which the sex worker's performance of normative femininity allows the customer to relax completely. As sex workers imagine it, they see the customer as ultimately craving recognition as someone hard-working, desirable, and fun to be around, and searching for the sense that the woman would like them even outside of the space of the transaction. Every action is carefully composed so as to underscore normative ideals of femininity, especially maternal care. Sex workers' skill is naturalized within these performances—in other words, these performances convey the notion that sex workers are good at the work *because* they are women. A sex worker who appears clumsy can be attractive if she creates the right impression of cheerful inexperience mixed with sincere effort.

As with other forms of emotional, intimate, caring, and affective labor, what makes *iyashi* effective is the appearance that it derives from authentic feeling rather than calculated and deliberate labor—from what Kathi Weeks calls "spontaneous eruption rather than cultivated display."[49] Women in the sex industry cannot present themselves as skilled experts who deliberately and self-consciously cultivate their proficiency in producing *iyashi*. Rather, to be valued, the work that goes into producing *iyashi* must be concealed.

Sites of Sexual Intimacy

From their vantage point, sex workers theorized marital relations as quickly growing cold sexually. Erina, whom we met in Chapter 3, was one sex worker who offered a pessimistic assessment of conjugal intimacy. She observed that many of her customers, especially older men, came to the sex industry because their marriage had grown "sexless." Erina explained: "Men prefer young women. So when their wife ages they lose interest and their wife just becomes the mother. They don't necessarily get along well with their wife, so they're lonely. Their hearts are lonely." She continued, laying bare the parameters of the emotional involvement she offered: "I used to think that those men were cheating on their wives but I don't think that anymore. It's not like I'm in love with the guy—there's nothing romantic or emotional about it. I'm just cleaning up his needs." Erina's reference to the provision of sexual release as "cleaning up" (*katazukeru*) a man's "needs" suggests that sex work is, in part, a type of manual (and menial) maintenance work that is devoid of any further emotional involvement on sex workers' part, in spite of their performance of authentic intimacy. The even more functional term, *shori*— meaning, "to deal with" or "to dispose of"—is often used, too. These terms relegate sex work to the most instrumental function possible and suggest that, in spite of these same women's assessments of the significance of their healing labor, sex workers themselves draw clear boundaries in terms of their intimate connection with their customers.

From the perspective of many sex workers, marriage is a site that produces a particular kind of intimacy. This was a topic that often came up in my conversations with sex workers, as it did when I asked Sayaka what she wanted Americans to understand about commercial sex in Japan. After a few moments of silence, Sayaka began talking about normative ideas of the excessive work ethic of Japanese men, linking this to home and family relations:

> You know that Japanese men are under extreme amounts of pressure, right? Americans and Europeans get a month of summer vacation, but for Japa-

nese men, once you graduate from university, there's no more vacation. Only Saturdays and Sundays. You do overtime every day and always have to work your hardest. The longest break you get is at New Year's, or maybe for Obon [a three-day holiday in mid-August]. But even then, it's only three or four days. If you can take a week off, you're lucky. But Japanese men are also under pressure because, well . . . rather than being under pressure, it's more like they're not being healed (*iyasarete inai*), and that's because marital relations tend to grow cold quickly. Sexlessness is a huge problem in Japan. And couples don't say, "I love you" to one another. Lovers might say it, but once you get married, after a year or two, no one says it anymore. If you have a child, you stop being a man or a woman and become a father or mother. This is what all my customers have in common—they all say this. So they come to the sex industry. It's the only place where they can be healed by a woman. Their wife isn't a wife anymore, but a mother, and that's why I think the demand for the sex industry is so high. Although an American woman might get angry if her husband went to the sex industry, in this kind of society, a Japanese wife might wonder whether her husband is going to the sex industry, but doesn't care so long as she doesn't have to know about it.

Sayaka's account captured numerous ideas that I heard repeated throughout my fieldwork, which linked the structure of middle-class labor with marital relations centered on a couple's role as parents rather than as romantic or sexual partners.

Many of the women in the sex industry that I spoke with took it for granted that, following the birth of a couple's first child, both the husband and wife would begin to emphasize the wife's new identity as a mother. Rather than the new mother simply being too tired from taking care of her infant to have sex, my interlocutors commonly implied that with motherhood comes a fundamental shift in a woman's primary self-identity away from being an erotic or sexual subject. This results in a freezing, or a de-emphasis, of conjugal intimacy—to which some husbands respond by seeking intimacy elsewhere, such as in the sex industry.[50] Although some women qualified to me that they thought their generation might be more invested in new notions of conjugal romance,[51] others emphasized that motherhood itself desexualizes a woman.[52]

For example, based on sex workers' conversations with their customers, many seem to take it for granted that, as wives age, they do not want to have sex anymore.[53] Shiori recounted one such case to me over dinner one night, which involved a man in his forties whose wife refused to have sex with him. Based on the way her customer spoke about his wife, Shiori said that it was clear that "in his heart" he really loved her. But, she explained, he was suffering because of his wife's stubbornness. From how Shiori recounted the story, it was apparent that she thought the wife to be selfish. In an extension of the attentive empathy she offered customers in their encounters, Shiori appeared highly sympathetic with her customer, seemingly accepting his perspective without considering that of his wife.

More broadly, popular ideas of what constitutes adultery seem to see no conjugal betrayal in a husband's visits to sex workers so long as his responsibilities to his family are not compromised. Researchers Kaname Yukiko and Mizushima Nozomi, for instance, cite a survey from the now defunct Tokyo evening paper, *Naigai Taimuzu*, in which 79.5 percent of respondents stated that it was *not* infidelity to go to the sex industry.[54] Kaname and Mizushima also queried the 126 female sex workers they surveyed in their own research on whether going to the sex industry—or working there—was considered "cheating." Of their respondents, 79.4 percent did not think that it constituted an infidelity for a man to go to the sex industry even if he was in a relationship, and a slightly higher number—81.7 percent—did not think that working in the sex industry constituted "cheating."[55]

The difference in how infidelity and extramarital (or extrarelational) sex are understood seems to be based on the nature of the personal relationship itself. The assumption is that the exchange of money for sex establishes a distance between two people, which distinguishes it from infidelity.[56] As respondents noted in Kaname and Mizushima's survey, "If [the customer] develops feelings for one woman, that would be cheating," and, "It's okay if it's just a breather, but not if you go all the time."[57] Among the *Naigai Taimuzu* respondents, comments included, "You're paying money, so it's not cheating. If you're just going to fulfill your sexual desire, then you're not emotionally betraying your wife," and, "Things that you deal with using money are business transactions. Where there's a bill, there are no emotions."[58]

In line with these survey responses, when I spoke with my interlocutors about whether they thought that going to the sex industry was considered "cheating" (*uwaki*) or not, the consensus seemed to be that it was in a different category. This reflects a distinction often made between *uwaki* and *furin* ("adultery"). Although the former alludes to an acting out of what is regarded as a natural male desire, the latter assumes a gravity that can serve as the basis for divorce. As the scholar Tanabe Seiko notes, "If you come home, it's *uwaki*. But if you think hmm, tonight, I'm not coming home, it's *furin*."[59] Although *uwaki* is not necessarily seen as unproblematic, it does not have the weight attached to it that *furin* does. *Furin*, then, is a relationship that threatens a man's obligations to his wife and family, while *uwaki* is understood as being about sex and essentialized ideas about the nature of male desire.

Although attitudes are changing and generational differences are important as well, it still seems to largely be the case that men's sex industry visits are categorized differently than the types of emotional relationships marked by a longer-term attachment that might threaten home and family life. In a survey of three hundred men published in *Nikkei Woman*, a magazine for female professionals, approximately 40 percent of respondents reported having been to the sex industry.[60] Although most of the respondents (73.6 percent) denied ever having had sex with someone who was not their lover/partner, about 60 percent stated that they had no problem (in theory) with having an affair, including 20.9 percent who answered, "It's okay as long as you love your wife or partner."[61] One respondent commented that he often went to the sex industry with his colleagues from work: "When men go to the sex industry together, the feeling of solidarity between them strengthens. So I go both for the relationship between coworkers and for my own sexual desire."[62] This response clearly recalls the company men depicted in Anne Allison's ethnography of early 1980s corporate entertaining, who underscored the masculine bonding that this entertainment made possible.[63]

Conclusion

Women working in Tokyo's sex industry often speak with great pride about their work. For them, the stress and exhaustion of their customers is self-evident, just as it is understood that the labor these men do is important. Against the backdrop of pervasive anxieties around an imperiled white-collar masculinity, sex workers value the healing labor that they deploy to repair the capacity of these men to be productive. They invest considerable effort in making their intimate encounters emotionally authentic and in doing so implicate aspects of their "real" selves in the work. At the same time, as Gregory Mitchell reminds us, in contexts of limited labor opportunity, sex workers' "ability to navigate and perform in the complicated affective terrain of desiring subjects" often entails considerable stakes.[64] In shaping their intimacy and gendered performances around what they assume to be the needs of men who are facing new economic pressures and challenges, sex workers experience in an embodied way the larger shifts in the national political economy, as well as, more generally, the exclusion of women from the labor market.[65]

Discourses of *iyashi* in the Japanese sex industry demonstrate that ideas about who plays a productive role in the economy shape how sex workers imagine and engage their customers' desires. The centrality of male laboring identities and questions of who is a productive worker in a context that might otherwise seem disconnected from such considerations illustrates that intimate encounters in the sex industry are never divorced from the terms of a gendered economy. Feminized affective labor is deeply implicated in regimes of male precarity in postindustrial capitalism. At a moment of perceived socioeconomic decline, sex workers' performances of gender and intimacy emphasize a reparative, maternal care that understands middle-class, white-collar men as hard-working producers who labor to the limits of their physical and psychological capacities, and whose search for relief is met with the reenactment of a relationship of care and indulgence.

Feminist scholars have long been interested in rethinking categories of labor to account for the unacknowledged economic roles of women. By thinking through gendered discourses of productivity that reflect hierarchies of the value of labor, we can see how it is that women may centrally assess the value of their work in terms that foreground its contributions to men's work. Adult Japanese women working in the sex industry imagine "the economy" as a fundamentally masculine space, thereby "eclipsing" their own forms of feminized productivity.[66] Examining how sex workers narrate their industry's contribution to society thus powerfully demonstrates the enduring truth that there is no way to even begin to talk about "the economy" outside of how the concept of productivity is implicated in gendered assumptions. In other words, *how* people imagine the relationship of gender to economic value continues to constitute the basic terms of how they think about economic activity under neoliberal capitalism. Despite the movement of middle-class women into the full-time workforce in many postindustrial contexts, conventional gender norms and ideologies of intimacy continue to be reproduced, thereby obscuring the roles of women in service-based industries and elsewhere as professionals. Whatever else may have changed in the realities of the labor market, the gendered division of labor is still one of the most defining elements of the nature of work at present. Although questions of productivity and value might seem ideologically separate from intimate performances in the sex industry, the point is precisely that they are not—the performance of an eroticized and maternal care that is understood to enable men's productivity, in other words, *is* the gendering of the economy.

Although sex workers regard their healing labor as socially and economically essential, this labor occurs in conditions of marginalization—from the grayness of regulation to the lack of recognition of sex work as an "ordinary" category of work and the associated stigma and discrimination. How do women in the sex industry view attempts to address the forms of vulnerability and abuse they may face? In the last two chapters, I will explore the rhetoric and interventions of two rights-based campaigns attempting, in different ways, to address circumstances in the sex industry. Sex workers' understanding of their work as healing labor deeply affects their attitudes toward these campaigns. Although sex workers feel great pride in their healing labor and see sex and the economy as fundamentally bound together, over the past decade and a half, a group of young and cosmopolitan anti-trafficking activists with visibility disproportionate to their numbers has begun to challenge the normalization of the sex industry. This organization, as we shall see, sees nothing positive about women's participation in commercial sex.

5   Victims All

IN FALL 2008, the Tokyo-based anti–human trafficking organization that I refer to by the pseudonym Let's Fight Slavery Japan (LFSJ) published a booklet for social service providers that succinctly stated their view on barriers to widespread recognition of this crime. The slim volume informs readers that

> most victims of human trafficking[1] are forced to work in the sex industry. Members of the public often assume that people in the sex industry are working because they want to or because they made a decision to based on their circumstances, and conclude that their exposure to things like rape, violence, or the risk of STIs or [HIV] can't be helped. Such prejudices mean that people overlook signs of harm, thinking, "It's because they're selling their bodies," and even blame women who have been trafficked for what happens to them. Men who buy these victims are also oblivious that they have been trafficked.[2]

The organization proposed that these misconceptions about the degree of freedom women have in the sex industry had inured the public to abuses around commercial sex. Adolescent girls who got mixed up with selling sex—runaways, abused children, teenagers involved in "compensated dating" (*enjo kōsai*)—were victims of human trafficking but so were adult women. Although the booklet provided plentiful information on the trafficking of foreign migrant women, what stands out most about its appeal is the focus on *Japanese* women and children as sexually vulnerable subjects and as individuals who might be working "like slaves" (*dorei no yō ni*) in and around the familiar settings of urban space.

Making claims about the exploitation and forced labor of Japanese women in the sex industry is not easy in a national context in which the industry operates in plain sight and its existence and necessity are widely accepted. Although the rhetoric of slavery in the sex industry has been a powerful rallying cry elsewhere,[3] in Japan the absence of a widespread sense that commercial sex is inherently exploitative paired with a general impression of the lucrative potential of sex industry work means that this rhetoric is largely not culturally meaningful. Nevertheless, through the conflation of sex work and human trafficking, LFSJ staff suggest that all sex industry work is either nonvolitional or, at best, the outcome of social pathologies that demand greater attention.[4] Although anti-prostitution causes generally attract relatively little attention in Japan, this influential organization skillfully applies the internationally mediated discourse of human trafficking in order to problematize the sex industry labor of adult Japanese women.

As with the healing labor of sex workers, the human rights advocacy of the staff and supporters of LFSJ is also a form of feminized care set against the backdrop of a restrictive female labor market. The individuals involved in LFSJ are deeply concerned with the vulnerabilities of adolescents and young adults in Japanese society and with how forms of neglect, marginalization, or lack of social connection may lead them into situations in which they can be taken advantage of by others. Influenced by an American-backed anti–human trafficking "rescue industry,"[5] this group seeks to reframe the normalization of women's work in the sex industry as exploitation by male management and customers. This chapter contrasts the organization's anti-prostitution rhetoric with the responses of sex workers who describe these activists as fundamentally misrecognizing who they are and what they do. Although women in the sex industry are greatly concerned with the risks they may face in their work, they describe feeling marginalized by the anti-trafficking activists who claim to act on their behalf.[6] These activists view sex and the economy as mutually exclusive categories and disregard the perspectives of sex workers, who maintain that what they offer is a meaningful social contribution.

Anti-Trafficking Energy

When Kanno Akiko established Let's Fight Slavery Japan in 2004 as an international branch office of the American organization, Alliance, it was a fertile time for anti–human trafficking advocacy.[7] The United Nations' adoption of the 2000 Protocol to Prevent, Suppress and Punish Trafficking in Persons (hereafter "the Palermo Protocol") generated funding streams and government-grassroots partnerships that led to the establishment of many new organizations.[8] Alliance, founded just two years earlier by two students who had learned about forced migrant labor occurring near their elite university, was a product of the energy produced by the new anti-trafficking discourse. Kanno, who had moved to the United States for her college education and would soon graduate, became interested in the organization.[9] Her university experiences had made her increasingly conscious and critical of aspects of mainstream Japanese society—especially the sex industry—and opened her up to the power and possibility of social action. After an interview with Alliance's directors fanned her enthusiasm, Kanno moved across the country to start an internship with the organization.

Kanno's internship occurred at a time of ambitious organizational expansion at Alliance. Around the time that Kanno proposed opening a Tokyo office, Japan was depicted as having a severe problem with human trafficking. Human rights and media reports portrayed a grim picture of the forced prostitution of foreign migrant women—especially Philippine, Thai, and Colombian nationals—in sex and entertainment districts across Japan.[10] With few nonprofits engaged with this issue locally, the Alliance leadership sensed a strategic opening.

Politically, the timing of LFSJ's establishment was fortuitous. In June 2004, the Trafficking in Persons (TIP) Report released annually by the US State Department's Office to Monitor and Combat Trafficking in Persons listed Japan on its Tier 2 "watchlist" ranking, essentially a warning that Japan was headed to Tier 3 (lowest) status. This ranking made Japan a priority country within the State Department and Kanno was able to secure US government funds to launch LFSJ. "Watchlist" status also galvanized political and legislative action in Japan; in December 2004, the government released an Action Plan of Measures to Combat Trafficking in Persons.

As an American organization establishing its presence in Japan, in the early years of its existence LFSJ was sustained largely by its American ties. The US embassy, which exerted pressure on the Japanese government to act on human trafficking throughout the 2000s, provided key support and facilitated communication with Japanese officials.[11] Moreover, LFSJ actively solicited expatriate supporters. A network of well-connected Anglophone donors, benefactors, and media concerned with what was widely perceived to be a rampant sex industry run by organized crime responded enthusiastically to LFSJ's activities. Even years later, during my internship in 2011, the organization still had a parallel event calendar for Japanese- and English-speaking audiences and separate publicity and fundraising mechanisms. As LFSJ's activities diversified and Kanno established herself in local nonprofit and social welfare networks, the organization began to attract local audiences and supporters as well as media attention. Not long after I returned to the United States from long-term fieldwork, for instance, I learned that Kanno had been profiled as a "person to know" in several high-circulation national news publications. Over the course of LFSJ's first decade, it gradually gained a separate "Japanese" identity and today it operates independently of Alliance.

Although there are other organizations in the greater Tokyo area involved in anti-trafficking advocacy—including several private women's shelters (both secular and Christian) and a handful of nonprofits—LFSJ was the most active and influential group in Japan during the time of my fieldwork. It was the only organization dedicated to offering a variety of services and activities, including a hotline, client services, public outreach activities, training workshops for professionals, and government advocacy.[12]

The extent of LFSJ's influence is disproportionate to its small size. Although the organization has only a handful of regular staff, Kanno quickly cultivated an impressive base of temporary staff (interns and volunteers) each bound by several months-long commitments.[13] By the time that I joined, there had already been thirty-odd interns, with two more following me in rapid succession. These were mostly college-aged women or recent graduates, many of whom were from the United States or western Europe. A large volunteer network assisted in the running of LFSJ's public events, including a monthly seminar series and special events, such as a Diet hearing and an international conference. Many of the short-term Japanese staff had worked or studied abroad, lending a decidedly cosmopolitan, outward-oriented outlook and bringing professional savvy and bilingual capacity to the organization. At the completion of my internship in 2011, LFSJ was recruiting a larger full-time staff and aspired to significant growth in the organization's capabilities over the next several years.

Initially, LFSJ focused their advocacy on foreign migrant women trafficked into the sex industry. Around 2007–8, however, following numerous inquiries to their hotline, the staff began to center their activities on the "domestic trafficking" of Japanese women and children. This pivot in focus has allowed the organization to carve out a unique position for itself within the Japanese anti-trafficking community. In Japan, the conversation about who can be a victim of human trafficking—and what constitutes this crime—was largely limited during the time of my fieldwork to foreign migrant women working in the sex industry.[14] Government rhetoric and victim identification reflected this focus, and the advocacy of an older cohort of anti-trafficking activists, many of whom had been active in dealing with issues around the exploitation of foreign migrant women since the 1980s and 1990s, likewise framed human trafficking as constituted by movement across borders and by a unique set of vulnerabilities tied to the intersections of cultural difference, racism, and sexism.[15] This older generation of activists recognizes the unique circumstances of Japanese citizens popularly known as "JFC" (Japanese-Filipino children)—children born to Filipina migrant women and Japanese men, who are often raised in the Philippines but who can easily migrate to Japan as adults—but they largely do not consider contemporary forms of trafficking as a problem facing Japanese. Instead, together with feminist scholars and activists, this older cohort has theorized a powerful historical critique of the trafficking and exploitation of Asian and Japanese women's bodies by Japanese men via both imperialism and capitalism from the late nineteenth century to the present.[16]

In contrast, LFSJ staff and supporters consistently bypassed preexisting historical and feminist discourses of human trafficking, instead framing it as an international issue of recent emergence and only vaguely alluding, if at all, to a longer history of exploitative practices involving commercial sex. For them, trafficking is mediated by a transnational discourse validated in the year 2000—the year of both the Palermo Protocol and US passage of federal anti-trafficking legislation. That LFSJ sees itself as part of the post–Palermo Protocol world, as opposed to the continuation of a Japanese anti–human trafficking movement, is abundantly clear. For instance, it is telling that in a presentation timed to immediately follow the 2012 release of the TIP Report, LFSJ included a timeline of "major events in human trafficking in Japan" that began in 2000, creating the impression that the anti-trafficking movement emerged just at this time out of a prior vacuum. Similarly, a timeline of newspaper articles covering human trafficking in the first edition of LFSJ's service providers' handbook likewise begins in 2000.[17]

By focusing on Japanese women and children as victims of human trafficking, LFSJ staff are attempting to increase public consciousness of who can be a victim of forced labor and of the relationship between exploitation and commercial sex. Although this focus has created a generational divide between them and an older cohort of activists, and created challenges for government partnerships, it has also constituted a major intervention in the field of Japanese anti-trafficking advocacy.[18]

Intimacy, Vulnerability, and Exploitation

The subject of the sex industry as a magnet for and a creator of traumatized women is one that a network of advocates involved in the Japanese social welfare system has long taken up. Kanematsu Sachiko, a guidance counselor at a publicly funded women's counseling center in Shinjuku for over thirty years, described the women she encountered as suffering from destitution, drugs, unstable family environments, mental illness, addiction, violence, and social isolation.[19] "It is highly significant," Kanematsu wrote, "that 64 percent of the women now in rehabilitation centers for prostitutes are emotionally unstable, have past records of psychological problems, are elderly, or suffer from some other kind of psychological or physical handicap. Poverty, then, is not the sole or fundamental cause of prostitution. Women take to the streets and soaplands and pink salons because of their low social and economic status and their uninformed, unformed sexual morality."[20]

At a Diet hearing in May 2011 organized by a coalition of mostly social welfare and Christian aid-based women's organizations (*Baibaishun Mondai to Torikumu Kai*) for the fifty-fifth anniversary of the Prostitution Prevention Law's passage, this perspective was fully on display. Shimojo Akemi, a college student interning at LFSJ, and I were the youngest attendees by at least a generation. Among such advocates, the anti-prostitution law is often critiqued as a *zaruhō*—a law with as many holes in it as a colander, which has effectively allowed prostitution to continue under a new name. The advocates present called for revisions to the law both to crack down on the legal sex industry and to strengthen support for issues relating to women's human rights.[21] Tanaka Mariko, the longtime director of one of Tokyo's five publicly funded women's shelters, declared that the circumstances of the women coming to these shelters had not changed much since the anti-prostitution law's passage in 1956. At that time, she explained, many women had entered prostitution to support their families; today, dysfunctional families filled with abuse or neglect drove women into the sex industry, but otherwise the outcomes were the same. Tanaka described how the women at her shelter who had previously been prostitutes were depressed, unstable, victims of violence and discrimination, ashamed of themselves, and left traumatized by the work: "To say they're doing it because they like it couldn't be further from the truth!" she exclaimed.

From the perspective of these anti-prostitution advocates, all women in the sex industry are victims—women who have fallen through the cracks of society in some way and, seeing few opportunities available to them and/or lured by the promise of fast cash, have landed in commercial sex. Kanno shared a similar perspective. In the summer of 2008, early into LFSJ's transition to focusing on domestic trafficking, Kanno told me,

> Both [sex workers and victims of human trafficking] are victimized by society. Sex workers might be single mothers or pimped out by a bad boyfriend, [or] they can be addicted to drugs. But even so, no one helps them. A lot of them were abused in their childhood. The situation of victims is harsh. There are so many people like that. They might think that they decided to do [sex work], but there isn't much difference between them and trafficking victims.

Even if Kanno allowed for a distinction (in theory, at least) between sex workers and victims of human trafficking, she also believed that women entered the sex industry only under severely constrained conditions that effectively undermined their agency.

Kanno greatly respected Tanaka and occasionally spoke to the staff about a visit she had made to her shelter. The shelter's archive of records held particular fascination for her and she wondered out loud what would be found if someone had the time to organize and transcribe the masses of hand-written notes. In Kanno's eyes, this archive held a hidden history of domestic trafficking that was tragically obscured by the handful of bureaucratic categories assigned to shelter residents—mental illness, sexual assault, familial abuse, self-harming behavior—and whose true nature was recognized only by the caring and patient shelter staff.

Although LFSJ staff members are generally sympathetic with openly anti-prostitution perspectives, in a context of widespread acceptance of the sex industry they are also aware that advocating an explicitly anti-prostitution stance could alienate potential supporters and allies. In practice, however, Kanno, the staff, and the guest seminar speakers regularly conflated sex work and human trafficking, and highlighted stories of trauma in the sex industry to construct all sex work as inherently exploitative.

Although sex workers understand sex as an activity that is productive of economic life, the young and cosmopolitan anti-trafficking activists of LFSJ view sex and the economy as mutually exclusive categories, adopting a framework that Viviana Zelizer calls "hostile worlds."[22] From this perspective, sexuality should be limited to an intimate sphere untouched by economic exchange. LFSJ staff regard this sphere as one circumscribed by monogamous, noncommercial relationships and, ideally, by marriage, and Kanno often suggested that improving romantic relations between couples would eliminate male demand for commercial sex. "Hostile worlds" constructs the sex industry as an illegitimate mixing of what should properly be kept separated, and LFSJ staff identify this market for intimacy—marked by a desire for instant gratification and by the commodity value of the body—as fundamentally alienating to and exploitative of the self.

To make their case about the exploitation of adult Japanese women in sex work, the staff rely mostly on stories about children and adolescents. These accounts express the ways in which LFSJ staff regard young people as made vulnerable by not having the right kinds of social relations. Young people, the activists suggest, are shaped by social pathologies such as neglect, marginalization, and lack of social connection, which make them susceptible to human trafficking.

This logic was illuminated, in particular, at one of LFSJ's monthly seminars. At a crowded event space on the third floor of one of the central Tokyo retail locations of an international cosmetics company, I sat among thirty-something attendees one weekend afternoon and listened as a medical doctor spoke about the crisis of sociality that he observed among the adolescents he came into contact with through his work.[23] The speaker was a male physician in his fifties who had made a name for himself promoting sex education to middle and high school students across the country. A self-branded "condom expert" whose personal website was full of information geared toward teenagers, he wore a tie with multicolored condoms personified with smiling faces wriggling their way across the black background. He was an engaging speaker whose performative capabilities were on full display in the frequent hearty laughter of the audience, their rapid-fire responses to the questions he posed them, and the occasional gentle teasing he doled out. At several points in the talk, when reaching significant aspects of his message, he would speak over a stirring pop song, perfectly timed to his presentation. But for all the entertaining exterior, his carefully packaged message that day was nevertheless a serious one: young people today are made vulnerable by their inability to effectively express—or even know—their own needs and to communicate empathetically with one another.

Kanno introduced the speaker prior to his lecture. Audience members, she said, might be wondering why LFSJ—an anti-trafficking organization—was hosting a doctor specializing in sex education. She defined trafficking as a crime in which someone controls another person for their own profit, regardless of whether an international border has been crossed. Many of the individuals who are most at risk of becoming trafficking victims, Kanno continued, are Japanese women and children. We needed to think about why this was happening in Japan, about the social environment of children and young people, and about the commodification of their sexuality. In the home for delinquent youth where she volunteered in her free time, Kanno told us, many of the adolescents had no *ibasho*. This is a commonly used term at LFSJ and within social welfare discourse in Japan more generally. *Ibasho* roughly refers to a place or a set of social relations where one feels "at home." Kanno informed us that it was just a small step for many of these adolescents—bereft of guidance or trusted relationships and ridden with insecurity—to enter the sex industry, where they were aware of the high market value that their young bodies would command. Why? She hoped that the doctor, whose materials she often used when working with young people, could explain more about this to us.

The doctor's talk, it turned out, was only superficially about sex education. Rather, it was about how we could get young people to both know themselves better and to think more about others. Drawing on numerous anecdotes of cases he had treated and interactions with sexually active adolescents who had spoken with or written to him, the doctor interpreted high rates of sexually transmitted infections and cases of teenage pregnancy and abortion as problems of interpersonal communication, diagnosing a deeper pathology around meaningful social connection.[24] According to the doctor, young people were unable to express what they themselves wanted and needed, or to read this in others. They had sex mechanically because they thought that was what they *should* want. For example, the doctor spent some time talking about the difference between saying, "This is good" and "I'll be fine with this," two phrases that in Japanese are differentiated by only one particle. The distinction he was drawing was meant to characterize how some young people just went along with things (like having sex) without really considering if it was what they truly wanted. He argued that constant attention to screens and technologically mediated relationships rather than to facial expressions, tone, and body language was leading to a generation of emotionally isolated young people. The doctor urged all of us to be more caring, more attuned to those around us—especially the young—and to their thoughts and feelings. That way, the doctor explained, we could reach out to and help those whose spirits were "ill."

The doctor's inclusion within a seminar lineup that otherwise featured lawyers, social workers, advocates, and researchers linked the more quotidian forms of vulnerability associated with adolescents and young people to the exploitative nature of human trafficking. *These* young people, he implied, who were unable to know themselves or their vulnerabilities, were the ones who might easily fall into situations where they had little control—these young people without proper sociality, in other words, might end up as victims of abuse.

Similarly, in their accounts of human trafficking, representatives of LFSJ spoke of adolescents who were deceived, bullied, or led astray by friends or strangers whom they had deemed trustworthy. One story Kanno often told involved a fourteen-year-old girl who was pressured by her friends to engage in *enjo kōsai*. The girl's friends posted her contact information on a website advertising underaged girls and arranged for her to meet older men for money at hotels across the city. This went on for a month before the police got involved, at which point LFSJ was contacted. In her narrative, Kanno highlighted the emotional fallout and ongoing issues of low self-esteem that the girl (now a young woman) still harbored years later. These included an inability to say "no" to men, feelings of revulsion toward her body, and inexplicable outbursts of crying. At sixteen, Kanno told audiences, the girl began (illegally) working at a hostess club. As with the language of passivity and inevitability—of women "flowing" into the sex industry—introduced in Chapter 3, the implication of Kanno's account was that even she believed that the girl would eventually end up in the sex industry, as the inevitable next step in a trajectory of self-harm.

A representative case in LFSJ's 2008 service providers' booklet describes a fictional teenaged girl who runs away from home, taking a bus to Tokyo to visit a man she met online. The man had always listened to her troubles concerning her family and school friends. She meets him in person for the first time when she arrives at his suburban apartment, and he tells her she can stay as long as she wants—there is currently another girl her age staying there, too.

Before long, the money the girl brought with her runs out, at which point the man tells her that it is time for her to contribute to the rent. He embraces her and begins to touch her. Terrified, she does not resist. The next day, he tells the girl that she is going to go to work, explaining that he found someone online who will pay her for sex. He tells her, "It's simple, you don't have to do anything. Just let the customer do what he wants." The girl meets the stranger and goes with him to a love hotel. Later on, the man takes the money she received and tells her that, from then on, she will earn money that way. He threatens her, saying that he will tell her family what she did if she runs away. She learns that the other girl at the house is also sleeping with strangers for money. Her cell phone is taken away. Although the man keeps a close eye on her, when she sees an opportunity, she manages to escape.[25]

Such stories of isolated adolescents lacking *ibasho* and self-knowledge who are taken advantage of by others form the great majority of LFSJ's narratives of domestic trafficking. They reflect the deep concern of the organization's staff and supporters with the circumstances of young people who may be bullied, insecure, self-abusing, or victims of dysfunctional family environments and whose needs are not being addressed by families, schools, or a limited juvenile welfare system. Problematically, however, LFSJ staff regularly linked these stories to the situations of adult women in the sex industry without providing firsthand accounts, thereby implying that all sex workers are really just the grown-up versions of the vulnerable children they were trying to protect. This slippage between adolescents and adults neatly avoided the need to give concrete data on adult women, and effectively negated the possibility of agency or moral complexity on the part of sex workers.

Classification

To quantify the scale of a problem—in the context of many causes competing for attention and resources—is to make a claim for its significance. This is especially true, and especially problematic, with underground practices, such as human trafficking. As Peter Andreas and Kelly Greenhill point out, "Difficult to observe phenomena are not perceived to be 'real' until they are quantified and given a number."[26] LFSJ staff perhaps felt this quandary especially keenly as, in their words, the "number one misconception" around human trafficking in Japan was a basic incredulity about its existence (for example, "*That's happening in Japan?*"). Although Kanno knew well the inherent difficulties in calculating the number of victims of an underground practice, pragmatically she also understood the efficacy of numbers. "Numbers make things easy for people to understand," she explained one day, pointing to a bundle of English-language promotional materials on a cluttered desk in the corner of the office. LFSJ had distributed these a few weeks earlier at a donor cocktail party celebrating the visit of Alliance's director. Kanno drew one pamphlet out of the bundle and read out loud: "We've trained over 5,000 people to identify trafficking victims, we've received over 1,500 phone calls, and we've helped over 100 victims." These figures broke down the group's diverse activities into discrete categories corresponding to easily digestible, satisfying, and auditable performance metrics.[27] Whenever Kanno wanted to talk about LFSJ's accomplishments, she quantified them in this way.

The organization's use of numbers occasionally led to conflict. A tense moment occurred at the closed-door session for anti-trafficking professionals at a conference organized by LFSJ during my fieldwork when a representative from the National Police Agency challenged Kanno in front of everyone assembled. Four days earlier, an article promoting the conference had appeared in the *Asahi Shimbun*, one of Japan's major national newspapers. This article reported that LFSJ estimated that there were 54,000 victims of human trafficking nationwide, both Japanese and non-Japanese. The police official wanted to know the source of the organization's data, which, he added, had come as a shock. His tone was unmistakable. He was accusing LFSJ of circulating fabricated or inflated numbers.[28] Already, the police were not particularly receptive to many of the organization's claims. Appearing calm and confident, Kanno explained that these numbers had been estimated based on research that used the Palermo Protocol definition of human trafficking.[29] Most of the victims, she continued, were in the sex industry. The police representative, although clearly skeptical of Kanno's answer, silently let the matter pass without further comment. LFSJ staff have repeated this same number many times since then.

Quantification is always also fundamentally about definitions—how one regards the scale of a problem like human trafficking is based on how one defines it.[30] Reflecting their concern for the diverse forms of vulnerability facing adolescents and young women in Japanese society, LFSJ staff and supporters believe that there are many cases of human trafficking in Japan that are not recognized as such due to prejudice and misconceptions about the legitimacy of the sex industry. In attempting to transform public consciousness of what constitutes human trafficking, the anti-trafficking activists applied an expansive politics of recognition that reclassified cases interpreted in other ways by the police or immigration authorities, the press, or the public.

For example, the organization's website featured a regularly updated page dedicated to human trafficking news. The webpage featured news stories covering topics ranging from foreign migrant women in forced prostitution to school teachers arrested for soliciting sex from students to North Koreans escaping from forced labor to China. Whether the reporting identified it in that way or not, a news story's inclusion on this webpage indicated that LFSJ staff classified it as human trafficking. In particular, anything related to minors and sexual commerce was immediately classified as human trafficking, as the Palermo Protocol stipulates that individuals under age eighteen cannot consent to commercial sex.[31] Cases involving the distinct Japanese legal-juridical labels of child prostitution (*jidō kaishun*) and child pornography (*jidō poruno*), forced prostitution (*kyōsei baishun*), and sexual exploitation (*seiteki sakushu*) were all identified as human trafficking (*jinshin torihiki*) and the staff questioned the basis by which forced prostitution was distinguished from trafficking.

Although many of LFSJ's reclassifications dealt with cases that had already been identified by the authorities as involving a crime, in other cases, their classificatory logic collided with very different framings of an event. This is most apparent when we look at the LFSJ staff's approach to *enjo kōsai*, which has been a topic of intense debate in Japan for three decades. Beginning in the early 1990s, the Japanese media fixated on middle and high school–aged girls who were said to be exchanging dates and sexual favors with older men in exchange for cash or brand-name goods.[32] Media coverage and commentary on *enjo kōsai* largely did not regard this phenomenon as characterized by force or exploitation and instead focused on what was billed as an assertive female sexuality paired with a crass materialism. The sociologist Miyadai Shinji, for example, famously argued that adolescent girls engaging in *enjo kōsai* were undermining patriarchal authority.[33]

Although the 1999 Anti-Child Prostitution and Child Pornography Law (*Jidō Kaishun Jidō Poruno ni Kakaru Kōitō no Kisei oyobi Shobatsu narabi ni Jidō no Hogotō ni kansuru Hōritsu*) identified sexual transactions between adults and minors as crimes, public attitudes toward *enjo kōsai* have tended to foreground the agency of the schoolgirls themselves. Sharon Kinsella, for instance, has noted that "while legislation originally sought to criminalize male customers rather than schoolgirls, the National Police Agency and [ruling Liberal Democratic Party] politicians worked to rapidly overturn this legal position, with further legislation clearly identifying young women as guilty parties in their own purchase."[34] Similarly, today, the crackdown on *joshi kōsei* ("high school girl"; abbreviated as "JK") businesses, in which adult men pay to spend time with an adolescent girl, represents the newest manifestation of these debates. On July 1, 2015, Aichi Prefecture became the first in the nation to prohibit all aspects of these businesses, citing their potential harm to minors. But although adolescent girls involved in JK businesses and their managers may face penalties, their customers do not, suggesting ongoing ambivalence about who is to blame for the commodification of adolescent girls' bodies. Thus, although LFSJ staff might classify *enjo kōsai* as a form of sexual harm and human trafficking, following the Palermo Protocol, this position clashes with a national discourse that has often highlighted the sexual agency of adolescent girls and held that, if anyone is to blame for this phenomenon, it is the teenaged girls themselves and not their adult partners.

In some sense, much or even most of the ethnographic scholarship on anti–human trafficking advocacy can be read as the analysis of different classificatory schemes around who can be trafficked, by what criteria or organizing principles such judgments are reached, and what the implications and consequences of such classifications are. Although there is little disagreement that an egregious phenomenon termed human trafficking exists, there is also tremendous friction over the question of how it is constituted, what the implications are, and the practicalities of identifying victims and/or perpetrators. The language of the Palermo Protocol is intentionally vague so as to accommodate diverse legal approaches to labor laws and to commercial sex around the world. As scholars have pointed out, the very separation of "labor" trafficking and "sex" trafficking is itself an arbitrary distinction that has now become taken for granted.[35] In many ways, the definition of human trafficking operates as a boundary object: an object "for cooperation across social worlds" that is "able to both travel across borders and maintain some sort of constant identity."[36] Its "translation" is in the hands of local activists—like LFSJ—who make the transnational legal language around trafficking meaningful in local terms.[37]

Scrutiny

Shortly after I first met Kanno, in the summer of 2008, when LFSJ was still overwhelmingly focused on the trafficking of foreign migrant women, she

expressed her frustrations with a public that she saw as turning a blind eye
to abuse. Apathy was something she had come to see in generational terms:
"Japanese don't know about human trafficking because they've been made
complacent by peace (*heiwaboke*)." Kanno explained that because people of
her and her parents' generation had only ever experienced a safe, peaceful,
and well-ordered society, they had become inured to suffering. "When they hear
'human trafficking' they think, 'Huh? Oh, that thing with Filipino and Thai
women,' and move on." She suggested that a prevalent casual racism led many
members of the public to view foreign migrant women as "bad" and "dirty"
women who came to Japan to make money and who flirted with and married
Japanese men. Kanno saw this in the relatively higher number of foreigners calling LFSJ's hotline:

> They're more aware that something's wrong in this community, something's
> wrong in this apartment, something might be happening to this young woman
> living in this small apartment. So, they call us because they think this might
> be trafficking, it may be some kind of exploitation. I'm sure that Japanese
> people also know about the signs of exploitation—the signs of trafficking—
> but this is a society where they just let it go.

Kanno referred to this as *miteminufuri* ("pretending not to see")—overlooking
what is right in front of one in order to avoid involvement with the social relations and attendant obligations that might follow. Her accusation was also
a diagnosis of a wider social pathology: the unwillingness, as she saw it, of
ordinary Japanese to help others even when they sensed that something was
wrong.

To counter such apathy, LFSJ staff emphasized the cultivation of forms of
affect and behavior that would allow supporters to vigilantly scrutinize their
social interactions for evidence of how strangers and loved ones alike might
be caught up in relations of coercion and control. When Kanno led awareness-
raising seminars on human trafficking for the public, she encouraged audiences to think of themselves as always potentially in the proximity of someone
in need of their help. The help that supporters could provide was, first of all,
"recognizing the signs" of suffering. This was sometimes articulated in seminars through the verb *kizuku*, which connotes suddenly perceiving something
that you had not paid attention to until then—such as things about a legal sex
industry that you had never considered previously. The staff's message was

that through greater awareness supporters could ask themselves, "Could that person be a victim?" and act accordingly.[38]

For example, during the Q&A of another public seminar, a full-time staff member, Arao Hiroshi, told audience members that he and a Belgian intern had been walking to the train station together one day recently while speaking in English when they attracted the attention of a homeless man. The man interrupted them to announce that his Filipino wife spoke English but that he had not seen her in a while. "That's when I felt the first inkling of suspicion," Arao told the audience. Striking up a conversation, Arao had asked the man about his wife and her present whereabouts, to which the man replied that he had no clue, shrugging at a question about the state of their marriage. Arao said that he suspected this must be a case of so-called fake marriage (*gisō kekkon*), in which a woman wishing to migrate to Japan for work married a Japanese man on paper so as to secure a spousal visa and eliminate all work restrictions. Relying on widely circulating stereotypes of Filipino migrant women in Japan, Arao suggested that the absent Filipino wife was likely working as a hostess or sex worker—only that whereas these stereotypes implicitly suggest the criminality of migrant women, Arao explained this marriage contract as a mechanism of human trafficking.

Kanno chimed in and brought up a conversation she had recently had with a middle-aged American volunteer. The woman, Cynthia, who had relocated to Japan many years previously, was in the audience that day and Kanno asked her if she would share their conversation with the group. Cynthia said that she had recently been sitting at a coffee shop next to two teenaged girls. They were chatting away happily while applying makeup. Not long after, a young man whom the American woman described as fitting her image of a yakuza, or member of an organized crime group, came in and joined them at their table. He asked the two teenagers what they were doing and why they weren't at work yet. He wasn't unfriendly and the girls didn't appear intimidated, but the woman thought she could detect an implicit threat in his question. Because they did not expect her to understand Japanese, Cynthia told us, she was able to listen in on their conversation without attracting notice. The nature of the work or the man's identity or relation to the girls was never made clear, but Cynthia believed that the dynamic indicated an unsavory relationship and had to point to underaged sex industry work. Kanno announced that this was likely the case of a "pimp" pushing two minors to get to work. If Cynthia's appraisal of him as a "yakuza type" was on point, she suggested, what else could the interaction signify?

In these two anecdotes given by LFSJ staff and supporters, seemingly unremarkable and innocuous circumstances are interpreted as bearing dark possibilities. Although neither Arao nor Cynthia acted on their suspicions, they shared their anecdotes to convey the message that audience members' everyday interactions could include encounters that warranted more scrutiny and attention. A heightened awareness of this possibility would allow them to notice if they encountered someone in need of their help. Andrea Muehlebach, writing about an unwaged affective labor regime in post-Fordist Italy, has described "the creation of a public that [binds] strangers to strangers through proper affect and ameliorative action."[39] This is similar to how supporters of LFSJ were encouraged to align themselves with an ethics toward those who, the staff argued, might be unable to help themselves. Absolute certainty about a situation was not necessary, the staff reassured audience members. One could feel comfortable relying on instinct, even if it was just a shadow of a suspicion that "maybe there's something going on there." The appropriate mode of action in such cases, the staff instructed audiences, was to call the organization's hotline and describe the circumstances to the staff, who would be able to judge whether they warranted further intervention.[40]

If a crisis of sociality is at the root of what LFSJ staff believe allows domestic trafficking to flourish, then the response of LFSJ is to extend care via an attentive scrutiny to the possible nature of unknown social relations. Staff and supporters, the message was, had the ability to see into otherwise opaque circumstances and seemingly quotidian exchanges to recognize the possible signs of abuse that might lie hidden therein. Scrutiny that might otherwise seem inappropriate and intrusive, as a form of policing or implicit bias, was recast as a caring and responsible act toward strangers potentially in desperate need of help.[41] Others, including progressive social activists, left-leaning researchers, and, especially, sex workers, have been critical of this policy of *kizuku* as fostering a "surveillance society" (*kanshi shakai*) in tandem with the marked increase of surveillance cameras and other technologies of observation and control. After the outing of a public school teacher in Osaka who was working in a sex industry business after her day job (see Chapter 3), one sex workers' rights advocate wondered out loud whether LFSJ hadn't somehow been responsible. She grumbled, "I bet their hotline is just people calling to tattle on others."

In these examples, the absence of overt evidence of human trafficking is productive of an alternative evidentiary regime.[42] In the face of what the staff and their supporters view as a widespread ignorance or lack of awareness of human trafficking among the general public, the absence of particular forms of "hard" data engender the creation of new rhetorics about what signs could index human trafficking. Otherwise tenuous claims about chance encounters and overheard conversations are compelling to the staff and their audiences in terms of how they distinguish the awareness and appropriate affect of the organization's supporters in recognizing the signs of a serious problem from that of an unaware public.

Misrecognition

"Do they think sex workers are total idiots?" the former *deriherujō* Hiromi asked, her voice flat but her tone suddenly piqued. "What are they trying to achieve by saying women and children are deceived into the work and calling us victims?" We had been talking about LFSJ's advocacy. It was apparent that for Hiromi, the organization's rhetoric confirmed what she believed to be the prejudicial assumptions harbored by the public toward sex workers. She continued: "They must look down on us to say that we're tricked. I made a decision to enter the industry and for someone to say that I didn't know what I was doing . . ." Hiromi left her sentence unfinished but her irritation was obvious.

In his ethnography of male Brazilian sex workers, Gregory Mitchell describes what happened when he asked one of his interlocutors about exploitation in prostitution. The man earnestly, and rather gravely, answers that many of his peers are shameless at extracting every penny they can out of their clients. He explains, "We have to love people and not things, but nowadays I, too, love more things than people," expressing self-consciousness at how his consumerist desires were displacing what he felt should rightly be an emphasis on the person. When Mitchell clarifies that he was actually asking whether the sex workers are exploited, the man laughingly assures him that "the only exploitation he can recall is what he inflicts on his clients, which he says is starting to weigh on his conscience."[43]

When I asked sex workers open-ended questions about exploitation (*sakushu*) or human trafficking (*jinshin baibai*) in the sex industry, there were almost always moments of misrecognition. Most often, the woman I was speaking with would simply not comprehend what I was asking. Hiromi was one such case. When I asked her about her familiarity with the term *jinshin baibai*, she told me that she had heard it in conjunction with cases of Chinese and Southeast Asian women who had been deceived and forced to work in the sex industry against their will. But when I followed up and asked if she thought trafficking bore any relation to Japanese women working in the legal sex industry, Hiromi appeared baffled. After a few moments pause during which she scrutinized me, Hiromi said she thought they were separate issues—why had I asked? When I explained that I was attending a hearing that afternoon by anti-prostitution activists for whom all sex workers are exploited, she signaled at once that she understood my meaning: "I chose to do this work of my own will and have a totally different experience of it from someone who was tricked and forced to work. When people talk about these two things as if they're the same, they can't see anything clearly anymore."

In other cases, when I filled the moments of puzzled silence with a further explanation of my question—namely, that over the past decade the government, media, and various nonprofits had given a lot of attention to the issue of human trafficking as a problem of the sex industry, and did they see any connection to Japanese women working there—my interlocutors would quickly assure me that although human trafficking was an issue that foreign migrant women might face, they, as adult Japanese women, did not—*could* not possibly—have to worry about it. Shiori looked annoyed when I asked her if she saw any connections between her work and trafficking. She sighed. It was one of many moments when she seemed exasperated with me, having thought that I understood more than I evidently did. Assuming an air of patience, she explained to me that as a Japanese woman she could not be forced to work.

Other sex workers likewise disassociated the possibility that human trafficking might affect them as Japanese women and instead spoke of the vulnerability of foreign migrant women. It was clear that they saw their own circumstances as bearing no relationship to those of foreign migrants in the sex industry, except insofar as how the market valued their services differently. Mika, the sex industry instructor, explained that the demand from male consumers who wanted to be able to purchase sex cheaply led to the illegal influx of foreign migrant women in the sex industry. But her explanation situated Japanese sex workers as unconnected to this—as individuals in a larger market detached from what was happening at its fringes. Hiromi, too, explained that, as she saw it, human trafficking existed because of a relentless demand for cheaper services, which Japanese women were not willing to provide.

As these reactions illustrate, when the common Euro-American assumption of the intrinsically exploitative nature of commercial sex is not taken as self-evident, a question about the relationship between human trafficking and the sex industry is jarring and appears to come out of nowhere. It makes little sense. Hiromi, Shiori, Mika, and others did not accept the basic premise of LFSJ's advocacy that Japanese women could be forced to work. There was a basic disassociation between cultural belonging and the possibility of forced labor, and even more so with the premise that exploitation is intrinsic to commercial sex. My interlocutors found it difficult to fathom that someone might think them duped or forced to work—doing something widely assumed to be undesirable, yes, and the subject of stigma and discrimination, yes, but not *forced*. Yumi mulled over the meaning of "being sold": "You sell your body [in sex work] but I never once had the feeling that I was selling myself. The compensation I got was for the service I provided. It didn't feel any different to me from my experiences as a massage therapist." Megumi, the former civil servant, commented, "The stereotype is that sex workers are all women who have no choice but to work because of debt or something else. If you express any kind of everyday complaint about the work to someone, they'll immediately ask, 'So why don't you quit?'" Among those whom Megumi had confided in about her work, she still identified an unwillingness to recognize that there could be positive aspects about the work; complaints were read against assumptions that no one would willingly engage in sex work.

Sex workers' misrecognition of themselves in anti–human trafficking rhetoric was also evident in how women spoke about the aspects of their work that they found problematic—which I will take up in the next chapter. Although many of the sex workers that I spoke with talked at great length about complaints about their workplace or customers, these women did not use the word *sakushu* (exploitation) to describe their circumstances or those of their peers or of the industry more generally. Even while some of the women spoke quite bitterly about systemic problems in the sex industry, they did not characterize these in the terms of a predatory and abusive power relation conveyed by the concept of exploitation. Instead, they characterized these problems as inseparable from the nature of the work as short-term labor with high turnover, as labor in a stigmatized industry, as labor in an only partially legal industry, or as part-time work, points that painted issues in the sex industry as one of a kind with workplace or labor issues more generally in Japan. The exception to this was Aimi, who did use the word *sakushu* in our conversation. But Aimi saw the labor issues present in the sex industry as contiguous with problems related to the structure of work in Japan more generally. She thought that exploitation was endemic to work:

> There are similar kinds of exploitation at normal companies. So the fact that no one really says that something is strange is the same. People [at regular companies] don't complain when they don't get paid for overtime or if they are sexually harassed because they'll be fired. That's the same as a woman in the sex industry being upset about being told she can't use a condom but feeling like she can't say anything about it. People might be more willing to say something at a soapland, but at a company, people would just say that something is to be expected. So, I don't think that this exploitation is anything particular to the sex industry.

As with Hiromi's immediate reaction when I mentioned anti-prostitution activists, to these women, terms like *anti-prostitution activist* or *feminist* indexed something very specific. To them, these were individuals who made distorted claims about and looked down on sex workers, with little interest in sex workers' actual experiences or opinions, reflecting the tense relationship that mainstream Japanese feminism continues to have with women in the sex industry.[44] When I repeated some of LFSJ's rhetoric to them, their attitude often changed to scorn and even hostility. They dismissed such rhetoric, saying, "That has nothing to do with me." The response of even politically apathetic women toward claims of their exploitation in the sex industry was contempt or ridicule. Normally good-natured Shiori observed, "People like [a famous anti-prostitution lawyer] don't know the industry at all and are mistaken. The sex industry is the subject of a lot of prejudice and discrimination. They should make some friends in the sex industry before making claims like that." Just a few minutes earlier, Shiori had been telling me about daughters sold into prostitution by their families in the Meiji period and later. She was familiar with this history of Japanese trafficking (and frank about what she saw as its exploitative nature) but saw the contemporary transnational discourse as having nothing to do with her. It is clear that my interlocutors thought that anti-prostitution advocates fundamentally misunderstood their work—everything from the conditions under which they had entered to their experiences of the work to what they were concerned or anxious about in their daily lives as a result of that work. Sex workers saw these activists as individuals unfamiliar with their circumstances as they themselves experienced them and who could not speak to their reality.

Likewise, sex workers' rights advocates were concerned about the effects of LFSJ's rhetoric. Kazue, an advocate who had previously conducted research on human trafficking in Southeast Asia, underscored that sex workers are themselves against forms of exploitation and human trafficking in the sex industry.[45] However, they are rarely included under the rubric of anti-trafficking activists. Kazue criticized the conflation of sex work and human trafficking:

> Fundamentally, I think that if you don't want to do sex work, then you shouldn't, and if you do want to do it, then you should. I'm against human trafficking, against people being forced to have sex against their will or being tricked into coming to Japan to work. That should not happen. But among people who are against human trafficking, there are those who want to get rid of sex work altogether. When they say "human trafficking," they use a broad definition that includes many things outside of marriage. I think that people who are being forced to have sex should be helped. That needs to be stopped. But you can't conflate victims of human trafficking with people who decide to do sex work. You have to keep those things separate. What I want to know is why those activists are so eager to get rid of sex work. Why do they look down on sex workers and think of them as pitiful? They just say, "It's bad, it's dangerous, let's get rid of the sex industry," but they don't bother to find out what circumstances in the sex industry really are. It's easy to say, "Let's get rid of the sex industry," without offering an alternative.

Kazue sharply criticized anti-prostitution activists for what she saw as their fundamentally discriminatory attitudes. Tomoko, on the other hand, linked the rhetoric of LFSJ and other anti-prostitution activists to widespread attitudes that dismiss the dignity and humanity of sex workers.

To be clear, sex workers themselves are well aware that their labor occurs in conditions of marginalization and that a male-centered industry, including managers and customers, benefits from this marginalization. When women in the sex industry encounter risks or abuses in their work, they must cope with them largely—even entirely—on their own, compounding feelings of isolation. At the same time, it is telling that the women in the sex industry whom I spoke with reacted so strongly to the rhetoric of LFSJ.

Anti–human trafficking organizations around the world that focus on the human right to freedom while disregarding the human right to work paradoxically embrace the universal subject of human rights while under-mining potential claims of sex workers to rights. Alice Miller has powerfully argued that this focus emphasizes the "protection of women" rather than the "protection of women's rights."[46] Miller describes how attempts by interna-tional activists in the late 1980s to achieve broad recognition of women's rights among the global human rights community failed to gain traction. Instead, it was a focus on sexual violence that put women's rights on the radar of inter-national human rights. As Miller elaborates, however, this inordinate focus on the sexual vulnerability or violation of women and girls abnegates the pos-sibility of promoting more agentive rights while reinforcing the conservative belief that "the most important thing to know about a woman is her chas-tity."[47] Although attention to sexual violence is vital, it can also serve to un-dermine the more empowering emphasis on assuring the conditions in which women can agentively exercise their rights in the first place.

Conclusion

Despite the many differences between NGO work and sex work, the human rights advocacy of the staff of LFSJ can also be understood as a performance of care set against the backdrop of a gendered economy. Although the organ-ization's staff typically came from privileged and cosmopolitan class and edu-cational backgrounds, the overwhelmingly young and feminized group was, in many ways, also marginalized from the labor market. Deeply concerned with what they see as a host of problems involving adolescents and young people, the grassroots efforts of these activists to transform awareness of the forms of sexual exploitation that Japanese women and children may face and to mobilize public action are another form of women's work as the provision of care—albeit care that manifests here in political action.[48]

Entering the activist space of a human rights organization—particularly one they perceived as speaking to important issues in a gender unequal society—afforded these young women opportunities to engage in politics in ways that might otherwise have been inaccessible to them. Kanno, for instance, felt great pride in her achievement in establishing and growing the organization and would occasionally remark that it was really "her" organization. Kanno was in her early thirties during the time of my fieldwork and directing LFSJ allowed her an exceptional role for a woman of her age—one who was invited to speak as an expert across Japan as well as overseas, who was recognized by the US embassy and by Japanese government officials, and who was profiled in the media as a "person to know." Similarly, the interns and volunteers that I worked with—mostly women in their twenties or early thirties—served as MCs at public lectures, attended hearings at the Diet, met local politicians and liaised with the staff of foreign embassies, and organized an international conference on human trafficking. This nonprofit work was deeply meaningful to them and embodied a form of care work on behalf of other women.[49]

However, if *care* is the operative term for what LFSJ staff and supporters are extending to women in the sex industry, then it is an unwelcome care that is resisted or refused by those at whom it is directed. Even as they spoke frankly about the forms of vulnerability they face in their work, the women working in the sex industry whom I conducted research with did not see themselves as victims of exploitation; did not find LFSJ's rhetoric to be relevant or useful to them; and, among the more politicized women, even saw their advocacy as detrimental to a sex workers' rights campaign. Crucially, sex workers' own sense of the value of what they offer to their customers clashes with activists' assertions that they are manipulated, abused, and/or traumatized. LFSJ rhetoric sharply contrasts with their own experiences and understandings of what they are offering and why it matters. Thus, spaces of overlap between the aims of the anti-trafficking activists and sex workers—such as a shared concern with how the public blames sex workers for the abuses they may face, for instance—appear untenable and unpalatable to sex workers and remain unrealized as potential areas of collaborative action.

The rhetoric of the anti–human trafficking advocates of LFSJ causes misrecognition on the part of the sex workers they claim to help. But what about the advocacy of those explicitly aligned with sex workers? In the next chapter, I will explore some of the issues that Japanese sex workers themselves express concern about and the rhetoric and interventions of a group of activists who use a labor rights framework to address working conditions in the sex industry. As we shall see, in a context in which male productivity is understood as being dependent on female care, sex workers' rights advocates are finding that claims to rights as laborers can only clash with the understanding of sex workers as caregivers.

6 Risk and Rights

SAYAKA WANTED TO SEE the new beds. We were walking through Kabukichō early on a weekday afternoon, when most people in this neighborhood where day and night are often reversed were, as Sayaka remarked, "still asleep." We had just passed outside the reception of the *deriheru* where Sayaka occasionally worked, when she said that we were close to the rental room (*rentaru rūmu*) business where she often met customers. Rental rooms are spaces that can be rented for sex. Averaging about ¥2,000–3,000 for a one-to-two-hour stay, they are a modest alternative to love hotels.[1] The affordable pricing comes at the expense of comfort, but the sluggish economy has made them a popular option among sex industry customers. After receiving several complaints, the establishment had recently bought new furniture. We turned down a short alleyway and entered the business. An older man at the reception stood up and Sayaka explained what she wanted. "Room 6 is occupied," the receptionist said gruffly, directing us among the handful of rooms. "But you can look in on Room 5." Even in the dimmed lighting, the small room looked dingy. It was bare save for a single-sized bed covered in black pleather. On the side of the room, a plastic fold-in door concealed a small shower. Without expression, Sayaka pushed her fists down on the mattress but it barely gave way. It was only a marginal improvement. She said, "It's not clean." As a working space, it left much to be desired, but customers were less willing to spend money than they used to be.

As nonregular workers in stigmatized labor, women in Tokyo's sex industry have little control over the conditions of their work. The room that

Sayaka and I visited, for instance, was uncomfortable and unclean. But the real issue—left unspoken between us that day—was that whatever conditions a sex worker might encounter when she meets a customer, she does so almost entirely on her own. Recently, this has become more acute. Rental rooms such as the one Sayaka and I visited are the by-products of a transformation in the form of commercial sex in Japan over the past two decades that is the combination of regulatory changes, new business opportunities, and the effects of recession on consumer spending (see Chapter 1). The overwhelming industry-wide shift to *deriheru* since the 2000s has exacerbated the risks to sex workers.[2] Although women working at brick-and-mortar businesses can rely on male staff to intervene in the case of a troublesome customer, *deriherujō* face customers alone in hotel or rental rooms and private apartments.[3] Numerous women I spoke with told me that they would never consider working at anything but a brick-and-mortar business, reducing their aversion to *deriheru* to a single word: *Kowai* ("I'm afraid"). What if something were to happen, they wondered out loud. They would be all alone in an unknown space with just the customer. Who would help them? Sayaka herself, self-assured and confident from many years in the industry, said that she felt more anxious and apprehensive working at a *deriheru*. But with over twenty thousand such businesses registered nationwide in 2018, the vast majority of women in the sex industry are *deriherujō*.[4] All women in the Japanese sex industry, however, wherever they work, share risks of unsafe sex and sexually transmitted infections (STIs), aggressive or violent customers, secret video recordings, harassment, crime, and/or assault.

In 1997, Momoka Momoko, an activist and the first Japanese sex worker to come out publicly, pointed out that there is nothing intrinsically violent about the exchange of sexual services for money. "Why is our work called 'dangerous'?" she asked. "Sex work itself is not dangerous. It's not helpful in the least when people tell you, 'You should quit because it's dangerous.' Why is all prostitution called 'violence'? Prostitution itself is not violent. The problem is that *it ends up becoming violent.*"[5] A market-based exchange itself does not produce violence—something we each know intuitively from the numerous exchanges we participate in daily, but that often seems to be forgotten when the topic is sex work. The question is, following Momoka, why does commercial sex *become* violent?

In many contexts around the world, individuals involved in commercial sex endure police harassment and/or abuse, arrest, violence (including verbal abuse, physical assault, rape, and murder), and/or theft.[6] This is due to the frequent social marginalization of those who transact sex and to dehumanizing and discriminatory attitudes that construct them as legitimate targets of abuse, violence, and crime. In Japan, widespread acceptance of the sex industry, its legal status, its high degree of organization, and low crime rates overall create an environment in which sex workers do not generally face the degree of violence that women involved in commercial sex elsewhere do. But the industry is hardly absent of problems. Although the rewards of working in the sex industry can be high, especially for young women, the risks of the work may also be high, particularly for those same young women with little social experience. Despite widespread perceptions of the industry's social necessity and sex workers' own understanding of the social value of their labor, to engage in sex work in Japan is to engage in a relationship with risk.[7]

In this chapter, I follow Momoka to explore why sex work *becomes* violent and look at the issues that women working in the sex industry themselves identify as subjects of concern. Although women in Tokyo's sex industry benefit from some of the conditions deriving from sex work's place in the gendered economy (such as high earnings), the grayness of regulation, the work's distinction from normative forms of labor, and stigma and discrimination toward sex workers produce conditions of risk and vulnerability. A sex workers' advocacy campaign that uses a labor rights framework to demand legal protections and benefits is working to improve the everyday conditions of sex workers. These advocates recognize the value of sex workers' healing labor and regard sex as an activity that is productive of economic life. Women working in the sex industry, however, are largely uninterested in engaging with the rhetoric or interventions of this campaign. I argue that sex workers' healing labor creates an impediment for labor rights in this context.

Engaging Risk

Sexual Health

"No one—neither the managers nor the customers—thinks about the health of sex workers," Aimi, who had worked five years as a dominatrix and five as a *sōpujō* while raising a daughter on her own, grimly summed up. We were talking about sexual health and the possibility of contracting an STI—an everpresent concern in an industry centered on intimate contact between strangers. Every sex worker I spoke to felt some degree of anxiety about her health.

But as Aimi's comment suggests, within the sex industry, sex workers are not the subjects of concern.

Rather, Tokyo's cisheteronormative sex industry is a market organized around the pleasure and preferences of customers. As such, responsibility for sexual health is placed squarely on the shoulders of individual sex workers, who must concern themselves both with the health of their customers and protecting their own. In a context of steep competition, however, many businesses discourage sex workers from using condoms, making managing one's sexual health a less than straightforward issue.

The grayness of the sex industry's status presents an obstacle to the collection of adequate information on the prevalence of STIs. For example, because the anti-prostitution law prohibits commercial exchanges involving penile-vaginal intercourse, for the government to fund research on STI transmission from intercourse would be to acknowledge that the law is being broken.[8] Thus, there is little information available on how widespread intercourse (*honban*) is throughout the industry and under what conditions it is happening, including at businesses such as soaplands, where, due to a legal loophole, it is open knowledge that intercourse is a standard service.

The available data, however, suggests that condom usage is relatively low for services at nonintercourse businesses. In a study of over three hundred sex workers mostly working at *deriheru* in Tokyo and neighboring prefectures, respondents reported *not* using condoms for services at the following rates: dry-humping (54% of 326); fellatio (56% of 330); ejaculation in the mouth (70% of 322); anal sex (21% of 95); and penile-vaginal intercourse (14% of 56).[9] Dry-humping and oral sex are standard services at *deriheru* and it is notable that over half of the women in the study engaged in them without a condom. Among 201 respondents who had not used a condom at their most recent encounter with a customer, 81 percent gave their reason as, "These are not services necessitating a condom"—reflecting a widespread misconception that STIs can only be transmitted through genital intercourse—while others noted the preferences of customers or pressure from managers.[10] Oral sex without a condom appears to be a fairly standard practice throughout the industry, given that only the sex worker—and not the customer—is put at risk. Some businesses discourage the use of condoms while others may outright forbid their use (except in cases in which a customer has visible symptoms of an STI). Sex workers also face pressure from customers themselves, who may protest or resist using condoms.

Despite the low self-reporting of occurrences of intercourse in the above study (56 out of 347), managers who were interviewed for the same study estimated that as many as half of *deriherujō* provide it at their discretion, suggesting that respondents underreported their willingness to offer this service.[11] It is even more difficult to obtain accurate information on how many women who are offering intercourse are using condoms. Based on her experiences working at a soapland, however, Aimi commented:

> [At soaplands,] a lot of customers want intercourse without a condom and so a lot of women end up not using them. On the websites of businesses, women who are willing to do it without a condom have special symbols on their profile so that customers know, although they might be written in code so that it's not too obvious. Of course, there are also women who always insist on a condom, but they won't be popular. That will only appeal to some customers. The first thing that needs to be done is to get rid of the belief that sex without a condom is better.

Sex workers identify a general lack of knowledge about sexual health and STIs in Japan as a key reason for the relatively low rates of condom usage in the sex industry. Japanese sex education programs focus primarily on family planning rather than on providing generalized sexual health information.[12] Some of the women I spoke with could not remember if they had even been taught about STIs at school. For many, it was only after they began working in the sex industry that they began to feel knowledgeable about their sexual health. Sex worker advocates have noted that STIs and sexual health are not an acceptable topic of conversation in Japan generally, and even veteran sex workers may have inaccurate knowledge.[13] The widespread misconception, for instance, that condoms are not necessary for acts that do not include genital intercourse stands in opposition to the reality that STIs may be transmitted in numerous ways. Sex workers and their advocates also report a lack of knowledge about STIs on the part of management and customers. Megumi, who had worked at about twenty different businesses, told me that none of her managers had ever given what she considered to be adequate health information: "Not a single one. Many managers don't know much about it or are misinformed. They don't really know anything about transmission or how you can get infected. The staff don't either." As for her customers, Megumi said: "Maybe one customer out of a hundred asks for a condom. It's so rare that, when it happens, I think, 'Wow, what a great customer!'" Megumi said she thought that these were men who were either conscientious husbands or who thought that using a condom would prolong their pleasure.

Sex worker advocates are aware that access to accurate information about sexual health is an issue for many women in the sex industry and much outreach and peer support activity focuses on collating useful information in convenient and easily digestible form. Available in hard copy as well as online, these materials explain how to identify STI symptoms and provide suggestions for how to manage situations when a customer appears symptomatic. The information is often presented in creative ways and draws on the "strategic use of cuteness" to mitigate the serious nature of the information being conveyed.[14] During the time of my fieldwork, free sex industry employment magazines and their websites also offered regular columns on sexual health.

STI testing remains stigmatized in Japan. Dr. Okazaki, a general health practitioner who operates a bustling practice in central Tokyo, told me that he only rarely receives requests for routine testing. Instead, to his frustration, patients usually come in for testing only once their symptoms have already progressed. Okazaki suspected that a general low awareness of STIs was compounded by prejudicial beliefs that testing is only for individuals who have been engaging in so-called abnormal behaviors, meaning same-sex contact, promiscuity, or sex work.[15] The structure of the national health system, which is based on a treatment model rather than a preventive care model, further discourages routine testing as national health insurance covers an STI exam only when an individual complains of symptoms and not when someone simply wants to check their health status.

Although customers face no obligation to know their STI status, sex workers' bodies are regulated through monthly or bimonthly checkups. The bill for the standard four tests that sex workers receive—gonorrhea, chlamydia, syphilis, and HIV—amounts to around ¥10,000–12,000. This translates to a significant financial burden for sex workers, who must bear the full cost of these regular tests. Should an STI test return positive, a woman cannot return to work until her symptoms have cleared; nor will her business offer her worker's compensation during this period. Participation in this system of medical surveillance is enforced as some managers prohibit women who do not submit regular health certificates from working.

In addition to the financial cost, sex workers may receive unwelcome attention from medical personnel. Some sex workers have reported being lectured to by clinic staff who wonder about their need for frequent STI exams.[16]

Those women who divulge the nature of their work to their doctor may be told, "But this is a clinic for ordinary married women . . ." and be turned away, or be questioned about their reasons for working in the sex industry.[17] For this reason, many women prefer to go to clinics near sex industry districts, whose staff are accustomed to catering to sex workers. Megumi, for instance, had been going to a doctor whose practice was just a short walk from the Kabukichō sex and entertainment district for a few years. The doctor had many patients who were sex workers and Megumi felt she could talk to him about her work without being judged. She praised his kindness, telling me that he often found ways to get her insurance to cover her tests. Aimi, on the other hand, went to a "normal" doctor and paid ¥30,000 each month for four tests. It was more expensive for her because her manager required that she get a certificate from the doctor declaring that she was healthy.

This regular testing that sex workers undergo is ultimately for the convenience of their customers. It is a means of controlling women's bodies in order to protect the health of customers while doing little to prevent risks to either sex worker or customer.[18] Of course, women in the sex industry benefit from finding out as early as possible if they have contracted an STI, especially as untreated infections can increase the likelihood of contracting (or spreading) other STIs and can lead to other health problems, such as pregnancy complications or infertility. STI testing itself, however, does nothing to protect sex workers from contracting an infection in the first place.

In the context of market demand for sexual services without a condom, women may make financially based decisions not to use a condom, just as they may make financially based decisions to offer intercourse. The unpredictability of economic opportunity in this nonregular work makes at least some women reluctant to create hard-and-fast rules about what they will or will not do, even if they are fully aware of the risks. Aimi explained the economic imperative behind women's calculations of risk and reward:

> At a company, you get a fixed salary, but at a soapland, if you work hard and are popular, you might go home with ¥100,000 that day or the next. Not many women will be willing to say that they will absolutely only have sex [intercourse] with a condom if the best way for them to make money is through not using one. Women will think in terms of a "balance." Of course they know that it's better to wear one and that if they catch something it would show up on a test and then they'd have to take a month off from work, which could be

hard for them. But when you're faced with a customer who will pay a huge amount of money for 120 minutes, most women would decide not to wear a condom.

The need to attract repeat customers is another consideration. Under such circumstances, a woman may productively engage risk in ways that shape the market for all sex workers.[19] Sex workers "past their prime," who have seen their earnings decrease as they age, may be especially willing to do so and begin to negotiate on services that previously they would not have considered.

In the absence of requirements that customers themselves get tested or wear condoms, some women in the sex industry feel that, ultimately, whether they contract an STI or not is up to chance. As Chie explained,

> A bad point about this work is that it's scary to get sick. . . . I go to a clinic for a checkup once a month. I've been lucky and haven't gotten sick once. But it's not always something you can control. No matter how safe the business where you're working, you could still get sick. Or, you could work at a business with unsafe services and never once catch anything. I've been lucky.

To refer to one's luck, however, is merely another way of underscoring the basic fact of risk.

Managing Customers

Due to the stigma around sex work and the short-term nature of many women's engagement in it, many sex workers know little, in general, about the relevant laws that frame their labor. Having grown up aware of the industry's existence, many women simply assume that it is unambiguously legal. Megumi, who had worked at both businesses that illegally offer intercourse and those that adhere to the law, told me that even after five years in the sex industry she was only hazily aware of some of the recent legal changes affecting it, most of which she saw as disconnected from the day-to-day concerns of her work: "Just through working, there are no opportunities to get that kind of information. The staff don't talk about [the law] at all. The manager probably knows more because he has to deal with it, but that knowledge doesn't filter down to the women interacting with customers." She thought that newcomers were especially vulnerable: "The youngest women probably don't even know that intercourse is illegal [due to the anti-prostitution law]. Eventually, they figure it out but they still don't understand why it's allowed at soaplands." Yumi had a more blunt assessment: "You only learn about the law when something happens," by which she meant, when the police show up. "No one is telling women about the law." Although police practice has generally been not to arrest sex workers or hold them accountable for working at a business participating in illegal activities, beginning with the mid-2000s cleanup campaign, the first cases of sex workers being arrested for *hōjozai* (aiding in the carrying out of a crime) occurred.[20] Although it is still a relatively rare occurrence, advocates are concerned that the number of women arrested on this charge is on the increase.

Even if a sex worker is aware that her business is violating the law, there is generally little she can do about it besides changing her workplace. Ayano's decision simply not to worry about the law reflected her precarious position. Ayano had previously worked for several years at a *hoteheru* that offered intercourse and had known that this was illegal. But she had decided not to think about that fact—what good would worrying do her, she reasoned. "The law had felt very abstract to me," Ayano explained. "There's nothing you can really do if you're working at an illegal business—which you might not even be aware of—so there's no point in worrying about it." Ayano had put the possibility that she might be caught up in a raid and detained by the police far from her mind, but twice, suddenly, without warning, the business she had been working for had shut down. Later she learned that closing down only to reopen under a new name was a strategy commonly used by businesses to avoid police raids. After this happened for a second time, she realized that the managers looked out only for themselves. "I realized that I would have to be pragmatic, too," she told me—what I understood as her meaning that she, too, should be as ruthlessly strategic as possible in deciding where to work.

Regardless of whether a business adheres to the law or not, customers may individually pressure sex workers for intercourse. Although some women refuse customer demands altogether, at *deriheru* in particular other sex workers may take advantage of the lack of oversight and negotiate directly with a customer. Megumi told me that many of her customers pretended not to know that intercourse was off-limits in order to see how far they could get, and would protest their ignorance when she stopped them. "They're terrible actors!" she exclaimed. Ayano, on the other hand, described how the value of intercourse had decreased over the past decade. To her, it was an alarming trend that a more intense service was now worth less and often done unprotected. She described how, when she had formerly worked at a *hoteheru*, she could negotiate with customers for how much they would pay her for intercourse on top of the standard service. "You get used to offering it," she told me, shrugging and conveying her sense of the arbitrariness of the law. Ayano had asked customers, "How much extra will you pay for this?" but she confessed that she had never liked negotiating and had often found it intimidating. At a get-together, I watched Ayano and Megumi make fun of customers who pleaded with them for intercourse but were unwilling to pay for it. Mimicking such customers, Ayano clapped her hands together as if in prayer and bowed her head, letting out a high-pitched *Onegai!* ("Please!"), while laughing. Ayano told Megumi and me that she thought most *deriheru* in western Japan now offer intercourse. It was so expected, she said, that, due to store competition, women were not even paid extra for it anymore. Megumi gloomily chimed in, observing that she "hated" customers in town on business from western Japan because they took it for granted that intercourse was part of the service. Of course, she added, when a sex worker decides on her own initiative to negotiate, she may unwittingly lead customers to believe that all employees at her business are willing to offer intercourse. If another woman at the same business then refuses, the customer might accuse her of making up store policy. This was a nuisance at best, Megumi explained, and, at worst, a more serious issue.

Dealing with angry or aggressive customers is a not uncommon, and often anxiety-inducing, concern for sex workers, especially those working in *deriheru*, who are keenly aware that "it's just the two of us in the room." I was often told by the women I spoke with that one has to be very careful in managing situations where a customer misbehaves or requests a service that one refuses. "If you get mad at the customer, he could get angry, too, and his attitude might change in an instant," Yumi, the former aromatherapist, told me, explaining how an encounter could quickly turn volatile if a customer grew upset. Customers might become embarrassed, for example, at being refused intercourse and react by becoming defensive, resentful, or angry. This can lead to tense or dangerous situations and sex workers often do not have many options at their disposal if they are alone at a hotel with their customer. In the aforementioned study of over three hundred sex workers in the greater Tokyo area, 60.5 percent of respondents overall reported having had experiences with customers who became angry after they were refused intercourse and 42.1 percent reported having been forced to do something they did not want to do.[21] Yumi described to me an encounter in which a customer with the physique of a pro wrestler had been very drunk. She had been scared of him. With her petite frame, most customers could easily overpower her normally. Yumi managed to find an excuse to slip out and called the management to tell them she was on her way back to the office. The driver who took Yumi back was sympathetic and tried to commiserate with her, but Yumi found this annoying: "The staff hadn't actually done anything to protect me!" Businesses typically react after an incident with a customer has occurred instead of pro-actively creating the conditions in which sex workers can safely work. To in-stall safeguards against such problems in the first place would be to make their services less attractive to customers.

Yumi's approach to dealing with troublesome customers was to maintain the intimacy of the encounter. She explained that she had been secretly filmed (*tōsatsu*) by at least three customers. These were just the times she had noticed, although she thought it likely that there had been other times when she had not. "The first time, I saw a camera peeking out of the customer's bag." She described how the customer had become evasive and visibly uncomfortable after he realized that she had seen the camera. Concerned that he would get angry, she smiled and took on a cheerful but pouty attitude: "It bothers me, it's embarrassing!" she whined in a singsong voice. The best way to deal with the situation, Yumi explained, was to complain as a girlfriend might. Similarly, when a customer pushed her for intercourse, she would cheerfully announce, "There are more fun things we can do instead!"

Yumi's approach to managing a potentially volatile situation was not un-like the advice that Mika, the sex industry instructor, gave at the Q&A follow-ing the new employee training session described in Chapter 4. One audience member, who had just recently begun working at the escort sexual massage business that hosted the session, had asked Mika how to deal with unwanted touching by a customer. Nodding knowingly, Mika advised the assembled women to use the maternal character they were assuming to cheerfully but firmly admonish the customer, making him feel mildly embarrassed (for ex-ample, "You naughty boy!"). Here, assuming a maternal stance served as a strategy for pacifying customers and protecting oneself. Infantilization, ex-pressed in an indulgent maternal tone, could defuse a situation whereas an angry rebuke might make matters worse.

What the performed cheerfulness of these situations disguises, however, is how stressful they can be for sex workers, who worry that a customer's mood could suddenly swing. Chie spoke to me of her strategy for dealing with dif-ficult customers, which, she emphasized, she had not been taught by manage-ment but had learned on her own as she gained experience. At one business, a *fasshon herusu* where the staff were on the premises, Chie had been willing to have intercourse if a customer offered her extra money. In these cases, she negotiated herself. "But," she muttered, "there are always idiots who want intercourse without having to pay for it." If a customer persisted after she had already told him it was not possible, Chie would call the reception and ask a staff member to come and assist her. This had been fairly straightforward. Working at a *deriheru*, however, Chie felt the dangers that came with being completely alone with a customer.

> When it's just the two of you in a hotel room or a rental room and you do something clumsy that ends up angering the customer, it can be scary. As you get used to it, you get better at communicating so that things go uneventfully. You can suggest to the customer, "Okay, why don't you talk to the store and if it's okay with them, it's fine with me." In the meantime, you quickly get dressed and run. You don't stop to take a shower first, you just get out of there because your safety is more important. Most *deriherujō* wear clothing that is easy to take off and put back on again. Part of the reason for that is so that they can put it on in a flash if they need to get out. But it doesn't happen so often that it comes to that, that you have to leave all of a sudden. Unless a customer is violent, a drug addict, or very drunk, with most people there's something you can do. If you make an effort you can talk your way through most things. But sex workers hate drug addicts and drunks. It's difficult for them to get it up or to finish. Dull and straightforward customers are the best.

Sex workers may also face unscrupulous customers. For *deriherujō* who visit customers at their homes, being photographed or filmed without one's knowledge is always a risk. Megumi had once caught a customer secretly recording their encounter, and now she was always vigilant. They had been midway through the service at his apartment when the camera made a noise. She became very upset and called the *deriheru*'s reception, leaving immediately. The management had put the customer on a black list but this did little to make Megumi feel better. It was a very frightening experience for her. Since then, Megumi has always been on the lookout for hidden cameras. If, for example, she sees a bag that seems oddly arranged, she immediately becomes suspicious. Similarly, once when I met the sex workers' rights advocate Tomoko she had just been on the phone at length with a sex worker who discovered a video of her on the Internet posted by a customer. This woman—as with Megumi, Yumi, and others—had not consented to having her image recorded and was terrified of how the images might circulate and with what consequences.[22]

At stake in these encounters with troublesome customers is the risk of violence or of being outed, women's feelings of autonomy over their body, and the humiliation and demoralization of not having one's wishes respected and of being forced to do something one does not want to do. Most individuals working in the sex industry are young women with no training for what they might encounter who are put into situations where they are alone and have to rely on their own quick-wittedness and resourcefulness to keep them safe. Such situations create anxiety and a sense of isolation, and the lack of prior knowledge or social experience with which many women enter into the sex industry has obvious implications here.

Finally, although rates of violent crime are low overall in Japan and Japanese sex workers face relatively less violence than their peers in other contexts, violence does occur. With the shift to *deriheru*, women have become more isolated. Kaname Yukiko has observed that from 2000 to 2011 there were 2,043 reported cases of brutal crimes at motels and love hotels, including 76 murders and 531 robberies. "There isn't data on how many of these involved *deriherujō*," Kaname writes, "but the fact that so many brutal crimes are happening in the sites where they work demands attention."[23] Many of the women I spoke to in my research were aware of the murder of a woman who had transacted sex with a man she had met through a *deai kafe*, which happened not long after I began long-term fieldwork. Women working in underground circumstances—especially foreign sex workers—are particularly easy targets for crime.[24]

A Lack of Labor Protections

Women working in the sex industry mostly have little recourse when they encounter abuses in their work because sex work is not formally recognized as labor in Japan. Individuals engaged in commercial sex are not guaranteed minimum workplace standards, granted protections, or provided benefits. As several examples have already demonstrated, a woman's workplace bears little responsibility to her, especially in regard to off-premises meetings with customers. Although many sex workers are pleasantly surprised to learn that they do not need to file taxes—as they are not considered employees—they also do not receive a minimum guaranteed salary, are not granted paid leave (for example, sick days, menstrual leave, family leave), do not make pension contributions, cannot protest sexual harassment or withholding of payment at the local labor standards office, and do not receive worker's compensation (*rōsai hoken*). In an industry in which sex workers are often discouraged from using condoms, the latter is a particular source of frustration for many. When Yumi contracted an STI while working at a *hoteheru* that illegally offered intercourse, she went to her manager to request worker's compensation to cover her recovery period. "He laughed at me," she recalled bitterly. She did not receive anything from her business. When Yumi informed the staff that she would be taking time off to recover, she was ridiculed. "They told me, 'If your body is so weak [that you have to take time off], you should just quit.'" Yumi was keenly aware that she alone bore the consequences after contracting an infection under workplace conditions decided by management. Unfortunately, her experience is not unusual. During my fieldwork, I encountered only one woman who had taken out private insurance to protect herself from lost earnings in the event of injury or illness.

The gendered aspects of this labor insecurity become apparent when we consider that male management and staff are recognized as laborers within the structure of a formal economy. In contrast to sex workers, who, from a legal standpoint, are treated as independent contractors, managers and staff are considered regular employees who have their wages deposited to their bank accounts, contribute to pension plans, and pay taxes. They are also subject to the grayness of the laws—and, in fact, are most likely to be arrested in case of a violation—but there is no doubt that what they are doing is formally considered to be labor. In countless other minor ways, workplace practices suggest that it is the male staff—and not female sex workers—who are viewed as the "real" employees. At soaplands, for example, it is common for the sex workers to be asked to pool together money for year-end bonuses for the staff. "Usually, at a normal company," Aimi said, "it's the president who gives bonuses to the employees. But at a soapland, women collect money to give to the men. That really shocked me." This was on top of what Aimi had already enumerated as a substantial list of the various investments she had had to make to begin working at the soapland. Everything that she needed for the work was paid for out of her own pocket, from condoms to outfits to cigarettes for customers. Even the tea served at staff meetings was paid for by the women!

Although sex workers can go to the police to report crimes by customers, both their uncertain legal status and social stigma may make them reluctant to do so. Generally, the authorities' regulation of the sex industry is primarily

concerned with restricting its excesses, and the industry is not a high priority for the police. When I asked an official at the National Police Agency how
sex workers could better protect themselves from potentially violent customers, the official reacted with blank surprise. The grayness of the sex industry
places women in an insecure position vis-à-vis the law, and the police may
crack down on what they normally tacitly allow if a police report is filed. For
women illegally negotiating intercourse, this may be particularly true, and
they may thus hesitate to report customer violence for fear of how their own
behavior will be viewed.[25] Moreover, to go to the police would entail exposing themselves to unwelcome scrutiny. When I asked a lawyer familiar with
sex industry cases how sex workers can determine without a doubt that their
business is properly registered, she responded: "Well, they can go to the police and find out, can't they?"[26] She paused awkwardly for a second, taking in
what she had just said before giving an embarrassed laugh. The likelihood of
a young woman going to the highly masculinized space of a police station to
inquire about whether the sex industry business she is considering working at
has its papers in order is low. On another occasion, a sympathetic police officer from central Japan told me that he wished that more sex workers would
report small infractions by their businesses, saying that this would help the
police to punish unscrupulous managers and benefit sex workers, too. But he
acknowledged that for a young woman to willingly identify herself as a sex
worker to the police and file a report would take courage and determination.

In court, the grayness of sex workers' status materializes in invalidated
claims and discriminatory treatment. According to the high-profile feminist
lawyer Tsunoda Yukiko, "Because women in the sex industry entered the work
'of their own free will,' there is a strong pressure that prevents them from
making complaints, no matter what work conditions they encounter."[27] Tsunoda argues that an inconsistency lies at the heart of legal attitudes toward sex
workers—one that effectively blames them for their predicaments and places
them outside of the protection of the law.[28] For the most part, claims by sex
workers are voided on the basis that they entered into an illegitimate "prostitution contract" (baishun keiyaku) by engaging in sex work. Citing a case in
which a woman working at a soapland was injured in a traffic accident and
filed for compensation for her absence from work, Tsunoda notes that because
the court interpreted the woman's normal earnings as deriving from prostitution, her claim was denied. Instead, she was provided compensation calculated based on the average wages for a woman of her age—a figure presumably

much lower than her actual missed earnings. Similarly, in the unlikely case that a sex worker would sue for withheld earnings, Tsunoda speculates that a court would invalidate her claim on the basis that her work violates "public order and morals."[29]

This legal logic was inverted, however, in an infamous 1987 trial known among sex workers' rights advocates as the "Ikebukuro Case" (*Ikebukuro Jiken*)—after the name of the Tokyo neighborhood where the events in question occurred. In this case, a woman working for a *hotetoru* business was attacked by her customer in a hotel room, bound, and filmed while being sexually assaulted. Eventually, through pretending to enjoy the acts, the woman managed to escape her bonds and take the knife that had been used to threaten her. In the struggle that followed, she stabbed the man over thirty times. He fainted and later died from blood loss, and the woman was arrested for his murder two weeks later.[30] At the criminal trial, the judges convicted the woman of excessive self-defense, basing their ruling on the argument that the woman had brought the crime on herself (*jigō jitoku*) through knowingly entering dangerous work, and that, as a sex worker, she was not subject to the same protections as "ordinary women and children."[31] Tsunoda, who took part in the woman's legal defense, points out that in this case, the judges treated the "prostitution contract" as legitimate, arguing that because the woman had implicitly entered such a contract by showing up at the hotel, she had renounced some of her physical and sexual freedoms.[32] Sex worker advocates have highlighted this ruling as a discriminatory legal precedent that underscores how the law differentiates between violence against "ordinary" women and violence against sex workers.[33]

Advocating for Rights

Despite the rhetorical dominance of North American and western European sex worker activism within the global sex workers' movement since the 1970s, individuals engaged in commercial sex have collectively struggled for better conditions, for recognition of their rights, and against discrimination and those who would seek to define their experiences in many sociohistorical contexts. As Kamala Kempadoo has observed, "Sex workers' struggles are . . . neither a creation of a western prostitutes' rights movement or the privilege of the past three decades."[34] In Japan, organized activism among those engaged in commercial sex dates at least to the 1950s, when an association of women working in brothels agitated against the passage of the Prostitution Prevention Law.[35]

In an essay inaugurating the last two decades of Japanese sex worker advocacy, Momoka Momoko describes some of the obstacles that women working in both the legal and illegal sectors of the sex industry face in protecting their health and safety. Summing these up, she writes, "Every day we are confronted with decisions about having sex and working safely—not just whether to take the [birth control] pill, but whether to use a condom and what kinds of services to offer. The issue is, who gets to decide and how."[36] Adopting the transliterated term "sex worker" as well as a labor rights framework, Momoka underscores the need for sex workers themselves to determine the conditions under which they offer services. She ends her essay with a call for sex workers to come together and correct the record: "Recently, there's suddenly been an increase in discussion about sex work by people who are not—that is, who don't see themselves as—sex workers. But what we need is discussion and action among ourselves. For that reason, a network of sex workers is being born in Japan. We are the only ones who can know what we ourselves need."[37]

Momoka's mention of "an increase in discussion" by non–sex workers was a reference to academic and feminist debates about sex work following the 1993 translation into Japanese of Frédérique Delacoste and Priscilla Alexander's edited volume *Sex Work: Writings by Women in the Sex Industry*.[38] Discourse by non–sex workers, as Momoka notes, often treated women in the sex industry in one of two ways: "We're [either] pitied as victims resigned to violence or criticized as traitors to feminism who are complicit with violence."[39] Following the publication of Momoka's essay, individuals working in the sex industry and their supporters began to challenge the ways in which sex workers' experiences had been framed by those without firsthand knowledge of sex work, particularly Japanese feminists, with the publication of Matsuzawa Kureichi's edited collection of essays critiquing anti-prostitution arguments and, a few years later, Kaname Yukiko and Mizushima Nozomi's landmark survey of female sex workers.[40] In the art world, the artist and sex worker BuBu de la Madeleine confronted the rhetoric of anti-prostitution feminists and proclaimed the dignity of sex workers.[41]

Heeding Momoka's call at the 1994 International AIDS Conference in Yokohama for the development of a sex workers' support and self-help group, a handful of women came together to establish such a group in 1995 and began meeting monthly in Osaka and Tokyo.[42] Throughout the 2000s, several small groups formed to engage in short-term projects to promote sexual health among sex workers. These groups have emphasized the creation of support networks among individuals in the sex industry. In 1999, however, a sex workers' rights advocacy group was founded after government funding for HIV prevention activities among sex workers became available.

Adopting a labor rights framework, the members of this group argue that people engaged in commercial sex have a right to work safely and should have access to the same dignity afforded by legal protections and benefits as individuals in other categories of work. The group's activities include outreach to women (both cisgender and transgender) in the sex industry, research on sex industry conditions, lobbying, overseas networking, and public outreach. The group's membership remains relatively small—roughly a dozen or so individuals—because public exposure as an advocate brings its own hazards. Some members are very active, while others only participate in select activities, and the group includes both members who are current or former sex workers themselves and their supporters.

Although full decriminalization of the sex industry is the group's ultimate goal, on a day-to-day basis the advocates focus on pragmatic activities through which to support and improve the conditions of sex workers. As one advocate told me:

> We have to be practical. Most [members of the public] will agree with you if you talk about things like preventing STIs or minimizing the possibility of violence against sex workers. But if you talk about things like rights (*kenri*) or human rights (*jinken*), neither of which are well understood as concepts in Japan, people will think that you're being unrealistic and that your ideas are not implementable at all. So, instead, the group focuses on the practical things that we can do for the people who are working now, like educational outreach on STIs and seminars for sex industry business managers.

This advocate suggested that, while most members of the public would favor improving everyday conditions for sex workers, they would be less willing to change their basic attitudes toward women in the sex industry or toward sex work. For instance, the advocacy group receives some funding for HIV/AIDS prevention work, but there are no grants that support advocacy for sex workers. This mirrors an issue that sex workers in many contexts face—there is often public support for approaches that view the sex industry as a source of public health problems, crime, or violence against women, but not for approaches that center the rights and dignity of the individuals working there.

The sex workers' rights advocates recognize the social value of sex workers' healing labor and argue that the sex industry should be treated as a quotidian sector of the economy. Tomoko, a tireless advocate who has been involved in the activities of the group since its inception, articulated these positions to me over numerous meetings.

"I don't want people to think that there's only a choice between putting up with the sex industry as it is now or getting rid of it altogether," Tomoko said, explaining what she thought people concerned about abuses in the sex industry should know. Instead, she believed the focus should be on "how to improve things, how to make them better than they are now, how to decrease misfortune and crime in the industry—I want people to think practically like this." From her years of advocacy work, Tomoko holds a deep conviction that, although commercial sex will always exist in some form, its conditions will deteriorate with stricter regulation: "Even if you get rid of sex industry businesses, people would just work on their own. Commercial sex would just go underground." Tomoko referred to the September 2010 murder of a woman by a man who had paid her for sex after meeting at a *deai kafe* to explain how criminalizing the sex industry would mean that businesses would take even less responsibility over the women whose labor they profited from and that the risks for sex workers would increase.

> The *deai kafe* [management] just said that the woman and the customer decided on their own [to exchange sex for money], so it has nothing to do with them. [Their attitude was,] "She ended up being murdered, but because she selfishly decided to do it, she only had herself to blame and it couldn't be helped." Is this the kind of world we want to live in? Because what she was doing isn't recognized as work, she was held responsible for the actions that led to her murder. . . . Sex workers have a right to work safely and to protect their health, and for us not to say that it's fine if sex work goes underground and that we don't care if someone ends up killed.

Although Tomoko recognized how a male-centered industry benefits from the insecurity of sex workers, she directed her anger at anti-prostitution activists who advocated for criminalizing the sex industry. Tomoko accused these activists of irresponsibility for being blind to the consequences of their rhetoric, which she saw as worsening conditions for those in the sex industry. She and other advocates resented the feeling of being lectured to, being treated as though they are enabling sexism, and hearing sex work described as undignified and lowly work with no value by such activists. But, more fundamentally, Tomoko viewed anti-prostitution advocates as oblivious to how the gendered economy makes sex work attractive to some women:

> [These activists] just say it's best for women to quit sex work and that the sex industry should be cracked down on. I think this is irresponsible. Many women would suffer if the sex industry were to disappear. There are lots of women who are able to do various things because of the sex industry—like raising their children, finding time to spend with them and looking after them. . . . That's because this is the only work that allows you to work freely and to quickly earn a lot of money. There's nothing else.

Tomoko reiterated some of the elements of autonomy and flexibility that distinguish sex work from normative forms of work in Japan, granting opportunities to women who prefer it over their alternatives in mostly low-status and low-pay feminized labor.

At the heart of Tomoko's critique was the accusation that anti-prostitution advocates do not recognize how sex is always a part of the gendered economy. "[Anti-prostitution advocates] say that . . . sex work promotes sexism, but don't other forms of work do that, too? There are many forms of work that are wrapped up in the gender system, and many forms of feminized work." All work is gendered, Tomoko pointed out, but she thought that sex work was singled out because it involves what she referred to as "sex without love." She posed a question: What about sex *for* love? "If it's sex for love, feminists don't think about how chauvinism or the gender system is integral to it—they don't problematize that." Tomoko explained that romantic love is also a gendered and sexualized economy based on a capitalist value system in which who is considered to be a desirable partner rests on their adherence to normative standards of femininity or masculinity.

Why, Tomoko wondered, did anti-prostitution advocates not critique notions of romantic love in the same way that they critiqued sex work? The marital household and the sex industry, she explained, are maintained by a family structure and gendered division of labor in which housewives and sex workers share in the care of men. According to Tomoko, the household-based reproductive labor of wives allows men to focus completely on their work, and the healing labor of sex workers rejuvenates these exhausted men. An ideology of romantic love serves to naturalize this division between differ-ent forms of women's reproductive labor. "Japanese economic growth is sup-ported by patriarchy," she summed up—and she didn't see things changing. "It's a bad economy now, right? And what are young women doing? Everyone wants to get married. Instead of opening up their own path or finding their way independently of a man, most women want to find a rich man or a stable salaryman or bureaucrat to marry. So, if you think about the gender system in Japan, whether sex work exists or not, Japanese women have a low conscious-ness [of empowerment]." Young women were eager to find good marriages, Tomoko explained—they wanted a place in this sexual economy. "For many women, this is happiness—taking care of a household and raising children while their husband works. That's what many women want." In Tomoko's eyes, women are not *rejecting* a gendered division of labor based in the family unit but rather *embracing* it.

When I asked Tomoko whether it wouldn't be appropriate to oppose this division of women into wives and sex workers, she hesitated. "Oppose it . . . hmm, that's difficult. It gets inconsistent here but I don't think that overthrowing patriarchy is in the interests of supporting sex worker rights. That's not what we're pushing for. There are many sex workers who want to be housewives. So we can't oppose it, even though it's contradictory." As To-moko's hesitation expressed, such a view is ultimately also complicit with a male-centered economy and notions that center a feminized care anchored to the conjugal household as the source of women's moral personhood. As Tomoko articulated it, the goal of the sex workers' rights movement is not to dismantle the structures of a gendered economy but to do away with distinc-tions that differentiate between the work of women in the sex industry and those in other areas of the economy such that the value of their contributions can be formally acknowledged. The gendered economy, however, would re-main intact.

Rights and Care

Although women working in Tokyo's sex industry benefit from the activities of a small group of dedicated activists who are working to improve conditions in their industry, sex workers largely show little interest in or engagement with the rights rhetoric or interventions of this campaign. In many laboring contexts around the world, widespread vulnerabilities and problems in an in-

dustry may galvanize collective action. Why, then, do sex workers seem uninterested in precisely the types of labor rights that seemingly might be a step
toward dealing with such problems?

Most basically, a labor rights framework depends on individuals seeing
themselves as having a longer-term stake in their labor and associating or
identifying with the work they are engaged in. As I have argued, however,
women in the Japanese sex industry overwhelmingly do not associate with
their work. Instead, these women prefer to think of themselves as *shirōto*
("amateurs") no different from other, "ordinary" women, and as transient
workers who have "flowed" into the industry and will "flow" out again when
the time comes. To identify *as* a sex worker would powerfully affect their own
sense of their place within the moral economy in which they operate. A lack of
a sense of identification and of longer-term investment means that for many
sex workers, politicization feels irrelevant. As the former *hoteherujō* Ayano
observed, "Women in the sex industry don't have an identity as sex workers.
There's no labor movement there either."

In practice, the grayness of the sex industry—and women's status within
it—works against the ability and desire of many sex workers to engage with
rights rhetoric. As Tomoko pointed out, the public typically blames sex workers for their circumstances, even when they are murdered. Many women in-
ternalize stigma and believe that, because they made a choice to engage in
what is considered to be disreputable work, they cannot complain about the
conditions they encounter.[43] As several examples in this chapter have suggested, sex workers often simply resign themselves to their situation when
they encounter a problem at their workplace, feeling that there is little that can
be done. When it comes to disputes with a customer around secret recordings, for instance, "Even if a customer does not verbally threaten a woman,
she will know her weak position and give up without protesting."[44] Similarly,
many women are reluctant to complain to managers about workplace conditions out of fear over how they may retaliate. Management often retains cop-
ies of women's identity card or promotional photographs, and sex workers
may worry about what an unscrupulous manager might do with these materials. Concerns such as these can make a woman wary of "making trouble"
for management, leading to a situation in which it is easier to simply look for
a new workplace than to push for better working conditions. As sociologist
Aoyama Kaoru has noted, the legal insecurity of sex workers "makes it difficult for them to publicly assert their existence, claim rights or assistance,

or speak about their conditions, which might lead to them being accused as criminals."[45]

Moreover, the structure of the sex industry itself undermines opportunities to foster solidarity. At many businesses, high turnover and flexibility in determining one's work schedule mean that there is often little interaction between women working at the same business. Even at businesses with a communal waiting room for sex workers, women may feel disinclined to socialize with others and prefer to keep to themselves. Some managers also discourage socializing between employees based on the assumption that it will focus on information-sharing, industry gossip, or airing grievances.[46] Finally, divisions among sex workers in the legal and illegal sectors of the industry also hamper solidarity. As Aoyama writes, "Criminalization works to divide sex workers into different groups . . . preventing them from forming solidarity networks."[47]

It is telling that even some women with a more politicized identity feel ambivalent about what would be best for working conditions in the sex industry. The former *deriherujō* Hiromi's musings on whether decriminalization was the right goal capture the problem: "The industry has changed over the past few years but, no matter how it changes, the fact that women work at their own risk hasn't changed. When I consider that, I think that it would be best to decriminalize the industry so that sex work would be legally recognized as labor. Right now, if something [bad] happens, the store does not need to help. It's unimaginably irresponsible." But Hiromi expressed deep ambivalence as she weighed the contradictions of the work. Decriminalizing sex work would solve many problems in the industry, but it would also make it less attractive as the work's lucrative potential rests on its marginalization. As Hiromi put it:

> The people working in the sex industry need to be protected. But the work isn't socially recognized. If a law establishing the legality of the sex industry were enacted, the number of women working might go down because then sex work would be taxed. Because it's difficult work, if you don't make that much money it probably wouldn't be worth it to a lot of women. You have to worry about the danger of STIs, of having sex with strangers. . . . If you consider the risks, it makes sense to want to fully decriminalize the industry and see it as labor, but if you think of it in terms of the money, it might be better to keep it how it is now.

Hiromi squarely recognized the contradictions of the work and how, in a gendered economy, its rewards depended on its marginalization. Although decriminalization would allow women the benefits of guaranteed standards, protections, and benefits, the work would also become less lucrative—and likely take on more of the qualities of normative workplaces that many sex workers dislike.

Beyond these factors, however, sex workers' healing labor also helps us to understand the pervasive discourse of amateurism in the sex industry and to tie it to sex workers' lack of engagement with labor rights in two ways. The first of these has to do with how many sex workers think about their future roles. No different from many other young women in their twenties or early thirties (especially those not from privileged class backgrounds), many sex workers recognize marriage and motherhood as the route to social adulthood and aspire to marry and become housewives themselves, as Tomoko observed. Many sex workers, that is, aspire to provide the valorized version of the feminized care that they replicate through *iyashi* in their workplaces. The paradigmatic model of female care in Japan remains firmly anchored in idealized norms of conjugal household relations, and many of the women I spoke with saw themselves as housewives in the future. Demanding rights on the basis of a politicized identity *as* a sex worker would imperil this goal by socially marking women as not only sex workers but *professionals* and create problems for their marriage prospects.

Second, sex workers' embrace of the self-descriptor of *shirōto* is also about the importance they place on providing the most authentic kind of feminine care possible. As Elana Buch has noted, a key tension within commercial care practices is that in dealing with the needs of another person, a caregiver must put aside their own problems in order to create the atmosphere of seemingly genuine intimacy and affection that distinguishes "good" care from "bad."[48] The problems on sex workers' minds are of course most often those directly produced by their insecure and unprotected laboring conditions, which the customer himself is implicated in because he benefits from them.[49] To effectively provide healing labor, sex workers cannot let on their discomfort with the venue a customer has chosen, his attitude toward her, his refusal to use a condom or coaxing to engage in off-limits services, the possibility that there is a hidden camera somewhere, and so on. "Good" care is about the moral imperative to prioritize the needs of the customer by concealing one's own and offering a seemingly spontaneous and intuitive affection.[50] Women in Tokyo's sex industry see professionalization as undermining their ability to offer such care in its emphasis on the cultivation of expertise and in calling out the inadequacies of laboring conditions.[51] These women understand their healing labor, in other words, to be at odds with professionalization.

With no sense of identification with their work or of longer-term investment in it, and with a strong sense of the value of providing authentic care, women in Tokyo's sex industry thus far remain uninterested in politicization. For the time being, the contradictions that define sex work as well as the conditions of their healing labor work against a broader engagement by sex workers with labor rights in this particular context.

Conclusion

Women working in the sex industry engage in a relationship with risk in their everyday working lives. In an industry that prioritizes the pleasure and preferences of customers, sex workers take on responsibility for customers' and their own sexual health and must learn to manage whatever conditions they encounter in the spaces where they work, carefully handling a customer's mood whatever demands he may make while they are providing healing labor. Workplaces take little responsibility for problems that may arise as sex workers are considered independent contractors and not employees—unlike the male staff. Moreover, treatment by the authorities differentiates between women in the sex industry and "ordinary" women and further marginalizes sex workers. Although a long-standing discourse of necessity drives the state's regulation of the sex industry, the state is not particularly concerned with the health, safety, or rights of the women who work there, and the conditions of sex workers receive little public attention.[52]

Sex worker advocates pragmatically work to improve conditions in the sex industry and call attention to the contributions of sex workers to society. Their advocacy, however, has not overcome the contradictions implicit to the work, which make sex workers unwilling to see themselves as politicized subjects who can make political and economic claims. The forms of support and assistance that the advocates offer are, instead, geared toward enabling women to work safely in the sex industry and leave it without suffering repercussions or discrimination in the future. Although the sex worker advocates are dedicated to their cause and to advancing the collective status of individuals in the sex industry, sex workers themselves want to be free to "flow" out of this work when they decide the time is right and to move on, unencumbered, to other roles and possibilities.

Epilogue

I BEGAN THIS BOOK with the vignette of an anonymous young woman weighing the options in front of her. At her wits' end from scraping together a living on her "office lady" salary and anxious about whether she would ever be able to pursue her dream career, this young woman asked three powerful male politicians appearing on national television for advice about whether to enter the sex industry. The politicians each drew audience laughter for responses that seemingly demonstrated a casual familiarity with the world of commercial sex and gave diverging advice. Two of those three politicians have gone on to lead Japan as prime minister (and one is leading it at the time of this writing), while the third has assumed other illustrious positions in national government and his political party. Of course, we do not know what happened to the young woman—whether she remained in her low-paying but respectable job, found another opportunity, or decided to try out sex industry work, and, if she did, how this decision changed her life. But each participant in this vignette took the existence and basic importance of commercial sex for granted, even as the question of morality posed by the young woman signals how the women who provide this labor remain marginalized and largely invisible.

This book has argued that sex shows us something about how the economy is always gendered. It has done so by focusing on how women in Tokyo's sex industry experience and understand the contradictions that define female sex work in Japan. Peering closely at individuals' lived experiences of these contradictions is a way of probing how people define themselves in relation to questions that are always already deeply implicated in gendered assumptions, such as what counts as work and what makes it productive or moral? Whose work really matters? Should all work be protected? Is work a means of supporting oneself, a means of supporting one's family, or a sign of one's status in society? The complex ways in which individuals grapple with, embody, and live these questions reveal to us the socially and historically specific dynamics of how the concept of gender remains fundamental to the continual production of notions of "the economy."

What I have called the healing labor of sex workers, in particular, underscores the relationship between how sex workers think about what sex is and what it does, on the one hand, and the roles and possibilities that they imagine for themselves on the other. Or, to put it slightly differently, it highlights the linkages in a specific context between how people imagine what it is that they are up to and what its value is, and how this shapes what they believe is or is not possible or permissible. As a central illustration of many of the contradictions of cisheteronormative Japanese sex work, healing labor helps us to see both how sex is understood as a socially productive activity and the political and economic consequences of erotic life. We can see, for instance, how sex workers' understanding of the social value of the care they offer affects the claims that they are willing to make on their behalf. Despite laboring in insecure and risky conditions, and enduring isolation due to their participation in work widely understood to transgress norms of feminine respectability, women in the sex industry are nevertheless largely uninterested in and unengaged with both a human rights and a labor rights campaign because they regard other things—such as their imagined future roles as wives and mothers, or their authentic care—as more important.

Healing labor permits us to consider sex and care in the same frame. Doing so allows us to observe the shared modes of relationality that may underlie both. In Tokyo's sex industry, these shared modes have to do with asymmetrical gendered interdependencies of male necessity (for pleasure, gratification, well-being, and productivity, and against exhaustion and social disorder) and female provision of that necessity. These are asymmetrical because they rest on an inequality in which women are expected to set aside their own needs in order to provide care to men, and in which women's labor in doing so is often devalued or rendered invisible as a sign of its moral legitimacy as being genuine feminine care.[1] Sex and care both tell us some-thing about the underrecognized feminized labor that produces the Japa-nese political economy more generally, in a context in which commercial sex is widely accepted as an inevitable and necessary part of social life and in which, despite the mass movement of women into the workforce, a gen-dered division of labor continues to be one of the defining elements of the nature of work.

Over the past several years, the administration of Prime Minister Abe Shinzō has promoted a host of policies under the name "womenomics" to encourage women's labor market participation. Since 2012, roughly two mil-lion women have joined the workforce, but observers note that this increased participation has not resulted in higher status for women, that many of these new positions are in nonregular work, and that the administration's focus is on economic growth rather than gender equality.[2] Despite these changes in women's workforce participation and, since the 1990s, in men's relationship to employment, certain gendered aspects of economic life remain largely un-changed in contemporary Japan. On the whole, Japanese women continue to face assumptions that their "real" careers involve the care of family members. Considering the processes by which the gendering of the economy is continu-ally enacted and reenacted helps us to understand the seeming intransigence of women's exclusion from the professional economy. As the healing labor of sex workers demonstrates, widespread ideas about the centrality of care in defining moral femininity and, closely linked to this, about the significance of women's care in producing economic life, have ongoing salience. The pro-vision of care may be a source of pride, identity, and achievement for many women, but it is also one that, simultaneously, demands the concealment of their labor and its assessment in terms of its contributions to the successes of others—and may act as an obstacle to demanding a change in the status quo. Just as the labor of women in the Japanese sex industry is simultaneously important and marginalized, so the nature of women's work more gener-ally rests on asymmetrical gendered interdependencies and inequalities that deeply shape how individuals live their lives, relate to others, and reproduce social practices.

To be clear, all economies are gendered. It is not my claim that Japan is some-how unique. What is noteworthy, however, is understanding how that gen-dering happens under particular political-economic and social circumstances, such as within the logic of a market for commercial care in a postindustrial service economy. As forms of feminine care previously tied to the domestic sphere increasingly become subject to the market, the assumptions they carry with them about intimate and economic life expose how the basic categories of contemporary life are reproduced under new conditions. The lives and experiences of women working in Tokyo's sex industry help us to see some of these tensions at the heart of regimes of care.

Notes

Introduction

1. I thank the sex workers' rights advocate Tomoko for sharing a clip of this segment with me. To protect the identities of research participants, pseudonyms are used throughout this book. In a few cases, some identifying information has been altered for the same reason.

2. Tanigaki went on to serve in many high-ranking political and governmental positions, including president of the Liberal Democratic Party and minister of justice.

3. Abe served as prime minister from 2006 to 2007 and assumed this office again in 2012. At the time of this writing, he is still prime minister.

4. Asō was prime minister from 2008 to 2009. At the time of this writing, he is deputy prime minister and minister of finance.

5. See Norma Field ([1991] 1993: 21–25) for her account of *jishuku* in the period immediately before and after the death of the Shōwa emperor (Hirohito).

6. In fact, anecdotal and other data suggests that, following the March 11, 2011, disaster, there was significant demand for commercial sex, although sex workers were not always willing to return to work. Freelance writer Ono Ikkō (2016) has described how sex workers in the disaster-struck areas of northeastern Japan were deluged with customers, often serving at least twice as many per day as they had before.

7. Although my focus is on younger women, there are also some women in their forties and older working in the sex industry.

8. Appel 2017; Bear et al. 2015; Holmes 2014; T. Mitchell 2002.

9. The National Police Agency lists 31,925 businesses under the legal category of "sex industry" (*seifūzoku*) for 2018. However, this figure includes roughly 9,500 love hotels and motels, adult shops, "encounter-type" cafés, and adult video sites.

Women working at these businesses are not considered to be sex workers (*fūzokujō*) (Keisatsuchō 2019: 9–11).

10. As Peter Andreas and Kelly Greenhill (2010) point out in their discussion of quantification in relation to illicit activities, the production of statistics is often fraught. Similarly, in his classic study of American rhetorical claims surrounding threats to children, Joel Best (1990) has illustrated how statistics, once in circulation, often take on a life of their own, regardless of their provenance (see also Feingold 2010 in relation to human trafficking statistics). Aware of these politics of numbers, I have attempted to be as transparent as possible in my calculations of the scale of the legal, heteronormative sex industry.

11. The sex workers' rights activist Cheryl Overs (2012), for example, made this point effectively in her plenary speech at the 2012 International AIDS Conference in Washington, DC: "[Clients] are not hard to reach. I'm sure I'm reaching hundreds [of clients] in this very room right now."

12. Rowley 2002; Shiga-Fujime 1993; Shin Yoshiwara Joshi Hoken Kumiai 1989.

13. Since they do not involve heterosexual intercourse, same-sex commercial sexual services are not regulated by the anti-prostitution law.

14. In contrast, in other global contexts of sexual commerce, the uniformity and organized nature implied by *sex industry* make it an unproductive term. Svati Shah (2014: 15), for instance, writing about three distinct spaces in which migrant women in Mumbai, India, transact sex—brothels, the streets, and public day-wage labor markets—has observed that, "the term 'industry' was not helpful in the context of this research because the sale and trade of sexual services in the three ethnographic sites was highly irregular and did not produce the same outcomes for the individuals who participated in these transactions."

15. Ogiue 2012; D. Suzuki 2010.

16. In 2000, Japanese women made up only 4 percent of those arrested for street prostitution in Tokyo (3 of 68 arrests), being far outnumbered by non-Japanese women; in 2010, they made up over 70 percent of a larger number of arrests in Tokyo (93 of 130 arrests) (Tōkyō Shimbun 2010, 2011).

17. Aoyama 2011, 2013; Yagisawa 2006.

18. Both the Chinese and Korean communities are well established in Japan, and the existence of a visa exemption for South Korean tourists since 2006 has reportedly made the Japanese sex industry a popular destination for women with deep credit card debts. In 2010, the South Korean police estimated that there were 30,000 Korean women working in the Japanese sex industry (Searchina News 2010).

19. On same-sex and transgender sex workers in Japan, see McLelland 2002; McLelland, Suganuma, and Welker 2007.

20. On the types of sexual relationships that hosts may enter with their customers, see, for instance, Takeyama 2016.

21. Akiko Takeyama (2016: 3), writing about host clubs in Tokyo, has compellingly illustrated how what is produced and consumed in these sites "is based on a promised future wherein host and client build a dream world together and set one another's fan-

tasies into motion." According to Takeyama, it is not only customers who are seduced by their fantasies in these clubs but also the hosts themselves who draw women into spending large amounts of money on their behalf in the pursuit of their own hopeful desires for a self-realized and successful future.

22. Clennell 2006; Sawamura 2008.

23. A range of ethnographies and documentary films have explored host and hostess clubs, including Allison 1994; Clennell 2006; Faier 2009; Longinotto and Williams 1996; Parreñas 2011; Takeyama 2005, 2010, 2016.

24. For example, television programs—such as TV Asahi's 2007 summer drama *Jotei* (Empress), about a young woman who ascends the ranks of a hostess club in Tokyo's Ginza neighborhood—and popular fashion magazines—such as *Koakuma Ageha* (Little Devil Swallowtail), which centrally features hostesses as models—make hostess work seem glamorous and desirable and allow the most elite hostesses a form of public success unimaginable to sex workers (Momoka and Yashiki 2009; Tabuchi 2009). In 2007, hostessing was listed as the ninth most popular dream profession among adolescent girls and women aged 15 to 22 (Miura and Yanauchi 2008: 15).

25. The same is true of hosts who, as Akiko Takeyama (2016: 95–96) details, make distinctions between the forms of sexual labor they may engage in with high-spending clients and the forms of labor associated with male sex workers.

26. Ochiai 1997.

27. Brinton 1993.

28. Vogel 1963.

29. Brinton 1993.

30. Genda [2001] 2005.

31. Brinton 2011: 30.

32. Kadokura 2009; NHK 2010; Satō 2000; Yamada 2007.

33. Allison 2013: 14.

34. Cook 2016.

35. Brinton 2011: 30.

36. Shimizu 2013: 166.

37. Steinberg and Nakane 2012: 19.

38. Asia-Japan Women's Resource Center 2009; Fujiwara 2009.

39. Kōseirōdōshō 2012.

40. Fujiwara 2008.

41. Additionally, 28.3 percent of first-time (married) mothers were still employed at their child's first birthday and had taken parental leave, while 10 percent were still employed but without having taken leave (Naikakufu Danjo Kyōdō Sankakukyoku 2018: 118).

42. Mun and Brinton 2015.

43. Osaki 2014.

44. These percentages include both those who responded "agree" and "somewhat agree." In the same survey taken in 2012, 55.1 percent of male respondents and 48.4 percent of female respondents agreed with the statement, while in the 2014 survey,

46.5 percent of male respondents and 43.2 percent of female respondents agreed (Nai-kakufu Danjo Kyōdō Sankakukyoku 2018: 117). The decline in respondents agreeing with the statement over a relatively short period of time reflects the success of Prime Minister Abe's "womenomics" policy push in encouraging women's continued partici-pation in the labor force even after marriage.

45. McCurry 2018; Yomiuri Shimbun 2018.

46. Reiter 1975; Rosaldo and Lamphere 1974.

47. Weiner 1976.

48. Strathern 1988.

49. Mahmood 2005.

50. Engels [1884] 1978.

51. K. Weeks 2011: 26.

52. Federici [1975] 1995: 190–91.

53. Rubin 1984.

54. As Gayle Rubin (1984: 279) observes, "Sexual acts are burdened with an excess of significance."

55. Hochschild 1983: 7.

56. Boris and Parreñas 2010: 2.

57. Hardt 1999; Hardt and Negri 2004.

58. Buch 2013; Hardt 1999; Muehlebach 2011; K. Weeks 2007.

59. G. Mitchell 2016.

60. Delphy 1984; Kuhn and Wolpe 1978; Malos [1980] 1995.

61. Donzelot [1977] 1997; Uno 1991.

62. Constable 2009.

63. Cooper and Waldby 2014: 5.

64. Koch 2016a.

65. Morgan [1870] 1997, [1877] 1964; Trautmann 1987.

66. Lévi-Strauss 1969: 43, emphases in the original.

67. Rubin 1975: 204.

68. As Rubin has articulated elsewhere, "In a Lévi-Straussian sense, kinship is a way of generating a social and political structure from manipulations of marriage and descent" (Rubin and Butler 1994: 86).

69. Groes-Green 2013; Ramberg 2014; Wardlow 2006. See also Roberts 2012 for a discussion of exchange, kinship, and social relations through what she calls "a traffic *between* women."

70. Rubin 1984: 275.

71. Abelove [1989] 2007; D'Emilio [1983] 1993; Foucault [1978] 1990; McIntosh 1968; Rubin 1984; Walkowitz 1980; J. Weeks 1977, 1981.

72. *Sexual economy* is a capacious term that can account for many different kinds of economies. For example, George Paul Meiu (2017: 33) has coined the far more spe-cific term *ethno-erotic economy* to refer to the "extensive circulations of money, goods, and desires that, while anchored in the commodification of ethnosexuality, move far beyond sexual transactions to shape subjectivities, identities, and social worlds."

73. Bernstein 2007b; Brennan 2004; Cabezas 2004; Hoang 2010, 2015; Parreñas 2011; Zheng 2009.

74. Boris and Parreñas 2010; Rivers-Moore 2016.

75. Takeyama 2016.

76. Allison 1994.

77. Allison 1994: 65, emphasis in the original.

78. Allison 1994: 42.

79. Allison 1994: 9. In other contexts, women's sexual(ized) entertainment is similarly recruited as part of male after-hours work practices. Kimberly Kay Hoang (2015) describes how an ascendant Vietnamese business elite uses the labor of bar hostesses—who may choose to negotiate on their own with men for sex—to impress clients through conspicuous consumption. Tiantian Zheng (2009) and Elanah Uretsky (2016) show how the fraternizing that attends elite male work culture in China, and which often involves commercial sex, plays a crucial role in building personal relations.

80. Frühstück 2003, 2015; Y. Matsui 1993; Soh 2008; Yoshimi [1995] 2000.

81. In his comments to the press, Hashimoto reported that he had told the US military commander, "In Japan there are places [sex industry businesses] that are regulated and where you can legally go to release your sexual energy. If you don't make use of such places, you won't be able to control the sexual energy of hot-blooded marines" (Asahi Shimbun 2013). US Department of Defense regulations place sex industry businesses off-limits to service members stationed overseas.

82. See Bell 1987 and Nagle 1997 on the exclusion of sex workers from mainstream North American feminism. For Japan, see Matsuzawa 2000 for pro-sex work critiques of anti-prostitution feminists.

83. Leigh 1997: 230. As political theorist Kathi Weeks (2011: 67) observes, "Rather than a character flaw that produces a moral crisis, sex work is reconceived as an employment option that can generate income and provide opportunity.... For those involved in sex worker advocacy, the term can serve not only as a way to foreground the economic dimensions of such labor practices, but as a way to insist on their essential worth, dignity, and legitimacy." Weeks goes on to caution, however, that the validation of sex work on the basis of its categorization as work valorizes, rather than challenges, the dominant discourse of work as virtue (67–68).

84. Work is, of course, not the only basis on which sex workers' rights can or should be recognized. Human rights are another basis and "sex workers' rights are human rights" is another slogan used by an international sex workers' advocacy movement. Entrenched stigma against sex workers, however, has made this effort less successful in places like Japan. As one sex worker advocate explained to me, it is much easier to get members of the public to agree with improving working conditions for sex workers than for them to embrace an idea of the human rights of sex workers.

85. Delacoste and Alexander 1987; Kempadoo and Doezema 1998.

86. Haha no Kai 2005; Matsuzawa 2000; Momoka 1997; SWASH 2018.

87. Merry 2006a, 2006b.

88. Koch 2016b.

89. Agustín 2007; Cheng 2010; Hoang and Parreñas 2014; Kempadoo, Sanghera, and Pattanaik 2005; Zheng 2010. For discussion of questions of agency and exploitation in relation to migrant women's work more generally, see also Constable 1997; Ehrenreich and Hochschild 2003; Parreñas 2001.

90. Parreñas 2011.

91. Parreñas 2011: 7. See also Aoyama 2009 on migrant Thai women in the Japanese sex industry.

92. Although I do not discuss this further, women working in the male-centered sex industry also represent diverse gender and sexual subjectivities, which may diverge starkly from those they perform at work. As one sex worker explained to me, "As a lesbian, it's easier to be clear-sighted about what's necessary to do well at the work." In other words, sex worker's gendered and sexual performances are part of the service they provide. See also G. Mitchell 2016.

93. *Honban* can be translated as "the central performance itself," as opposed to a rehearsal or practice session.

94. NHK 2002: 152–153.

95. See, for example, Allison 2001. See Alexy (2019: 1–2) on representations of intimate relations in Japan by the Anglophone media.

Chapter 1

1. In contrast, the former police investigator Matsuki Takashi suggests a connection between crime and lack of access to commercial sex when he describes how incidences of sexual assault increased in the Ishikawa Prefecture town where he was working when the anti-prostitution law was fully enacted in 1958 (Matsuki 2011: 47–49).

2. Makino 2013. See also C. Burns 2005 on judicial decision-making in cases of sexual assault.

3. See Dower 1999; Frühstück 2003, 2015; Lie 1997; Soh 2008; Yoshimi [1995] 2000.

4. Nishiyama 1997: 41.

5. Stanley 2012.

6. Stanley 2012; Nagai 2002.

7. De Becker [1905] 1971: 8–11; Fowler 1996: 36–37.

8. Sone 1999: 171.

9. Seigle 1993.

10. Stanley 2012.

11. Stanley 2012: 7.

12. Stanley 2012: 70.

13. Sone 1999; Stanley 2012.

14. S. Burns 1998; Fujime 1997. See De Becker [1905] 1971 on Meiji-period licensed prostitution in Yoshiwara.

15. Frühstück 2003; Fujime 1997.

16. Colligan-Taylor 1999; Mihalopoulos 2011; Yamazaki [1972] 1999.

17. Frühstück 2003, 2015; Soh 2008; Yoshimi [1995] 2000.

18. Dower 1999: 127, 124–32. See also Lie 1997; Yoshimi [1995] 2000: 179–85.

19. These were called "red-line districts" (akasen chitai), so named for how the police colored the borders of these areas on maps (Dower 1999: 130–32).

20. Dower 1999; Kovner 2012; Kramm 2017; Sanders 2012.

21. Given the anti-prostitution law's narrow definition of "sex," same-sex commercial sexual services are not regulated by this law.

22. Nagai 2002.

23. With a 1984 revision, the Fūeihō underwent a name change to Fūzoku Eigyōtō no Kisei oyobi Gyōmu no Tekiseikatō ni kansuru Hōritsu (commonly abbreviated as Fūtekihō). However, to reflect the practice of my interlocutors and for the sake of simplicity, I will refer to both as the Fūeihō.

24. Nagai 2002.

25. Nagai 2002: 20–21. See Nagai for a detailed overview of how the postwar state has sought to regulate different forms of adult recreation.

26. Matsuki 2011. See also Adelstein 2009.

27. Fujinaga [1996] 2005: 302.

28. Tsunoda 2010: 4.

29. A police handbook obliquely declares that "harmful effects" would follow if the state were seen as authorizing prostitution (Fujinaga [1996] 2005: 302).

30. Outside of Tokyo, the necessary paperwork can be found on the respective prefectural police website.

31. Keishichō 2018a.

32. Keishichō 2018b.

33. See, for example, Sawada 2002, Tachikawa 2010.

34. Sociologist Aoyama Kaoru similarly observes, "The sex industry has been both normalized through legislation under the [Fūeihō] and ostracized through criminalization under the Prostitution Prevention Law. This combination makes it difficult for sex workers not to be at the mercy of the whims of the police" (Aoyama 2015: 283).

35. Adelstein 2009: 154.

36. Utsunomiya 2003.

37. Kobayashi 2006. According to a government survey, almost 90 percent of respondents felt less safe in 2004 than they had a decade earlier (Kobayashi 2006). Kubo Hiroshi, a former senior bureaucrat in the Tokyo metropolitan government who was directly involved with the anti-crime efforts, has argued that the rhetoric of the public safety campaign served to strengthen government authority by encouraging residents to feel less safe (Kubo 2006).

38. See, for instance, Adelstein 2009; Lee 2005a; Yagisawa 2006.

39. Kaplan and Dubro 2003.

40. Lee 2005b; T. Suzuki 2005.

41. Leheny 2006.

42. Asahi Shimbun 2005.

43. Asahi Shimbun 2005.

44. See Matsuzawa 2005 for an account of the clean-up campaign's first year.

45. T. Yoshida 2005: 54–55.

46. NHK News 2004, 2005.

47. Okinawa Times 2011.

48. See, for example, Matsuzawa's (2005: 84) discussion of the casino rumor. Cybriwsky (2011: 196–197) also discusses the possibility that redevelopment interests may have been at least partially behind the spate of closures of Roppongi nightclubs in the mid- and late 2000s.

49. See T. Yoshida 2005 for one interpretation of Ishihara's personal motives.

50. T. Yoshida 2005.

51. Nagai 2002.

52. In collating this data from police statistics, I included soaplands, *fasshon herusu*, and strip theaters (Categories 1–3 of brick-and-mortar sex industry businesses as regulated by the *Fūeihō*) in the brick-and-mortar businesses. For the mobile businesses, I included just *deriheru* (Category 1 of the non–brick-and-mortar businesses as regulated by the *Fūeihō*). Of course, this data does not account for unregistered businesses. Many businesses targeted in the mid-2000s crackdown were not registered with the authorities to begin with and thus are not reflected here.

53. Women who transact sex on their own with men that they meet through "encounter-type" (*deaikei*) websites or "encounter cafés" (*deai kafe, deai kissa*) are also implicated in this broader movement off premises, away from brick-and-mortar businesses (Kaname 2012). The *Fūeihō* has recognized *deai kafe* as sex industry businesses since 2011.

54. Tōkyōtochō n.d.

55. See also Rubin 1991.

56. Cybriwsky 2011.

57. See, for instance, Tōkyō Shimbun 2006 on Yokohama's Koganechō neighborhood and Yomiuri Shimbun 2008a on the neighborhood around Saitama Prefecture's Nishi Kawaguchi Station.

58. Hashimoto 2009: 134–36.

59. Yomiuri Shimbun 2005.

60. Yomiuri Shimbun 2008c.

61. Yomiuri Shimbun 2008a.

62. Yomiuri Shimbun 2008a, 2008b, 2008c.

63. Yomiuri Shimbun 2008c.

64. Bernstein 2007b; Delany 1999; Warner 2002.

65. See, for example, Hashimoto 2009.

66. See also Aoyama 2015.

Chapter 2

1. Bernstein 2007b: 78.

2. See Kanematsu 1987 for an older account of marginalized women in the sex industry.

3. Needless to say, the same is not true for men, who occasionally eagerly shared with me their experiences of or opinions on the sex industry.

4. When I visited Tokyo in 2016 and 2017, the magazines had mostly disappeared from the streets and completely transitioned to their associated Internet portals, which are gateways of information about the sex industry.

5. The magazines are distributed rather indiscriminately to female pedestrians because the individuals handing them out—typically young men in their twenties—are motivated by a distribution quota. Although I am phenotypically Euro-American, I was also offered the magazines on numerous occasions. Similarly, I once observed as a pair of women in their sixties were handed the magazines. They looked at the cover and exclaimed, "High-paying work for girls?!" before laughing and marching back to return the magazines to the now blushing young man.

6. Bengoshi Dottokomu Nyūsu 2017.

7. AKB48 is a wildly popular all-girls pop group formed in the mid-2000s.

8. The magazine's name is onomatopoeic, evoking the sound of an engine being revved (the equivalent of "vroom, vroom"). It suggests that the magazine is a vehicle for women to jumpstart their ambitions.

9. LunLun Work 2010: 1.

10. Momoco 2008: 9.

11. Hanamaru Work 2011: 17.

12. Frühstück 2007: 136.

13. Bisuche BB Kyūto 2008: 166–67.

14. Kakuma 2017: 8.

15. SWASH 2013.

16. Kōseirōdōshō 2011.

17. Kōseirōdōshō 2016; Mainichi Shimbun 2016.

18. Mainichi Shimbun 2016.

19. Nakamura 2015: 32–37.

20. Walters 2016b: 105.

21. There is, however, some discrepancy in this freedom depending on the type of business. Soaplands generally allow less freedom to set one's own schedule.

22. Nakane 1970.

23. There is no alimony or joint custody in Japan and the parent without custody is not required to pay child support.

24. Tōkyō Shimbun 2012.

25. Nagasawa 1999; Sakai 1998, 2006.

26. See also Hoang 2015; Zheng 2009.

27. A common contrast, as if these are the only two viable or meaningful options for women.

28. Nakamura and Teshigawara 2015: 115–16.

29. Sakai 1998.

30. In addition to splitting the earnings, some stores also deduct miscellaneous fees from a sex worker's share, making it closer to a 40:60 distribution. When a customer selects a specific sex worker, that woman also receives the "designation fee" (*shimeiryō*) paid by the customer—typically around ¥2000. Additionally, she receives the amount paid by the customer for any additional "optional" services not included within the basic set of standard services.

31. Tachikawa 2010: 101, 119.

32. Nakamura and Teshigawara 2015: 63–70.

33. K. Weeks 2011.

34. K. Weeks (2011: 68) notes how advocacy around treating commercial sex *as* work "usefully demoralizes the debates around the nature, value, and legitimacy of sex for wages in one way, but it often does so by remoralizing it in another; it shifts the discussion from one moral terrain to another, from that of a suspect sexual practice to that of a respectable employment relation."

35. Nakamura and Teshigawara 2015: 150–51.

36. Nakamura and Teshigawara 2015: 60–62.

37. Nakamura 2015. In contrast, men's tabloids and sports papers frame the entry of college students in the sex industry as an enticing development for male consumers.

38. Nakamura 2015; Nakamura and Teshigawara 2015: 159.

39. Nakamura and Teshigawara 2015: 62.

40. Nakamura and Teshigawara 2015: 137–38.

41. K. Weeks 2011.

Chapter 3

1. Hanamaru Work 2011: 246–47.

2. Nakamura 2015: 36.

3. Kaname and Mizushima 2005: 62–64. Kaname and Mizushima note that romantic partners were more likely to know about their lover's work either because they had met at the sex industry business (e.g., they were a staff member or customer), they were a close friend prior to becoming the woman's lover and had been told about the work, or it had been "outed" to them (63). The number of women who had spoken to family members was miniscule, but sisters were the most common family member confided to (256).

4. By "moral economy," I refer to how all forms of exchange can simultaneously be understood as moral actions. See also Fassin 2005; Scott 1976; Thompson 1971; Ticktin 2011.

5. That is, in Japan, women in the sex industry are seen as disreputable because they have sex "in the wrong ways—too much, with the wrong [people, and] for the wrong reason" (Mac and Smith 2018: 23).

6. See, for instance, Onnatachi no 21 Seiki 2012a: 40–47.

7. Onnatachi no 21 Seiki 2012a: 40–41, 43.

8. Osaka Yomiuri Shimbun 2013; Sankei Shimbun 2013.

9. Goffman 1963: 42.

10. Sakai 1998.

11. Onnatachi no 21 Seiki 2012a: 41.

12. Some sex industry businesses also explicitly discourage socializing between sex workers. One explanation I was given for this is that it prevents women from trading information about other businesses, which may lead them to seek better fortunes elsewhere.

13. Clennell 2006; Sawamura 2008; Takeyama 2016.

14. Women's use of stage names in their social networks occasionally causes confusion, as it did at several instances during my fieldwork when a third party and I who both knew different stage names for the same woman would try to figure out whether we were talking about the same person or two different people. While this was mostly innocuous and amusing, on one occasion it was a source of great frustration as a soapland manager refused to believe that I had been sent to him by one of his employees when I had accidentally been given a stage name different from the one he was familiar with.

15. Bessatsu Takarajima Henshūbu 1995: 4–5.

16. Soaplands are an exception to this as managers routinely expect newcomers to pay out of their own pocket for an experienced *sōpujō* to demonstrate the basics to them.

17. Whether they were expressed in terms of naiveté or inexperience, I took these professions as an element of a transition story. Emphasizing their initial lack of knowledge and subsequent developing insight was a way for women to express how they had changed over time through their engagement in sex work.

18. Hitt 2012: 3–5.

19. Morinaga 2005.

20. See Bernstein 2007b on demand for the "girlfriend experience" in postindustrial commercial sex.

21. Nakamura and Teshigawara 2015: 29.

22. Ogiue 2012: 325, 327; Onnatachi no 21 Seiki 2012b: 12.

23. Ogiue 2012, D. Suzuki 2010.

24. *Deai kissa* often have signs on the wall reminding patrons that prostitution is illegal, but media reportage notes that these are merely to absolve the business of any liability.

25. Sex workers are often unaware of the legal status of a business due, among other things, to a lack of knowledge of the law as well as to unscrupulous managers who may mislead employees. Illegal businesses include, for instance, those that are

not registered with the police, are outside of the zoning area, employ minors or those without the proper visa, or operate after legally designated hours.

26. Sex workers may be arrested for *hōjozai*, or aiding in the carrying out of a crime. Although still relatively rare, during the period of my fieldwork (2008–13), the number of female sex workers arrested for "aiding" crimes was on the increase, causing concern among advocates. Matsuzawa Kureichi describes some of the first such arrests in 2004–2005 (Matsuzawa 2005: 79, 82).

27. Anna Wilking (2014) similarly addresses how sex workers use locally available discourses of feminine sacrifice to mitigate stigma, both in the eyes of others and in regard to how they perceive themselves. In the deeply Catholic context of Quito, Ecuador, sex workers are scorned as women "living in sin." The street prostitutes that Wilking worked with, however, all of whom were mothers, emphasized their maternal sacrifice of their spiritual salvation, thereby redeeming themselves as exemplary and virtuous mothers, both in their individual relation to God and to other people.

28. Although today Yoshiwara is surrounded by residential zoning, it retains a distinctive character. In contrast to the dense integration of diverse sex industry businesses with entertainment, dining, and shopping venues that is characteristic of other sex industry districts, Yoshiwara is a monoculture of soaplands. Whereas a sex worker in another district will blend into the pedestrian crowd, women walking the streets in Yoshiwara are often approached and asked by strangers where they work, breaching the degree of anonymity and privacy available to sex workers elsewhere.

29. See, for instance, Stanley 2012. Although *miuri* is often treated as synonymous with the "sale" of women and girls into prostitution, the practice of debt bondage reflects a larger history of government-sanctioned exploitative labor arrangements. In the Meiji (1868–1912) and Taisho (1912–26) periods, for instance, daughters were bonded not only into prostitution, but into such industries as silk and cotton textile production, coal mining, and agriculture (Shiga-Fujime 1993: 14–15; Sievers 1983; Tsurumi 1990). Daughters' labor throughout these eras was not their own, but an asset to be managed by the household head.

30. See, for instance, Lock 1993.

31. See Holly Wardlow (2006) for an account of how anger is a central motivation for many Huli "passenger women."

32. Kaname and Mizushima (2005:71) note that women who stay longer in the sex industry than average tend to wait until an external factor outside of their control pushes them out of the industry, while those who stay shorter periods tend to have their sights trained on accomplishing a particular goal and quit once they have done so.

33. Hana-chan is a pseudonym for Shiori's stage name.

34. This was the combined total for both the bathing charge (*nyūyokuryō*) and the service charge (*sābisuryō*).

35. Sex workers' internalization of stigma and of sentiments that they are participating in "the lowest class of work" may intensify such feelings (Onnatachi no 21 Seiki 2012a: 44).

36. The language of "flowing" relates to the water imagery that has characterized metaphorical references to forms of women's commercial intimacy from the Edo period on (Dalby [1983] 2000: 274–75, 332–33 nn.1–2). The Edo-period metaphor of the "floating world" (*ukiyo*) referred to theater and the pleasure districts, while the contemporary term, the "water trade" (*mizushōbai*), refers to the diverse nightlife businesses that include, among others, cabaret clubs and host clubs. Water, floating, and flowing symbolically evoke the fickleness, uncertainty, and impermanence that characterize these businesses.

37. Similarly, in her study of place-making and nostalgia in an urban Japanese "bedroom town," Jennifer Robertson (1991a: 29–30) has illustrated how the intransitive *naru* (to become) is used to refer to the negative impact of external forces such as Westernization, while the transitive *tsukuru* (to make, to build) is used to denote positive, agential change by local residents.

38. In the aftermath of the March 11, 2011, disaster, anti–human trafficking activists voiced their concern over women from the disaster-struck areas "flowing" into the sex industry given that the local economy was in shambles. But this usage contains a different nuance of inevitability than the previous two examples—one of making do with the options available to one. When I repeated these comments to Shiori, she was skeptical over whether any woman who had been unwilling to do sex work previously would suddenly enter the sex industry.

39. Hill and Irvine 1993.

40. Walters 2016b.

41. Walters 2016b: 105.

42. Walters 2016b: 100.

43. Walters 2016b: 112.

44. See Esther Newton ([1972] 1979: 18) for her discussion of how drag queens in the American Midwest in the mid-1960s who identified as stage impersonators claimed respectability over street impersonators through carefully limiting their temporal commitment to drag by seeing it as work: "For if drag is work or a profession, a man might take some pride in doing it well; if it is work, it is not home, it is not where a man 'lives' in the deepest sense; if it is work, a man could always quit."

Chapter 4

1. Brennan 2004; Cabezas 2004; Hoang 2010, 2015; Parreñas 2011; Zheng 2009.

2. Bernstein 2007b: 103. Bernstein observes that "evidence of middle-class sex workers' efforts to manufacture authenticity resided in their descriptions of trying to simulate—or even produce—genuine desire, pleasure, and erotic interest for their clients. Whereas in some cases this involved mere 'surface acting' . . . it could also involve the emotional and physical labor of manufacturing authentic (if fleeting) libidinal and emotional ties with clients, endowing them with a sense of desirability, esteem, or even love" (103).

3. See also Frank 2002.

4. Dasgupta 2013; Roberson and Suzuki 2003; Vogel 1963.

5. Cook 2016: 3.

6. Allison 1994; Borovoy 2005.

7. Kushida, Shimizu, and Oi 2013; Rosenbluth and Thies 2010.

8. Allison 2013; Brinton 2011; Cook 2016.

9. Conrad 2013.

10. Shimizu 2013: 166.

11. Satō 2000.

12. Ronald and Alexy 2011.

13. Kadokura 2009.

14. Kitanaka 2012.

15. Kitanaka 2012: 131.

16. Ozawa-de Silva 2008: 536.

17. Allison 2013; NHK 2010.

18. Muehlebach 2013: 298.

19. AFP BB News 2012.

20. Ono 2016: 43.

21. Ozawa-de Silva 2008: 536.

22. Most recently, in late 2016 and the summer of 2017, I saw advertisements invoking *iyashi* to market vacation packages and yoga courses.

23. T. Matsui 2011.

24. It is telling that, when respondents in Kaname and Mizushima's (2005: 58–59, 250–54) survey of 126 sex workers were asked to compare their work to another occupation, around one-third categorized the work as similar to that of nurses, social workers, caregivers, or counselors. When responses giving massage therapist/esthetician and beautician are included, the number is slightly less than half. Even more telling is that, in response to a question about what they are selling in the work, approximately three-quarters of respondents gave replies pointing to the emotional, physical, and *reparative* aspects of the work (60–62, 254–56).

25. Allison 1994.

26. Some of the male hosts portrayed in Jake Clennell's (2006) documentary film, *The Great Happiness Space*, also articulated their service in terms of *iyashi*. In the context of a host club catering to a female clientele, however, it does not carry the same links to ideas about (masculine) productivity and maternal care—although it does demonstrate that not only women offer this feminized care.

27. The fluidity with which women circulate between different types of businesses in an industry with high turnover further suggests that *iyashi* forms the common denominator to what is offered in the sex industry while other distinctions (e.g., costume play, special services) exist only at the superficial level.

28. *Kaishun massāji* are businesses where women provide a sexualized prostate and anal/perineal massage that ends with bringing the customer to orgasm manually.

29. Through terms of address, I am trying to replicate the ways in which status and hierarchy are constructed between sex workers and clients. Although sex workers go by (fake) personal names as a way of demonstrating a lower and familiar relational status, customers are referred to deferentially by their surnames.

30. Brinton 2011; Cook 2016. Given anxieties around the precarity of white-collar masculinity, there is some irony in the fact that a nonregular worker stood in as a foil for a salaryman.

31. Although there is also perhaps a degree of incestuous role-playing involved, this was never alluded to. In the late 1970s and early 1980s, anxieties over the excessiveness of the housewife as micromanager of her (male) children's socialization and education manifested in stories of mother-son incest that circulated in the Japanese media (Allison 2000).

32. Doi 1973. See also Borovoy 2005.

33. At a later encounter, Mika reflected that what customers desire is an idealized femininity not unlike the Virgin Mary—benevolent, self-sacrificing, endlessly indulgent, and, oddly, sexless.

34. The genre of massage called *kaishun* refers to the "return of spring."

35. Allison 1994.

36. Nihon Keizai Shimbun 2013.

37. Butler 1990.

38. Buch 2013: 637.

39. Boris and Parreñas 2010: 4.

40. Robertson 1991b: 88 n.1.

41. Zelizer 2005: 14.

42. Stories of Number Ones abound in the sex industry. As symbols of success, they become objects of curiosity to other women working at the same business and, often, models against which to measure oneself. In many of the stories I heard, the punch line was that an older woman thought to be "past her prime" was in fact the most successful worker.

43. Sakai 2006: 11.

44. Nakamura and Teshigawara 2015: 126.

45. Nakamura and Teshigawara 2015: 128.

46. Maruyama 2007: 140–41; Yagisawa 2006.

47. Many women in the sex industry report feeling a deep sense of individual achievement when being thanked by their customers for how much better they now feel due to their efforts. I often heard from sex workers how simple expressions of gratitude and appreciation—which they perceived as representing customers' sincere thoughts (*honne*) and as shorn of any sense of obligatory pleasantry—elevated their feelings about the work and themselves.

48. See also Tanaka 2014.

49. K. Weeks 2007: 240.

50. Although from a very different historical context, this "common sense" is not unlike that of the Tokugawa period (1603–1868) when for women of a certain class

"marriage effectively was the rite of passage that . . . severed a woman from her sexuality" (Robertson 1991b: 97). Wives were relegated to the realm of procreation, and "sexuality proper was limited to concubines and courtesans" (97).

51. Hirsch and Wardlow 2006.

52. See Alexy 2011 on how the "intimate dependence" of married couples in Japan relates to notions of conjugal romance and intimacy.

53. Sandra Buckley notes that this construction of Japanese wives foremost as mothers denies them an autonomous sexual identity and institutionalizes their role in domestic labor (Buckley 1997: 140–41).

54. Kaname and Mizushima 2005: 66. As with other evening papers and sports newspapers, the *Naigai Taimuzu* frequently carried articles and advertisements related to the sex industry, meaning that its readership would not be unfamiliar with the industry.

55. Kaname and Mizushima 2005: 65.

56. Zelizer 2010.

57. Kaname and Mizushima 2005: 65.

58. Kaname and Mizushima 2005: 66. These responses seem to reflect a sentiment similar to what Viviana Zelizer (2010) calls "hostile worlds"—the notion that the economic and the intimate are separate realms that should not overlap. Despite deeply held beliefs in a "hostile worlds" framework in the United States, "intimate relations regularly coexist with economic transactions without being corrupted" (Zelizer 2010: 270; see also Zelizer 2005). In Japan, there is perhaps less sense—for men at least—that these two domains need necessarily be separated in the first place. Commercial sites of male "play" (*asobi*) have long been realms of intimacy where the confessions of an "unmasked" inner self may be selectively revealed (Allison 1994; see also Clennell 2006 and Takeyama 2016 on women's "play"). As activist and sex worker Momoka Momoko writes, for instance, "With a sex worker, [customers] talk about things which nobody in the family or workplace will listen to. Or they can talk about personal things because they are more able to relax with a sex worker than in front of their colleagues or their wives" (Momocca 1998: 180). Moreover, the distinction between "cheating" and "adultery"—as I discuss in the next paragraph—further suggests that it is also the level of attachment and future intent that matter in evaluating the nature of extrarelational sex.

59. Cited in West 2006: 266.

60. Nikkei Woman 2011a: 125.

61. Nikkei Woman 2011a: 125.

62. Nikkei Woman 2011b: 126.

63. Allison 1994. See also Uretsky 2016; Zheng 2009.

64. G. Mitchell 2016: 6.

65. Bernstein 2007b; Hoang 2015; G. Mitchell 2016.

66. Strathern 1988: 155. Marilyn Strathern responded to feminist debates concerning male exploitation of women's reproductive labor by proposing the notion of "eclipsing," wherein female labor is understood as implicit within male prestige-

earning activity. Although Japan is a postindustrial capitalist context rather than a gift economy, the metaphor of eclipse remains salient for elucidating how the concealment of sex workers' labor in producing *iyashi* is not locally understood as alienation.

Chapter 5

1. The LFSJ booklet used the term *jinshin torihiki* to refer to the transnational discourse of human trafficking. *Jinshin torihiki* is the term used by the Japanese government and within translations of international protocols. However, it is often perceived to be overly legalistic by anti-trafficking advocates and is not well known among the public. *Jinshin baibai*, in contrast, refers to a trade in humans. Although *jinshin baibai* is the term that is more familiar to the public, because of its associations with the historical practice of parents "selling" their children into indentured labor, its use occasionally causes confusion.

2. In order to preserve the organization's anonymity, I am not including a citation for the booklet.

3. See, for example, Bernstein 2007a.

4. See Rubin 2011 and Vance 2010 on the British and US history of the conflation of prostitution / sex work with human trafficking.

5. Agustín 2007.

6. See also Agustín 2007 for her critique of "social helpers" engaged in anti–human trafficking advocacy and Cheng 2010 for her analysis of a South Korean community-based organization working with Filipina migrant entertainers. See Ahmed and Seshu 2012 and Walters 2016a on the "rescue" of Indian sex workers by local anti-trafficking advocates.

7. The names of both organizations are pseudonyms.

8. The enthusiasm of governments for the protocol lay with its security focus, rather than for its implications for human rights.

9. I refer to LFSJ staff by (pseudonymous) family names to reflect the convention of Japanese workplaces.

10. Caouette and Saito 1999; Daily Yomiuri 2003a, 2003b, 2004; Dinan 2000; Kyōto YWCA and APT 2001. See also JNATIP and F-GENS 2005 and Y. Yoshida 2004, which came out shortly after LFSJ's founding, as well as JNATIP 2007 and The Asia Foundation 2008. For earlier works on grassroots efforts to assist and call attention to victims of human trafficking in Japan, see Asian Women's Association 1988; Babior 1993; Kanagawa Onna no Supēsu "Mizura" 2002; Y. Matsui 1999; Ohshima and Francis 1989. For ethnographic accounts that examine Thai and Filipina migrant workers' experiences of labor and migration in the Japanese sex and entertainment industry, see Aoyama 2009 and Parreñas 2011.

11. The US embassy in Tokyo occasionally intervened on the organization's behalf. For example, when LFSJ was organizing an international conference on human trafficking and having little success in securing commitments to attend from Japanese government

officials, the organization's liaison at the embassy instructed me to draw up a list of bureaus for embassy staff to contact.

12. The staff's energies were not evenly distributed among these, and at the time of my engagement with them LFSJ had only an inactive client services program. With the exception of a volunteer who assisted with Korean-language requests, Kanno was the only staff member who engaged in client services.

13. When I refer to LFSJ "staff" in this chapter, I refer collectively to both the full-time staff and interns and volunteers.

14. While anti-labor trafficking activists pushed for the recognition of foreign migrant laborers in other forms of forced labor as victims of human trafficking, through the end of my fieldwork the distinction between "labor" and "sex" trafficking continued to be a meaningful one among Japanese advocates.

15. Asian Women's Association 1988; Babior 1993; Caouette and Saito 1999; Ohshima and Francis 1989; Y. Yoshida 2004.

16. Ajia to Josei Kaihō 1977; Y. Matsui 1989, 1993, 1999. See also Ajia no Baibaishun ni Hantai Suru Otokotachi no Kai 1995.

17. Cf. Yamaguchi 2005.

18. The generational divide between LFSJ and this older cohort occasionally became manifest. As recently as 2011, when I interviewed the social worker at a consulate in Tokyo that had previously dealt with the serious problem of the trafficking of its nationals into forced prostitution, she had dismissed LFSJ as a newcomer late onto the scene. Within discourse on forced prostitution in Japan, the early to mid-2000s are routinely identified as the time point at which the trafficking crisis was at its most severe. The social worker told me that, at the height of the crisis, she had dialed the phone numbers of the three shelters that had managed all of the services for trafficking victims in the greater Tokyo area so many times, that her somatic memory could still reliably recall the numbers years later. To prove her point, she walked to a telephone at the side of the room and motion-dialed the numbers. The social worker's embodied memory communicated whom she saw as a legitimate actor in the anti-trafficking field.

19. Kanematsu 1987.

20. Kanematsu 1988: 88.

21. The Prostitution Prevention Law established public funding for a nationwide network of women's counseling centers (*fujin sōdanjo*) and women's shelters (*fujin hogo shisetsu*). Although originally intended as venues for aiding women involved in prostitution, these centers and shelters gradually came to offer public assistance to women dealing with diverse sorts of problems. With the 2001 passage of the Anti-Domestic Violence Law (*Haigūsha kara no Bōryoku no Bōshi oyobi Higaisha no Hogotō ni kansuru Hōritsu*), provisions have been made for female victims of intimate partner violence to access these centers.

22. Zelizer 2005, 2010.

23. Writing about the United States, Elizabeth Bernstein (2007a) has noted the decidedly pro-business rhetoric of much anti–human trafficking activism. This cosmet-

ics retailer hosted many of LFSJ's seminars as part of their corporate social responsibility activities. A company representative would be on hand during the seminar to distribute publicity materials and typically spoke briefly at the end of the event. The publicity materials included, among other things, information on which hand cream attendees could purchase to help combat human trafficking as consumers. This was an invitation by the retailer to participate in what the political scientists Lisa Anne Richey and Stefano Ponte (2008: 714) have referred to as "conscientious commerce," or "heroic shopping," whereby shoppers are constructed as consumer-citizens who are "fashion-conscious yet actively engaged and [ethically] reflexive."

24. It is interesting that the doctor highlighted a lack of social connection, which is also part of what drives the discourse of *iyashi*.

25. Once again, to preserve the organization's anonymity, I am not citing their booklet. LFSJ has imported US rhetoric about the central role played by "pimps" who manipulate adolescent girls. On the first day of our internship orientation, another intern and I were shown the US documentary film *Very Young Girls*, about the commercial sexual exploitation of adolescent girls in New York City.

26. Andreas and Greenhill 2010: 6. See also Feingold 2010, Merry 2016, and Warren 2010 on some of the issues around quantification specific to the production of human trafficking statistics.

27. Strathern 2000.

28. Joel Best (1990) is the classic source on how statistics, once produced and circulated, often take on a life of their own, regardless of their origins.

29. Article 3(a) of the Palermo Protocol states: "'Trafficking in persons' shall mean the recruitment, transportation, transfer, harbouring or receipt of persons, by means of the threat or use of force or other forms of coercion, of abduction, of fraud, of deception, of the abuse of power or of a position of vulnerability or of the giving or receiving of payments or benefits to achieve the consent of a person having control over another person, for the purpose of exploitation. Exploitation shall include, at a minimum, the exploitation of the prostitution of others or other forms of sexual exploitation, forced labour or services, slavery or practices similar to slavery, servitude or the removal of organs" (United Nations 2000).

30. Feingold 2010; Merry 2016; Warren 2010.

31. Articles 3(c) and (d) of the Palermo Protocol state: "The recruitment, transportation, transfer, harbouring or receipt of a child for the purpose of exploitation shall be considered 'trafficking in persons' even if this does not involve any of the means set forth in subparagraph (a) of this article," and, "'Child' shall mean any person under eighteen years of age" (United Nations 2000).

32. Cullinane 2007; Kinsella 2012; Leheny 2006; Miyadai [1994] 2006.

33. Miyadai [1994] 2006.

34. Kinsella 2012: 70.

35. Brennan 2014; Vance 2011.

36. Bowker and Star 1999: 15, 16.

37. Merry 2006b.

38. Whether via an attentive empathy of the kind described in Chapter 4 or via this attentive scrutiny, it is notable that both sex workers and the highly feminized staff and audiences of LFSJ center attentiveness to others.

39. Muehlebach 2011: 60.

40. This is not wholly unlike the "vigilante rescue" of evangelical anti-trafficking organizations in Los Angeles described by Elena Shih (2016), in which the most banal behaviors—looks of confusion, incredulity, a lone woman waiting for and then being picked up by a car filled with other people late at night—are viewed as suspect, with the effect of policing immigrant working-class neighborhoods. Although LFSJ staff certainly did not advocate for this kind of civilian vigilantism, they encouraged audiences to pay attention to the relations around them and to act if they noticed anything they felt might be unusual.

41. Implicit in this ethics of observing everyday interactions and reporting things that seem out of place with the aim of helping women is a form of "carceral feminism"—that is, a partnership with law enforcement as a solution to problems of violence against women (Bernstein 2010; see also Bumiller 2008).

42. See also Bernstein and Shih 2014 for their analysis of human trafficking "reality tours" in Thailand.

43. G. Mitchell 2016: 75–76.

44. See, for example, Matsuzawa 2000.

45. Kempadoo and Doezema 1998; Kempadoo, Sanghera, and Pattanaik [2005] 2012.

46. A. Miller 2004: 18; see also Ticktin 2011.

47. A. Miller 2004: 19.

48. See Fassin 2012 and Ticktin 2011 on the role of compassion and moral sentiment in contemporary politics.

49. There is much here that is reminiscent of early social reformers in the late nineteenth- and early twentieth-century United States (Agustín 2007).

Chapter 6

1. Love hotels, motels, and rental rooms are distinguished from "ordinary" hotels by the abbreviated nature of customers' visits. At love hotels, customers choose between short "rest" or overnight "stay" options, while rental rooms offer hourly rates. These businesses are regulated by the *Fūeihō*, which restricts their locations.

2. I also include the emergence of "encounter cafés" (*deai kafe, deai kissa*) and "encounter-type" (*deaikei*) websites here. *Deai kafe* and *deai kissa* have been categorized under the *Fūeihō* since 2011.

3. Although a driver may be waiting in a car outside, sex workers keenly feel this distance.

4. Keisatsuchō 2019: 10.

5. Momoka 1997: 60, emphasis mine.

6. Kempadoo and Doezema 1998; Overs and Hunter 2011.

7. Although I do not discuss the circumstances of foreign migrant women working in the Japanese sex industry, it is clear that the risks are often greatest for them (see, e.g., Aoyama 2011, 2012, 2013, 2015; Parreñas 2011).

8. E. Miller 2002: 16, 22; Momoka 1997: 55.

9. Higashi 2010: 29.

10. Higashi 2010: 29.

11. Higashi 2010: 30.

12. Castro-Vázquez 2007; Nihon Seikyōiku Kyōkai 2007; Runestad 2010.

13. Haha no Kai 2005: 34–35.

14. Frühstück 2007: 136.

15. Gay men and hemophiliacs constituted many of the earliest cases of HIV in Japan. E. Miller (2002) and Cullinane (2007), however, have illustrated how public discourse about HIV/AIDS from the late 1980s to the 2000s focused on non-Japanese women and female sex workers (or adolescent girls engaging in *enjo kōsai*) as vectors of the disease. Runestad (2010) points out that public perceptions of HIV continue to focus on Japanese and non-Japanese women despite the epidemiological reality that Japanese men who have sex with men vastly outnumber any other group in numbers of new infections.

16. Kaname and Mizushima 2005: 103–4.

17. Momoka 1997: 57.

18. Walkowitz 1980.

19. Cf. Zaloom 2004.

20. Matsuzawa 2005: 79, 82.

21. Higashi 2010: 31.

22. There is little one can do about this if it happens; see Onnatachi no 21 Seiki 2012a: 42.

23. Kaname 2012: 30.

24. See Kaname 2012.

25. See also Aoyama 2015.

26. Sex industry businesses do not generally demonstrate to their employees that they are properly registered with the police. Women who insist on seeing the registration during their interview may be viewed as troublesome and not taken on.

27. Tsunoda [2001] 2005: 131.

28. Tsunoda [2001] 2005: 133–34.

29. Tsunoda [2001] 2005: 131–32.

30. Burns 2005: xiv–xv.

31. Burns 2005: xvii; Haha no Kai 2005: 12.

32. Tsunoda [2001] 2005: 133.

33. Haha no Kai 2005: 12.

34. Kempadoo 1998: 21.

35. Rowley 2002; Shiga-Fujime 1993; Shin Yoshiwara Joshi Hoken Kumiai 1989.

36. Momoka 1997: 59.

37. Momoka 1997: 61.

38. Delacoste and Alexander 1987.

39. Momoka 1997: 60.

40. Matsuzawa 2000, Kaname and Mizushima 2005. See also Aoyama's (2009: 29–30) discussion of these key publications in Japanese debates around prostitution/ sex work in the 1990s and 2000s.

41. de la Madeleine 2005.

42. Momocca 1998: 180.

43. Tsunoda [2001] 2005: 131.

44. Onnatachi no 21 Seiki 2012a: 42.

45. Aoyama 2015: 289–90.

46. Onnatachi no 21 Seiki 2012a.

47. Aoyama 2015: 290.

48. Buch 2018.

49. Elana Buch (2018: 10) brilliantly makes this point in regard to American home care workers.

50. Buch 2013, 2018.

51. As sex worker activists Juno Mac and Molly Smith (2018: 33) write, "There is an obvious conflict of interest between a fantasy persona who loves their job and an activist who demands policy intervention to remedy the abuse of their human rights in the workplace. Using just one persona to assure your clients that you love your working conditions and *also* to highlight how inadequate they are is a difficult line to walk" (emphasis in original).

52. See also Tsunoda [2001] 2005: 127–35.

Epilogue

1. See Buch 2018 for a parallel argument about inequalities embedded in the structure of home care for the elderly in the United States.

2. Inagaki and Harding 2018; *The Economist* 2016, 2017.

Glossary

chatto redī   "chat lady"; woman who live chats with customers online

chon no ma   part of the illegal sex industry; small shopfronts masquerading as bars or restaurants at which women provide (illegal) penile-vaginal intercourse

deai kafe, deai kissa   "encounter cafés," "encounter coffee shops"; businesses at which men pay to meet women (who get in for free). If a man wants to talk to a particular woman, he pays an additional fee.

deribarī esute   callout ("delivery") sexual massage

deribarī herusu (deriheru)   "delivery health"; a callout business in which the sex worker goes to a hotel or the customer's home. The standard service involves oral sex and/or a hand job.

deriherujō   woman who works at a *deriheru*

enjo kōsai   "compensated dating"; adolescent girls who exchange dates and sexual favors with adult men in exchange for cash or brand-name goods

fasshon herusu   "fashion health"; a brick-and-mortar sex industry business at which the standard service involves oral sex and/or a hand job. Often abbreviated to *herusu*.

Fūeihō   common abbreviation for the Law Regulating Entertainment Businesses (both the 1948 *Fūzoku Eigyō Torishimari Hō* and the 1984 revision, renamed *Fūzoku Eigyōtō no Kisei oyobi Gyōmu no Tekiseikatō ni kansuru Hōritsu*)

fūzoku   colloquial term for *seifūzoku* (although technically, *fūzoku* refers to all businesses regulated by the Law Regulating Entertainment Businesses, including bars, pachinko parlors, and cabaret clubs, among others)

fūzokujō   woman who works in the sex industry

herusujō   woman who works at a *fasshon herusu*

honban   sex industry term for penile-vaginal intercourse; the term can be translated as "the central performance itself," as opposed to a rehearsal or practice session

hoteheru   "hotel health"; a callout business in which a sex worker meets a customer at a love hotel or rental room. The standard service involves oral sex and/or a hand job.

hoteherujō   woman who works at a *hoteheru*

imekura   "image club"; a brick-and-mortar business that offers costumes, role-playing, and rooms designed to cater to fantasy scenarios (e.g., a clinic, a train). The service involves oral sex and/or a hand job.

iyashi   healing; the key term through which women in Tokyo's sex industry narrate the social value of their labor

jinshin baibai   trade in humans; a term used to refer to the historical practice of parents "selling" their children into indentured labor, including indentured prostitution. Today, the term is also used to refer to the contemporary transnational discourse of human trafficking.

jinshin torihiki   the legal-juridical term for the transnational discourse of human trafficking

kyabakura   "cabaret club"; a hostess club

manshon herusu   an illegal form of sex industry business in which *fasshon herusu* services are sold from an ordinary apartment

mizushōbai   "the water trade"; refers to the diverse range of businesses offering forms of eroticized intimacy, flirtation, and conversation in Japanese nightlife (e.g., hostess and host clubs)

nanbā wan   "Number One"; the designation given to the highest-earning employee at a sex industry business

nyū hāfu   "new half"; a transgender woman working in the sex and entertainment industry

onakura   a business at which a sex worker watches a customer masturbate

onēsan   literally, "older sister"; woman with more experience

pinku saron   "pink salon"; a brick-and-mortar business at which the customer drinks beverages while receiving oral sex and/or a hand job

rentaru rūmu   "rental room"; an inexpensive space used for sex that can be rented by the hour. Rental rooms are much cheaper than love hotels.

seifūzoku   the sex industry; a legal category under the Law Regulating Entertainment Businesses that refers to businesses at which women offer male clients a range of explicitly sexual services. Colloquially often abbreviated to *fūzoku*.

seikan herusu   a form of *fasshon herusu* at which customers receive a prostate and anal/perineal massage in addition to standard services

sekkusu wākā   "sex worker"

shirōto   "amateur"; this term highlights innocence and authenticity and its use by sex workers bears little relationship to how long a woman has been engaged in sex work

SM kurabu   "S&M club"; a brick-and-mortar business at which S&M services are offered

sōpujō   woman who works at a *sōpurando*

sōpurando   "soapland"; a brick-and-mortar business at which a woman bathes the customer; their services are widely known to include (illegal) penile-vaginal intercourse

teikō   resistance or aversion

yakuza   a member of an organized crime group; the Japanese mafia

yoru no sekai   "the night world"

yūkaku   government-licensed pleasure district

Bibliography

Abelove, Henry. [1989] 2007. "Some Speculations on the History of 'Sexual Intercourse' During the 'Long Eighteenth Century' in England." In *Beyond the Body Proper: Reading the Anthropology of Material Life*, edited by Margaret Lock and Judith Farquhar, 217–23. Durham, NC: Duke University Press.

Adelstein, Jake. 2009. *Tokyo Vice: An American Reporter on the Police Beat in Japan*. New York: Pantheon Books.

AFP BB News (Agence France-Press). 2012. "Tōkyō Gorin Shōchi ga 'Nihon o Iyasu,' Takeda Gorin Shōchi'i Rijichō [Olympic Bid for Tokyo Would "Heal Japan," Says Bid Chairperson Takeda]." November 14. http://www.afpbb.com/articles/ -/2910151.

Agustín, Laura María. 2007. *Sex at the Margins: Migration, Labour Markets, and the Rescue Industry*. London: Zed Books.

Ahmed, Aziza, and Meena Seshu. 2012. "'We Have the Right Not to Be "Rescued" . . .': When Anti-Trafficking Programmes Undermine the Health and Well-Being of Sex Workers." *Anti-Trafficking Review* 1: 149–65.

Ajia no Baibaishun ni Hantai Suru Otokotachi no Kai. 1995. *Ajia no Baibaishun to Nihon no Otokotachi* [Prostitution in Asia and Japanese Men]. Tokyo: Ajia no Baibaishun ni Hantai Suru Otokotachi no Kai.

Ajia to Josei Kaihō. 1977. "Tokushū: Kaishun Kankō o Yurusuna! [Theme Issue: We Won't Allow Prostitution Tourism!]." *Ajia to Josei Kaihō*, no. 2 (October).

Alexy, Allison. 2011. "Intimate Dependence and Its Risks in Neoliberal Japan." *Anthropological Quarterly* 84 (4): 895–917.

———. 2019. "Introduction: The Stakes of Intimacy in Contemporary Japan." In *Intimate Japan: Ethnographies of Closeness and Conflict*, edited by Allison Alexy and Emma E. Cook, 1–34. Honolulu: University of Hawai'i Press.

Allison, Anne. 1994. *Nightwork: Sexuality, Pleasure, and Corporate Masculinity in a Tokyo Hostess Club*. Chicago: University of Chicago Press.

———. 2000. *Permitted and Prohibited Desires: Mothers, Comics, and Censorship in Japan*. Berkeley: University of California Press.

———. 2001. "Memoirs of the Orient." *Journal of Japanese Studies* 27 (2): 381–98.

———. 2013. *Precarious Japan*. Durham, NC: Duke University Press.

Andreas, Peter, and Kelly M. Greenhill. 2010. "Introduction: The Politics of Numbers." In *Sex, Drugs, and Body Counts: The Politics of Numbers in Global Crime and Conflict*, edited by Peter Andreas and Kelly M. Greenhill, 1–22. Ithaca, NY: Cornell University Press.

Aoyama, Kaoru. 2009. *Thai Migrant Sex Workers: From Modernisation to Globalisation*. New York: Palgrave Macmillan.

———. 2011. "Migrants and the Sex Industry." In *Transforming Japan: How Feminism and Diversity Are Making a Difference*, edited by Kumiko Fujimura-Fanselow, 284–301. New York: Feminist Press at the City University of New York.

———. 2012. "'Atte wa Ikenai Sekkusu Wāku': Gaikokujin Sekkusu Wākā to Fukashika no Kiken ["Sex Work That Should Not Exist": Foreign Migrant Sex Workers and the Dangers of Invisibility]." *Onnatachi no 21 Seiki* 72: 34–39.

———. 2013. "Moving from Modernization to Globalization: Migrant Sex Workers in Japan." In *Asian Women and Intimate Work*, edited by Emiko Ochiai and Kaoru Aoyama, 263–88. Leiden: Brill.

———. 2015. "The Sex Industry in Japan: The Danger of Invisibility." In *Routledge Handbook of Sexuality Studies in East Asia*, edited by Mark McLelland and Vera Mackie, 281–93. New York: Routledge.

Appel, Hannah. 2017. "Toward an Ethnography of the National Economy." *Cultural Anthropology* 32 (2): 294–322.

Asahi Shimbun. 2005. "Shinjuku Kabukichō, Kyakuhiki Gekigen, Susumu 'Jōka,' Hyōjō Henka [Progressing Clean-Up in Shinjuku's Kabukichō Leads to a Drop in Touting and a Change in Expression]." April 2, evening edition: 14.

———. 2013. "Ianfu Mondai Fūzokugyō o Meguru Hashimotoshi no Hatsugen Yōshi [Hashimoto's Comments on the Comfort Women and the Sex Industry]." May 14. http://www.asahi.com/politics/update/0514/OSK201305130144.html.

Asia-Japan Women's Resource Center. 2009. "Security in Solidarity: As Women and Poor." *Voices from Japan*, no. 23 (September): 4–12.

Asian Women's Association. 1988. *Women from Across the Seas: Migrant Workers in Japan*. Tokyo: Asian Women's Association.

Babior, Sharman. 1993. "Women of a Tokyo Shelter: Domestic Violence and Sexual Exploitation in Japan." PhD diss., University of California, Los Angeles.

Bear, Laura, Karen Ho, Anna Tsing, and Sylvia Yanagisako. 2015. "Gens: A Feminist Manifesto for the Study of Capitalism." *Society for Cultural Anthropology*, March 30. https://culanth.org/fieldsights/652-gens-a-feminist-manifesto-for-the-study-of-capitalism.

Bell, Laurie. 1987. *Good Girls / Bad Girls: Feminists and Sex Trade Workers Face to Face*. Toronto: Seal Press.

Bengoshi Dottokomu Nyūsu. 2017. "'Bānira' to Kodomo ga Utaidashi Oya wa Konwaku: Tōkyōto Jōrei no 'Nukemichi' o Hashiru Ado Torakku [Parent Bewildered by Child Singing the First Bars of "Vanilla": Ad Trucks Use Loopholes in Tokyo City Ordinances]." *Bengo4.com*, September 8. https://www.bengo4.com/internet/n_6635.

Bernstein, Elizabeth. 2007a. "The Sexual Politics of the 'New Abolitionism.'" *differences: A Journal of Feminist Cultural Studies* 18 (3): 128–51.

———. 2007b. *Temporarily Yours: Intimacy, Authenticity, and the Commerce of Sex.* Chicago: Chicago University Press.

———. 2010. "Militarized Humanitarianism Meets Carceral Feminism: The Politics of Sex, Rights, and Freedom in Contemporary Antitrafficking Campaigns." *Signs: Journal of Women in Culture and Society* 36 (1): 45–71.

Bernstein, Elizabeth, and Elena Shih. 2014. "The Erotics of Authenticity: Sex Trafficking and 'Reality Tourism' in Thailand." *Social Politics* 21 (3): 430–60.

Bessatsu Takarajima Henshūbu. 1995. "Baishun ga Shirōtoka Suru Shakai ni Ikiru to iu Koto [Living in a Society of Amateur Prostitution]." *Bessatsu Takarajima* 224: 4–5.

Best, Joel. 1990. *Threatened Children: Rhetoric and Concern About Child-Victims.* Chicago: University of Chicago Press.

Bisuche BB Kyūto. 2008. "Zettai Yakudatsu Shigoto Navi [An Absolutely Useful Work Navigator]." *Bisuche BB Kyūto* (July) 322: 166–67.

Boris, Eileen, and Rhacel Salazar Parreñas. 2010. "Introduction." In *Intimate Labors: Cultures, Technologies, and the Politics of Care*, edited by Eileen Boris and Rhacel Salazar Parreñas, 1–12. Stanford, CA: Stanford University Press.

———, eds. 2010. *Intimate Labors: Cultures, Technologies, and the Politics of Care.* Stanford, CA: Stanford University Press.

Borovoy, Amy. 2005. *The Too-Good Wife: Alcohol, Codependency, and the Politics of Nurturance in Postwar Japan.* Berkeley: University of California Press.

Bowker, Geoffrey C., and Susan Leigh Star. 1999. *Sorting Things Out: Classification and Its Consequences.* Cambridge, MA: MIT Press.

Brennan, Denise. 2004. *What's Love Got to Do with It?: Transnational Desires and Sex Tourism in the Dominican Republic.* Durham, NC: Duke University Press.

———. 2014. *Life Interrupted: Trafficking into Forced Labor in the United States.* Durham, NC: Duke University Press.

Brinton, Mary C. 1993. *Women and the Economic Miracle: Gender and Work in Postwar Japan.* Berkeley: University of California Press.

———. 2011. *Lost in Transition: Youth, Work, and Instability in Postindustrial Japan.* Cambridge: Cambridge University Press.

Buch, Elana D. 2013. "Senses of Care: Embodying Inequality and Sustaining Personhood in the Home Care of Older Adults in Chicago." *American Ethnologist* 40 (4): 637–50.

———. 2018. *Inequalities of Aging: Paradoxes of Independence in American Home Care.* New York: New York University Press.

Buckley, Sandra. 1997. *Broken Silence: Voices of Japanese Feminism.* Berkeley: University of California Press.

Bumiller, Kristin. 2008. *In an Abusive State: How Neoliberalism Appropriated the Feminist Movement Against Sexual Violence.* Durham, NC: Duke University Press.

Burns, Catherine. 2005. *Sexual Violence and the Law in Japan.* London: RoutledgeCurzon.

Burns, Susan. 1998. "Bodies and Borders: Syphilis, Prostitution, and the Nation in Japan, 1860–1890." *U.S.-Japan Women's Journal,* English Suppl. 15: 3–30.

Butler, Judith. 1990. *Gender Trouble: Feminism and the Subversion of Identity.* New York: Routledge.

Cabezas, Amalia L. 2004. "Between Love and Money: Sex, Tourism, and Citizenship in Cuba and the Dominican Republic." *Signs: Journal of Women in Culture and Society* 29 (4): 987–1015.

Caouette, Therese, and Yuriko Saito. 1999. *To Japan and Back: Thai Women Recount Their Experiences.* Geneva: International Organization for Migration.

Castro-Vázquez, Genaro. 2007. *In the Shadows: Sexuality, Pedagogy, and Gender Among Japanese Teenagers.* Lanham, MD: Lexington Books.

Cheng, Sealing. 2010. *On the Move for Love: Migrant Entertainers and the U.S. Military in South Korea.* Philadelphia: University of Pennsylvania Press.

Clennell, Jake, dir. 2006. *The Great Happiness Space: Tale of an Osaka Love Thief.* New York: Clennell Films and Pimlico Pictures. DVD.

Colligan-Taylor, Karen. 1999. "Translator's Introduction." In Tomoko Yamazaki, *Sandakan Brothel No. 8: An Episode in the History of Lower-Class Women,* xiii–xxxix. Armonk, NY: M. E. Sharpe.

Conrad, Harald. 2013. "Converging to a Market-Based Type of Human Resource Management? Compensation System Reforms in Japan Since the 1990s." In *Syncretism: The Politics of Economic Restructuring and System Reform in Japan,* edited by Kenji E. Kushida, Kay Shimizu, and Jean C. Oi, 173–97. Stanford, CA: Walter H. Shorenstein Asia-Pacific Research Center.

Constable, Nicole. 1997. *Maid to Order in Hong Kong: Stories of Filipina Workers.* Ithaca, NY: Cornell University Press.

———. 2009. "The Commodification of Intimacy: Marriage, Sex, and Reproductive Labor." *Annual Review of Anthropology* 38: 49–64.

Cook, Emma E. 2016. *Reconstructing Adult Masculinities: Part-Time Work in Contemporary Japan.* New York: Routledge.

Cooper, Melinda, and Catherine Waldby. 2014. *Clinical Labor: Tissue Donors and Research Subjects in the Global Bioeconomy.* Durham, NC: Duke University Press.

Cullinane, Joanne. 2007. "The Domestication of AIDS: Stigma, Gender, and the Body Politic in Japan." *Medical Anthropology* 26 (3): 255–92.

Cybriwsky, Roman. 2011. *Roppongi Crossing: The Demise of a Tokyo Nightclub District and the Reshaping of a Global City.* Athens: University of Georgia Press.

Daily Yomiuri. 2003a. "Human Trafficking Becoming a Hot Topic." October 5: 1.

———. 2003b. "Japan Urged to Stamp Out Trafficking in Women." November 29: 4.

———. 2004. "Laws Provide Little Help for Sex Slaves." February 12: 3.

Dalby, Liza. [1983] 2000. *Geisha.* London: Vintage.

Dasgupta, Romit. 2013. *Re-Reading the Salaryman in Japan: Crafting Masculinities*. London: Routledge.

De Becker, J. E. [1905] 1971. *The Nightless City, or the History of the Yoshiwara Yūkwaku*. Rutland, VT: Charles E. Tuttle.

Delacoste, Frédérique, and Priscilla Alexander. 1987. *Sex Work: Writings by Women in the Sex Industry*. Pittsburgh: Cleis Press.

de la Madeleine, BuBu. 2005. *BuBu de la Madeleine: Art Works 1993–2005*. Tokyo: Ota Fine Arts.

Delany, Samuel R. 1999. *Times Square Red, Times Square Blue*. New York: New York University Press.

Delphy, Christine. 1984. *Close to Home: A Materialist Analysis of Women's Oppression*. Translated by Diana Leonard. Amherst: University of Massachusetts Press.

D'Emilio, John. [1983] 1993. "Capitalism and Gay Identity." In *The Lesbian and Gay Studies Reader*, edited by Henry Abelove, Michèle Aina Barale, and David M. Halperin, 467–76. New York: Routledge.

Dinan, Kinsey. 2000. *Owed Justice: Thai Women Trafficked into Debt Bondage in Japan*. New York: Human Rights Watch.

Doi, Takeo. 1973. *The Anatomy of Dependence*. Translated by John Bester. Tokyo: Kodansha International.

Donzelot, Jacques. [1977] 1997. *The Policing of Families*. Translated by Robert Hurley. Baltimore: Johns Hopkins University Press.

Dower, John W. 1999. *Embracing Defeat: Japan in the Wake of World War II*. New York: W. W. Norton.

Ehrenreich, Barbara, and Arlie Russell Hochschild, eds. 2003. *Global Woman: Nannies, Maids, and Sex Workers in the New Economy*. New York: Metropolitan Books.

Engels, Friedrich. [1884] 1978. "The Origin of the Family, Private Property, and the State." In *The Marx-Engels Reader*, 2nd ed., edited by Robert C. Tucker, 734–59. New York: W. W. Norton.

Faier, Lieba. 2009. *Intimate Encounters: Filipina Women and the Remaking of Rural Japan*. Berkeley: University of California Press.

Fassin, Didier. 2005. "Compassion and Repression: The Moral Economy of Immigration Policies in France." *Cultural Anthropology* 20 (3): 362–87.

———. 2012. *Humanitarian Reason: A Moral History of the Present*. Berkeley: University of California Press.

Federici, Silvia. [1975] 1995. "Wages Against Housework." In *The Politics of Housework*, edited by Ellen Malos, 187–94. Cheltenham, UK: New Clarion Press.

Feingold, David A. 2010. "Trafficking in Numbers: The Social Construction of Human Trafficking Data." In *Sex, Drugs, and Body Counts: The Politics of Numbers in Global Crime and Conflict*, edited by Peter Andreas and Kelly M. Greenhill, 46–74. Ithaca, NY: Cornell University Press.

Field, Norma. [1991] 1993. *In the Realm of a Dying Emperor: Japan at Century's End*. New York: Vintage Books.

Foucault, Michel. [1978] 1990. *The History of Sexuality*. Vol. 1. Translated by Robert Hurley. New York: Vintage Books.

Fowler, Edward. 1996. *San'ya Blues: Laboring Life in Contemporary Tokyo*. Ithaca, NY: Cornell University Press.

Frank, Katherine. 2002. *G-Strings and Sympathy: Strip Club Regulars and Male Desire*. Durham, NC: Duke University Press.

Frühstück, Sabine. 2003. *Colonizing Sex: Sexology and Social Control in Modern Japan*. Berkeley: University of California Press.

———. 2007. *Uneasy Warriors: Gender, Memory, and Popular Culture in the Japanese Army*. Berkeley: University of California Press.

———. 2015. "Sexuality and Sexual Violence." In *The Cambridge History of the Second World War*. Vol. 3, *Total War: Economy, Society, Culture at War*, edited by Michael Geyer and Adam Tooze, 422–46. Cambridge: Cambridge University Press.

Fujime, Yuki. 1997. "The Licensed Prostitution System and the Prostitution Abolition Movement in Modern Japan." Translated by Kerry Ross. *positions: east asia cultures critique* 5 (1): 135–70.

Fujinaga, Yukiharu, ed. [1996] 2005. *Fūzoku, Seihanzai* [Entertainment Industry and Sex Crimes]. Tokyo: Tōkyō Hōrei Shuppan.

Fujiwara, Chisa. 2008. "Single Mothers and Welfare Restructuring in Japan: Gender and Class Dimensions of Income and Employment." *Asia-Pacific Journal: Japan Focus* 6 (1). http://japanfocus.org/-Fujiwara-Chisa/2623.

———. 2009. "The Impoverishment of Women Caused by Gender Discriminative Policies: Market, Welfare, Family, and Women in Poverty." *Voices from Japan*, no. 23 (September): 13–16.

Genda, Yūji. [2001] 2005. *A Nagging Sense of Job Insecurity: The New Reality Facing Japanese Youth*. Translated by Jean Connell Hoff. Tokyo: International House of Japan.

Goffman, Erving. 1963. *Stigma: Notes on the Management of Spoiled Identity*. Englewood Cliffs, NJ: Prentice-Hall.

Groes-Green, Christian. 2013. "'To Put Men in a Bottle': Eroticism, Kinship, Female Power, and Transactional Sex in Maputo, Mozambique." *American Ethnologist* 40 (1): 102–17.

Haha no Kai. 2005. *Nihon no Sekkusu Wāku to STD: Sekkusu Wākā no Shiten de Miru* [Sex Work and STDs in Japan as Seen from Sex Workers' Perspectives]. Tokyo: Haha no Kai.

Hanamaru Work. 2011. "Hanamaru Worker Jittai Chōsa [Fact-Finding Survey of Hanamaru Workers]." *Hanamaru Work* (May) 74: 14–17.

Hardt, Michael. 1999. "Affective Labor." *boundary 2* 26 (2): 89–100.

Hardt, Michael, and Antonio Negri. 2004. *Multitude: War and Democracy in the Age of Empire*. New York: Penguin.

Hashimoto, Gyokusen. 2009. *Iromachi o Yuku* [Walking the Red-Light Districts]. Tokyo: Saizusha.

Higashi, Yūko. 2010. "Seifūzoku ni kakawaru Hitobito no HIV Kansen Yobō, Kainyū Shuhō ni kansuru Kenkyū: Josei Sekkusu Wākā no Ishiki, Kōdō Chōsa [Research on HIV Prevention and Intervention Among Individuals in the Sex Industry: A Survey on Female Sex Workers' Awareness and Behavior]." In *Kobetsu Shisakusō (toku ni Seifūzoku ni kakawaru Hitobito, Ijūrōdōsha) no HIV Kansen Yobō Taisaku to sono Kainyū Kōka no Hyōka ni kansuru Kenkyū* [HIV Prevention Efforts and Intervention Results Among High-Risk Groups (Especially Individuals Connected to the Sex Industry and Migrant Laborers)], edited by Yūko Higashi, 25–40. Osaka: Osaka Prefecture University.

Hill, Jane H., and Judith T. Irvine. 1993. "Introduction." In *Responsibility and Evidence in Oral Discourse*, edited by Jane H. Hill and Judith T. Irvine, 1–23. Cambridge: Cambridge University Press.

Hirsch, Jennifer S., and Holly Wardlow, eds. 2006. *Modern Loves: The Anthropology of Romantic Courtship and Companionate Marriage.* Ann Arbor: University of Michigan Press.

Hitt, Jack. 2012. *Bunch of Amateurs: A Search for the American Character.* New York: Crown Publishers.

Hoang, Kimberly Kay. 2010. "Economies of Emotion, Familiarity, Fantasy, and Desire: Emotional Labor in Ho Chi Minh City's Sex Industry." In *Intimate Labors: Cultures, Technologies, and the Politics of Care,* edited by Eileen Boris and Rhacel Salazar Parreñas, 166–82. Stanford, CA: Stanford University Press.

———. 2015. *Dealing in Desire: Asian Ascendancy, Western Decline, and the Hidden Currencies of Global Sex Work.* Berkeley: University of California Press.

Hoang, Kimberly Kay, and Rhacel Salazar Parreñas. 2014. *Human Trafficking Reconsidered: Rethinking the Problem, Envisioning New Solutions.* New York: International Debate Education Association.

Hochschild, Arlie Russell. 1983. *The Managed Heart: Commercialization of Human Feeling.* Berkeley: University of California Press.

Holmes, Douglas R. 2014. *Economy of Words: Communicative Imperatives in Central Banks.* Chicago: University of Chicago Press.

Inagaki, Kana, and Robin Harding. 2018. "Japan's Culture of Discrimination Saps 'Womenomics.'" *Financial Times,* August 29. https://www.ft.com/content/2d05e910-a45e-11e8-8ecf-a7ae1beff35b.

Jinshin Baibai Kinshi Nettowāku (JNATIP). 2007. *"Jinshin Baibai Higaisha Shien no Renkei no Kōchiku: Chi'iki, Kokkyō o Koeta Shien ni Mukete" Chōsa oyobi Katsudō Hōkokusho* [Research and Activities Report on Constructing Alliances for Supporting Trafficking Victims: Toward Providing Support Beyond Regional and National Borders]. Tokyo: JNATIP.

Jinshin Baibai Kinshi Nettowāku (JNATIP) and Ochanomizu Joshi Daigaku 21seiki COE Puroguramu "Jendā Kenkyū no Furonteia" (F-GENS). 2005. *"Nihon ni okeru Jinshin Baibai no Higai ni kan suru Chōsa Kenkyū" Hōkokusho* [Research Report on Human Trafficking Victims in Japan]. Tokyo: JNATIP and F-GENS.

Kadokura, Takashi. 2009. *Sekkusu Kakusa Shakai* [Sexual Inequality Society]. Tokyo: Takarajimasha.

Kakuma, Jun'ichirō. 2017. *Fūzokujō no Mienai Koritsu* [The Out-of-Sight Loneliness of Sex Workers]. Tokyo: Kōbunsha.

Kanagawa Onna no Supēsu "Mizura". 2002. *Sherutā, Onnatachi no Kiki: Jinshin Baibai kara Domesutiku Baoirensu made "Mizura" no 10nen* [Shelter and Women in Crisis: From Human Trafficking to Domestic Violence, Ten Years of "Mizura"]. Tokyo: Akashi Shoten.

Kaname, Yukiko. 2012. "Fūzoku no Hitenpoka ga Motarasu Risuku [The Risks Brought by the Off Premises Movement of the Sex Industry]." *Onnatachi no 21 Seiki* 72: 30–33.

Kaname, Yukiko, and Nozomi Mizushima. 2005. *Fūzokujō Ishiki Chōsa: 126nin no Shokugyō Ishiki* [A Survey of Sex Workers: The Attitudes of 126 Sex Workers Toward Their Work]. Tokyo: Potto Shuppan.

Kanematsu, Sachiko. 1987. *Tojirareta Rirekisho: Shinjuku, Sei o Uru Onnatachi no 30nen* [Closed Curriculum Vitae: 30 Years of Women Selling Sex in Shinjuku]. Tokyo: Asahi Shimbunsha.

———. 1988. "The Women of Kabukichō." *Japan Quarterly* 35 (1): 84–89.

Kaplan, David E., and Alex Dubro. 2003. *Yakuza: Japan's Criminal Underworld*. Berkeley: University of California Press.

Keisatsuchō. 2004. *Heisei 16nen Keisatsu Hakusho* [Police White Paper 2004]. Tokyo: Keisatsuchō. https://www.npa.go.jp/hakusyo/h16/hakusho/h16/index.html.

———. 2009. *Heisei 20nenjū ni okeru Fūzoku Kankei Jihantō ni tsuite* [Crimes in the Entertainment Industry in 2008]. Tokyo: Keisatsuchō Seikatsu Anzenkyoku Hoanka.

———. 2014. *Heisei 25nenjū ni okeru Fūzoku Kankei Jihan no Torishimari Jōkyōtō ni tsuite* [The Regulation of Crimes in the Entertainment Industry in 2013]. Tokyo: Keisatsuchō Seikatsu Anzenkyoku Hoanka.

———. 2019. *Heisei 30nen ni okeru Fūzoku Eigyōtō no Genjō to Fūzoku Kankei Jihan no Torishimari Jōkyōtō ni tsuite* [Business Conditions and Crimes in the Entertainment Industry in 2018]. Tokyo: Keisatsuchō Seikatsu Anzenkyoku Hoanka. https://www.npa.go.jp/publications/statistics/safetylife/hoan/h30_fuzoku_jihan.pdf.

Keishichō. 2018a. "Seifūzoku Kanren Tokushu Eigyō [Sex Industry Businesses]." May 16. http://www.keishicho.metro.tokyo.jp/tetsuzuki/fuzoku/style/style2.html.

———. 2018b. "Seifūzoku Kanren Tokushu Eigyō, Shin'ya Shurui Teikyō Inshokuten Eigyō no Todokede [Registration for Sex Industry Businesses and Late Night Drinking Establishments]." May 16. http://www.keishicho.metro.tokyo.jp/tetsuzuki/fuzoku/todokede.html.

Kempadoo, Kamala. 1998. "Introduction: Globalizing Sex Workers' Rights." In *Global Sex Workers: Rights, Resistance, and Redefinition*, edited by Kamala Kempadoo and Jo Doezema, 1–28. New York: Routledge.

Kempadoo, Kamala, and Jo Doezema, eds. 1998. *Global Sex Workers: Rights, Resistance, and Redefinition*. New York: Routledge.

Kempadoo, Kamala, Jyoti Sanghera, and Bandana Pattanaik, eds. [2005] 2012. *Trafficking and Prostitution Reconsidered: New Perspectives on Migration, Sex Work, and Human Rights*. Boulder, CO: Paradigm Publishers.

Kinsella, Sharon. 2012. "Narratives and Statistics: How Compensated Dating (Enjo Kōsai) Was Sold." In *A Sociology of Japanese Youth: From Returnees to NEETs*, edited by Roger Goodman, Yuki Imoto, and Tuukka Toivonen, 54–80. New York: Routledge.

Kitanaka, Junko. 2012. *Depression in Japan: Psychiatric Cures for a Society in Distress*. Princeton, NJ: Princeton University Press.

Kobayashi, Kakumi. 2006. "Ishihara Crime Fight Serving Big Brother, Stoking Xenophobia?" *Japan Times*, August 29: 3.

Koch, Gabriele. 2016a. "Producing Iyashi: Healing and Labor in Tokyo's Sex Industry." *American Ethnologist* 43 (4): 704–16.

———. 2016b. "Willing Daughters: The Moral Rhetoric of Filial Sacrifice and Financial Autonomy in Tokyo's Sex Industry." *Critical Asian Studies* 48 (2): 215–34.

Kōseirōdōshō. 2011. *Chiikibetsu Saiteichingin no Zenkoku Ichiran* [Nationwide Minimum Wages Prefecture by Prefecture at a Glance]. Tokyo: Kōseirōdōshō. http://www.mhlw.go.jp/topics/seido/kijunkyoku/minimum/minimum-02.htm.

———. 2012. *Heisei 23nendo Zenkoku Boshi Setaitō Chōsa Kekka Hōkoku* [Results of the 2011 National Survey of Single-Mother Households]. Tokyo: Kōseirōdōshō Koyō Kintō / Jidō Kateikyoku Katei Fukushika. http://www.mhlw.go.jp/seisakunitsuite/bunya/kodomo/kodomo_kosodate/boshi-katei/boshi-setai_h23.

———. 2016. *Chiikibetsu Saiteichingin no Zenkoku Ichiran* [Nationwide Minimum Wages Prefecture by Prefecture at a Glance]. Tokyo: Kōseirōdōshō. http://www.mhlw.go.jp/stf/seisakunitsuite/bunya/koyou_roudou/roudoukijun/minimumichiran.

Kovner, Sarah. 2012. *Occupying Power: Sex Workers and Servicemen in Postwar Japan*. Stanford, CA: Stanford University Press.

Kramm, Robert. 2017. *Sanitized Sex: Regulating Prostitution, Venereal Disease, and Intimacy in Occupied Japan, 1945–1952*. Berkeley: University of California Press.

Kubo, Hiroshi. 2006. *Chian wa Hontō ni Akka Shiteiru no Ka?* [Is Public Safety Really Deteriorating?]. Tokyo: Kōjinsha.

Kuhn, Annette, and AnnMarie Wolpe, eds. 1978. *Feminism and Materialism: Women and Modes of Production*. London: Routledge and Kegan Paul.

Kushida, Kenji E., Kay Shimizu, and Jean C. Oi, eds. 2013. *Syncretism: The Politics of Economic Restructuring and System Reform in Japan*. Stanford, CA: Walter H. Shorenstein Asia-Pacific Research Center.

Kyōto YWCA and APT. 2001. *Jinshin Baibai to Ukeire Taikoku Nippon: Sono Jittai to Hōteki Kadai* [Human Trafficking and the Major Destination Country Japan: Realities and Legal Issues]. Tokyo: Akashi Shoten.

Lee, Xiao Mu. 2005a. *Kabukichō no Chūgokujo* [The Chinese Women of Kabukichō]. Tokyo: Basilico.

———. 2005b. "Nihon ni Habikoru Chūgoku Mafia no Shōtai [The True Colors of Japan's Chinese Mafias]." *NONFIX Nakkuruzu* 1: 60–67.

Leheny, David. 2006. *Think Global, Fear Local: Sex, Violence, and Anxiety in Contemporary Japan*. Ithaca, NY: Cornell University Press.

Leigh, Carol, aka Scarlot Harlot. 1997. "Inventing Sex Work." In *Whores and Other Feminists*, edited by Jill Nagle, 225–31. New York: Routledge.

Lévi-Strauss, Claude. 1969. *The Elementary Structures of Kinship*. Translated by James Harle Bell and John Richard von Sturmer. Edited by Rodney Needham. Boston: Beacon Press.

Lie, John. 1997. "The State as Pimp: Prostitution and the Patriarchal State in Japan in the 1940s." *Sociological Quarterly* 38 (2): 251–63.

Lock, Margaret. 1993. *Encounters with Aging: Mythologies of Menopause in Japan and North America*. Berkeley: University of California Press.

Longinotto, Kim, and Jano Williams, dirs. 1996. *Shinjuku Boys*. New York: Women Make Movies. DVD.

LunLun Work. 2010. *LunLun Work* (August) 87: 1.

Mac, Juno, and Molly Smith. 2018. *Revolting Prostitutes: The Fight for Sex Workers' Rights*. London: Verso.

Mahmood, Saba. 2005. *Politics of Piety: The Islamic Revival and the Feminist Subject*. Princeton, NJ: Princeton University Press.

Malos, Ellen. [1980] 1995. *The Politics of Housework*. Cheltenham, UK: New Clarion Press.

Mainichi Shimbun. 2016. "Saiteichingin: Zenkoku Heikin 823en, 02nendo Ikō Saidaiage [Japan's Average Minimum Wage Set at ¥823, the Biggest Increase Since 2002]." August 24, morning edition: 4.

Makino, Masako. 2013. *Keiji Shihō to Jendā* [Criminal Justice and Gender]. Tokyo: Inpakuto Shuppankai.

Maruyama, Yūsuke. 2007. *Zukai Ura Shakai no Karakuri* [Diagrams of the Tricks of the Underworld]. Tokyo: Saizusha.

Matsui, Takeshi. 2011. "How Was 'Iyashi' (Healing) Commercialized and Institutionalized in Japan? The Dynamic Interaction of Media Discourse and Marketing Behaviors." Paper presented at the German Institute for Japanese Studies Business and Economics Study Group, Tokyo, February 14.

Matsui, Yayori. 1989. *Women's Asia*. London: Zed Books.

———. 1993. *Ajia no Kankō Kaihatsu to Nihon* [Japan and Tourism Development in Asia]. Tokyo: Shinkansha.

———. 1999. *Women in the New Asia: From Pain to Power*. Translated by Noriko Toyokawa and Carolyn Francis. London: Zed Books.

Matsuki, Takashi. 2011. *Fūzoku no Mushi: Sōsakan ga Nozoita Nihon no Fūzoku 70nen* [An Insect in the Sex Industry: 70 Years of Japan's Sex Industry as Glimpsed by a Police Investigator]. Tokyo: Gentōsha Renaissance.

Matsuzawa, Kureichi. 2005. "Tōkyōto Jōka Sakusen: Sono Seijaku no Kage de [Tokyo's Clean-Up Campaign: In the Silence's Shadow]." *NONFIX Nakkuruzu* 1: 76–85.

———, ed. 2000. *Uru Uranai wa Watashi ga Kimeru: Baishun Kōtei Sengen* [I'm the One Who Decides Whether to Sell (Sex) or Not: A Pro-Prostitution Declaration]. Tokyo: Potto Shuppan.

McCurry, Justin. 2018. "Tokyo Medical School Admits Changing Results to Exclude Women." *Guardian*, August 8. https://www.theguardian.com/world/2018/aug/08/tokyo-medical-school-admits-changing-results-to-exclude-women.

McIntosh, Mary. 1968. "The Homosexual Role." *Social Problems* 16 (2): 182–92.

McLelland, Mark. 2002. "The Newhalf Net: Japan's 'Intermediate Sex' On-Line." *International Journal of Sexuality and Gender Studies* 17 (2–3): 163–75.

McLelland, Mark, Katsuhiko Suganuma, and James Welker, eds. 2007. *Queer Voices from Japan: First-Person Narratives from Japan's Sexual Minorities.* Lanham, MD: Lexington Books.

Meiu, George Paul. 2017. *Ethno-Erotic Economies: Sexuality, Money, and Belonging in Kenya.* Chicago: University of Chicago Press.

Merry, Sally Engle. 2006a. *Human Rights and Gender Violence: Translating International Law into Local Justice.* Chicago: University of Chicago Press.

———. 2006b. "Transnational Human Rights and Local Activism: Mapping the Middle." *American Anthropologist* 108 (1): 38–51.

———. 2016. *The Seductions of Quantification: Measuring Human Rights, Gender Violence, and Sex Trafficking.* Chicago: University of Chicago Press.

Mihalopoulos, Bill. 2011. *Sex in Japan's Globalization, 1870–1930: Prostitutes, Emigration, and Nation Building.* London: Pickering and Chatto.

Miller, Alice M. 2004. "Sexuality, Violence Against Women, and Human Rights: Women Make Demands and Ladies Get Protection." *Health and Human Rights* 7 (2): 16–47.

Miller, Elizabeth. 2002. "What's in a Condom? HIV and Sexual Politics in Japan." *Culture, Medicine, and Psychiatry* 26 (1): 1–32.

Mitchell, Gregory. 2016. *Tourist Attractions: Performing Race and Masculinity in Brazil's Sexual Economy.* Chicago: University of Chicago Press.

Mitchell, Timothy. 2002. *Rule of Experts: Egypt, Techno-Politics, Modernity.* Berkeley: University of California Press.

Miura, Atsushi, and Tamao Yanauchi. 2008. *Onna wa Naze Kyabakurajō ni Naritai no Ka?: "Shōnin Saretai Jibun" no Jidai* [Why Do Women Want to Become Cabaret Club Hostesses? The Era of "Wanting Approval"]. Tokyo: Kōbunsha.

Miyadai, Shinji. [1994] 2006. *Seifuku Shōjotachi no Sentaku: After 10 Years* [The Choices of Girls in School Uniforms: After 10 Years]. Tokyo: Asahi Bunkō.

Momocca, Momocco. 1998. "Japanese Sex Workers: Encourage, Empower, Trust and Love Yourselves!" In *Global Sex Workers: Rights, Resistance, and Redefinition*, edited by Kamala Kempadoo and Jo Doezema, 178–81. New York: Routledge.

Momoco. 2008. "Osaifu Check! [Wallet Check!]." *Momoco* (July, Kanagawa edition) 6: 8–9.

Momoka, Momoeri, and Yukari Yashiki. 2009. *Momoeri*. Tokyo: Take Shobō.

Momoka, Momoko. 1997. "Sekkusu Wākā kara Mita Piru [The Pill as Seen by a Sex Worker]." *Impaction* 105: 53–61.

Morgan, Lewis Henry. [1870] 1997. *Systems of Consanguinity and Affinity of the Human Family*. Lincoln: University of Nebraska Press.

———. [1877] 1964. *Ancient Society*. Cambridge, MA: Harvard University Press.

Morinaga, Maki Isaka. 2005. "Osanai Kaoru's Dilemma: 'Amateurism by Professionals' in Modern Japanese Theatre." *TDR: The Drama Review* 49 (1): 119–33.

Muehlebach, Andrea. 2011. "On Affective Labor in Post-Fordist Italy." *Cultural Anthropology* 26 (1): 59–82.

———. 2013. "On Precariousness and the Ethical Imagination: The Year 2012 in Sociocultural Anthropology." *American Anthropologist* 115 (2): 297–311.

Mun, Eunmi, and Mary C. Brinton. 2015. "Workplace Matters: The Use of Parental Leave Policy in Japan." *Work and Occupations* 42 (3): 335–69.

Nagai, Yoshikazu. 2002. *Fūzoku Eigyō Torishimari* [The Regulation of Entertainment Businesses]. Tokyo: Kōdansha.

Nagasawa, Mitsuo. 1999. *Fūzoku no Hitotachi* [People of the Sex Industry]. Tokyo: Chikuma Shobō.

Nagle, Jill, ed. 1997. *Whores and Other Feminists*. New York: Routledge.

Naikakufu Danjo Kyōdō Sankakukyoku. 2018. *Danjo Kyōdō Sankaku Hakusho Heisei 30nenban* [White Paper on Gender Equality 2018 Edition]. Tokyo: Naikakufu. http://www.gender.go.jp/about_danjo/whitepaper/h30/zentai/index.html.

Nakamura, Atsuhiko. 2015. *Joshidaisei Seifūzokujō: Wakamono Hinkon Taikoku Nihon no Riaru* [College Students Who Are Sex Workers: The Real World of Japan's Impoverished Youth]. Tokyo: Asahi Shimbun Shuppan.

Nakamura, Atsuhiko, and Mamoru Teshigawara. 2015. *Shokugyō toshite no Fūzokujō* [Sex Worker as Occupation]. Tokyo: Takarajimasha.

Nakane, Chie. 1970. *Japanese Society*. Berkeley: University of California Press.

Newton, Esther. [1972] 1979. *Mother Camp: Female Impersonators in America*. Chicago: University of Chicago Press.

NHK News. 2004. "Tōkyōto ga Chiiki Bōhan Katsudō no Rīdā Yōsei e [Tokyo Nurturing Leaders in Local Anti-Crime Activities]." May 18.

———. 2005. "Bōhan Boranteia [Anti-Crime Volunteers]." June 20.

NHK (Nippon Hōsō Kyōkai "Nihonjin no Sei" Purojekuto). 2002. *Dētabukku NHK Nihonjin no Sei Kōdō, Sei Ishiki* [NHK Databook on the Sexual Behavior and Attitudes of the Japanese]. Tokyo: Nihon Hōsō Shuppan Kyōkai.

NHK ("Muen Shakai Purojekuto" Shazaihan). 2010. *Muen Shakai* [A Society Without Connections]. Tokyo: Bungei Shunjū.

Nihon Keizai Shimbun. 2013. "Zeisei Kaisei no Pointo, Kōsaihi, Daikigyō mo 50% Sonkin ni [With Revisions to Tax Policy, Large Firms Can Deduct 50% of Entertainment Expenses]." December 13: 6.

Nihon Seikyōiku Kyōkai. 2007. *"Wakamono no Sei" Hakusho: Dairokkai Seishōnen no Seikōdō Zenkoku Chōsa Hōkoku* [White Paper on "Young People's Sexuality": A Report on the Sixth National Survey of Youth Sexual Behavior]. Tokyo: Shōgakukan.

Nikkei Woman. 2011a. "300nin Ankēto de Wakatta Otoko no Honne [Men's True Feelings as Revealed by a Survey of 300]." *Nikkei Woman* (November): 124–25.

———. 2011b. "6nin ga Sekirara Hakusho [Six Men Tell Us What They Really Think]." *Nikkei Woman* (November): 126–27.

Nishiyama, Matsunosuke. 1997. *Edo Culture: Daily Life and Diversions in Urban Japan, 1600–1868*. Translated and edited by Gerald Groemer. Honolulu: University of Hawai'i Press.

Ochiai, Emiko. 1997. *The Japanese Family System in Transition: A Sociological Analysis of Family Change in Postwar Japan*. Tokyo: LTCB International Library Foundation.

Ogiue, Chiki. 2012. *Kanojotachi no Warikiri: Shakai kara no Sekiryoku, Deaikei no Inryoku* [Women's "One-Night Stand" Prostitution: Excluded from Society, Attracted to Encounter-Type Sites]. Tokyo: Fusōsha.

Ohshima, Shizuko, and Carolyn Francis. 1989. *Japan Through the Eyes of Women Migrant Workers*. Tokyo: Japan Woman's Christian Temperance Union.

Okinawa Times. 2011. "Ginowanshi ga 'Ihō Fūzokuten Zero' Kanban [Signboards Posted Say "Zero Illegal Sex Industry Businesses" in Ginowan City]." March 28. http://www.okinawatimes.co.jp/article/2011-03-28_15960.

Onnatachi no 21 Seiki. 2012a. "Fūzoku de Hataraku Josei e no Sabetsu, Sutiguma [Discrimination and Stigma Toward Women Working in the Sex Industry]." *Onnatachi no 21 Seiki* 72: 40–47.

———. 2012b. "Shakai no Soba ni aru Sekiryoku: 'Warikiri' Josei e no Chōsa kara [Exclusion at Society's Edge: Results from a Survey of "One-Night-Stand" Women]." *Onnatachi no 21 Seiki* 72: 11–15.

Ono, Ikkō. 2016. *Shinsai Fūzokujō* [Earthquake Disaster–Struck Sex Workers]. Tokyo: Ōta Shuppan.

Osaka Yomiuri Shimbun. 2013. "Kōkō Kyōyu Fūzoku de Baito [High School Teacher Working in the Sex Industry]." May 3, morning edition: 29.

Osaki, Tomohiro. 2014. "Female Worker Scores Legal Win over Maternity." *Japan Times*, October 24: 1.

Overs, Cheryl. 2012. "The Tide Cannot Be Turned Without Us: HIV Epidemics Amongst Key Affected Populations." Plenary presentation at the International AIDS Conference, Washington, DC, July 26. https://www.kff.org/global-health-policy/event/aids-2012-plenary-dynamics-of-the-epidemic-in-context.

Overs, Cheryl, and Andrew Hunter. 2011. *Making Sex Work Safe*. Edinburgh: Global Network of Sex Work Projects.

Ozawa-de Silva, Chikako. 2008. "Too Lonely to Die Alone: Internet Suicide Pacts and Existential Suffering in Japan." *Culture, Medicine, and Psychiatry* 32 (4): 516–51.

Parreñas, Rhacel Salazar. 2001. *Servants of Globalization: Women, Migration, and Domestic Work*. Stanford, CA: Stanford University Press.

———. 2011. *Illicit Flirtations: Labor, Migration, and Sex Trafficking in Tokyo*. Stanford, CA: Stanford University Press.

Ramberg, Lucinda. 2014. *Given to the Goddess: South Indian Devadasis and the Sexuality of Religion.* Durham, NC: Duke University Press.

Reiter, Rayna R., ed. 1975. *Toward an Anthropology of Women.* New York: Monthly Review Press.

Richey, Lisa Ann, and Stefano Ponte. 2008. "Better (Red)™ than Dead? Celebrities, Consumption, and International Aid." *Third World Quarterly* 29 (4): 711–29.

Rivers-Moore, Megan. 2016. *Gringo Gulch: Sex, Tourism, and Social Mobility in Costa Rica.* Chicago: University of Chicago Press.

Roberson, James E., and Nobue Suzuki, eds. 2003. *Men and Masculinities in Contemporary Japan: Dislocating the Salaryman Doxa.* London: RoutledgeCurzon.

Roberts, Elizabeth F. S. 2012. *God's Laboratory: Assisted Reproduction in the Andes.* Berkeley: University of California Press.

Robertson, Jennifer. 1991a. *Native and Newcomer: Making and Remaking a Japanese City.* Berkeley: University of California Press.

———. 1991b. "The Shingaku Woman: Straight from the Heart." In *Recreating Japanese Women, 1600–1945,* edited by Gail Lee Bernstein, 88–107. Berkeley: University of California Press.

Ronald, Richard, and Allison Alexy, eds. 2011. *Home and Family in Japan: Continuity and Transformation.* London: Routledge.

Rosaldo, Michelle Zimbalist, and Louise Lamphere, eds. 1974. *Woman, Culture, and Society.* Stanford, CA: Stanford University Press.

Rosenbluth, Frances McCall, and Michael F. Thies. 2010. *Japan Transformed: Political Change and Economic Restructuring.* Princeton, NJ: Princeton University Press.

Rowley, G. G. 2002. "Prostitutes Against the Prostitution Prevention Act of 1956." *U.S.-Japan Women's Journal,* English Suppl. 23: 39–56.

Rubin, Gayle. 1975. "The Traffic in Women: Notes on the 'Political Economy' of Sex." In *Toward an Anthropology of Women,* edited by Rayna R. Reiter, 157–210. New York: Monthly Review Press.

———. 1984. "Thinking Sex: Notes for a Radical Theory of the Politics of Sexuality." In *Pleasure and Danger: Exploring Female Sexuality,* edited by Carole S. Vance, 267–319. Boston: Routledge and KeganPaul.

———. 1991. "The Catacombs: A Temple of the Butthole." In *Leatherfolk: Radical Sex, People, Politics, and Practice,* edited by Mark Thompson, 119–41. Boston: Alyson.

———. 2011. "The Trouble with Trafficking: Afterthoughts on 'The Traffic in Women.'" In *Deviations: A Gayle Rubin Reader,* edited by Gayle Rubin, 66–86. Durham, NC: Duke University Press.

Rubin, Gayle, and Judith Butler. 1994. "Sexual Traffic." *differences: A Journal of Feminist Cultural Studies* 6 (2–3): 62–99.

Runestad, Pamela. 2010. "What People Think Matters: The Relationship Between Perceptions and Epidemiology in the Japanese HIV Epidemic." *International Journal of Interdisciplinary Social Sciences* 5 (4): 331–44.

Sakai, Ayumi. 1998. *Nemuranai Onna: Hiru wa Futsū no Shakaijin, Yoru ni Naru to Fūzokujyō* [Women Who Don't Sleep: Ordinary Adults by Day, Sex Workers by Night]. Tokyo: Gentōsha.

———. 2006. *Fūzokujō, Sono Go* [Life After Being a Sex Worker]. Tokyo: Kawade Shobō Shinsha.

Sanders, Holly. 2012. "Panpan: Streetwalking in Occupied Japan." *Pacific Historical Review* 81 (3): 404–31.

Sankei Shimbun. 2013. "Sensei 'Hōkago' wa Fūzokujō [After School, Teacher Works as Sex Worker]." May 3, Tokyo morning edition: 23.

Satō, Toshiki. 2000. *Fubyōdō Shakai Nihon: Sayonara Sōchūryū* [Unequal Society Japan: Goodbye to the Mass Middle Class]. Tokyo: Chūō Kōron Shinsha.

Sawada, Takashi. 2002. *"Deriheru" Shōbai no Hajimekata, Mōkekata* [How to Open and Run a Profitable "Delivery Health" Business]. Tokyo: Paru Shuppan.

Sawamura, Takuya. 2008. *Fūzokujō Monogatari: Hosuto ga Mita Kanojotachi no Sugao* [Tales of Women in the Sex Industry: Their Real Faces as Seen by a Host]. Tokyo: Kawade Shobō Shinsha.

Scott, James C. 1976. *The Moral Economy of the Peasant: Rebellion and Subsistence in Southeast Asia*. New Haven, CT: Yale University Press.

Searchina News. 2010. "Shakkin o Kaesenai Josei o Nihon ni Uri, 'Ichinichi 10kai Ijō Baishun Kyōyō' [Women Who Can't Return Their Debts Are Being Sold to Japan, "Forced to Prostitute Themselves over 10 Times a Day"]." *Livedoor News*, October 22. http://news.livedoor.com/article/detail/5089015.

Seigle, Cecilia Segawa. 1993. *Yoshiwara: The Glittering World of the Japanese Courtesan*. Honolulu: University of Hawai'i Press.

Shah, Svati P. 2014. *Street Corner Secrets: Sex, Work, and Migration in the City of Mumbai*. Durham, NC: Duke University Press.

Shiga-Fujime, Yuki. 1993. "The Prostitutes' Union and the Impact of the 1956 Anti-Prostitution Law in Japan." Translated by Beverly L. Findlay-Kaneko. *U.S.-Japan Women's Journal*, English Suppl. 5: 3–27.

Shih, Elena. 2016. "Not in My 'Backyard Abolitionism': Vigilante Rescue Against American Sex Trafficking." *Sociological Perspectives* 59 (1): 66–90.

Shimizu, Kay. 2013. "The Survival of Regional Banks and Small and Medium Enterprises." In *Syncretism: The Politics of Economic Restructuring and System Reform in Japan*, edited by Kenji E. Kushida, Kay Shimizu, and Jean C. Oi, 147–71. Stanford, CA: Walter H. Shorenstein Asia-Pacific Research Center.

Shin Yoshiwara Joshi Hoken Kumiai. 1989. *Fujin Shinpū: Shin Yoshiwara Joshi Hoken Kumiai Kikanshi* [Women's Fresh Breeze: Bulletin of the New Yoshiwara Women's Health Preservation Union]. Tokyo: Akashi Shoten.

Sievers, Sharon. 1983. *Flowers in Salt: The Beginnings of Feminist Consciousness in Modern Japan*. Stanford, CA: Stanford University Press.

Soh, Chunghee Sarah. 2008. *The Comfort Women: Sexual Violence and Postcolonial Memory in Korea and Japan*. Chicago: University of Chicago Press.

Sone, Hiromi. 1999. "Prostitution and Public Authority in Early Modern Japan." In *Women and Class in Japanese History*, edited by Hitomi Tonomura, Anne Walthall, and Haruko Wakita, and translated by Akiko Terashima and Anne Walthall, 169–85. Ann Arbor, MI: Center for Japanese Studies.

Stanley, Amy. 2012. *Selling Women: Prostitution, Markets, and the Household in Early Modern Japan*. Berkeley: University of California Press.

Steinberg, Chad, and Masato Nakane. 2012. "Can Women Save Japan?" IMF Working Paper 12/248. Washington, DC: International Monetary Fund.

Strathern, Marilyn. 1988. *The Gender of the Gift: Problems with Women and Problems with Society in Melanesia*. Berkeley: University of California Press.

———, ed. 2000. *Audit Cultures: Anthropological Studies in Accountability, Ethics, and the Academy*. London: Routledge.

Suzuki, Daisuke. 2010. *Deaikei no Shinguru Mazātachi: Yokubō to Hinkon no Hazama de* [Single Mothers and Online Dating Services: Between Desire and Poverty]. Tokyo: Asahi Shimbun Shuppan.

Suzuki, Tomohiko. 2005. "Kabukichō no Yami, Teikō Seiryokutachi no Koe [Voices of the Opposition Forces in Kabukichō's Darkness]." *NONFIX Nakkuruzu* 1: 68–75.

SWASH. 2013. "Tōkyō, Saitama, Susukino no Tenpogata Herusuten no 'Heikinteki' Fūzokujō [The "Average" Sex Worker at Store-Based *Herusu* in Tokyo, Saitama, and Susukino]." http://swashweb.sakura.ne.jp/file/2013research.pdf.

———. 2018. *Sekkusu Wāku Sutadīzu* [Sex Work Studies]. Tokyo: Nihon Hyōronsha.

Tabuchi, Hiroko. 2009. "The Well-Paid Flirt: Young Japanese Women Vie for a Once-Scorned Job." *New York Times*, July 28: B1.

Tachikawa, Fumito. 2010. *"Fūzoku" Shōbai no Hajimekata, Mōkekata* [How to Open and Run a Profitable "Sex Industry" Business]. Tokyo: Paru Shuppan.

Takeyama, Akiko. 2005. "Commodified Romance in a Tokyo Host Club." In *Genders, Transgenders, and Sexualities in Japan*, edited by Mark McLelland and Romit Dasgupta, 200–215. New York: Routledge.

———. 2010. "Intimacy for Sale: Masculinity, Entrepreneurship, and Commodity Self in Japan's Neoliberal Situation." *Japanese Studies* 30 (2): 231–46.

———. 2016. *Staged Seduction: Selling Dreams in a Tokyo Host Club*. Stanford, CA: Stanford University Press.

Tanaka, Masakazu. 2014. "'Yatto Honto no Kao o Misete Kureta Ne!': Nihonjin Sekkusu Wākā ni Miru Nikutai, Kanjō, Kannō o Meguru Rōdō ni tsuite ["Finally, You've Shown Me Your True Self!": Physical, Emotional, and Erotic Labor Among Japanese Sex Workers]." *Contact Zone* 6: 30–59.

The Asia Foundation. 2008. *Trafficked Koreans to Japan: Who the Victims Are and How We Can Protect Them*. Tokyo: The Asia Foundation Japan Office.

The Economist. 2016. "More Glaring Than Shining: Women and Work in Japan." November 26: 51.

———. 2017. "Flower Power: Sexism in Japan." November 18: 51.

Thompson, E. P. 1971. "The Moral Economy of the English Crowd in the Eighteenth Century." *Past and Present* 50: 76–136.

Ticktin, Miriam. 2011. *Casualties of Care: Immigration and the Politics of Humanitarianism in France*. Berkeley: University of California Press.

Tōkyō Shimbun. 2006. "Datsu Fūzoku [De-Sex Industry]." March 10, morning edition: 28.

———. 2010. "'Yozakura Porisu' Kōsei mo Shidō ["Evening Cherry Tree Police" Offer Rehabilitation and Guidance]." December 25, evening edition: 1.

———. 2011. "Baishun Josei no Kōsei Tedasuke [Giving Female Prostitutes a Hand Toward Rehabilitation]." July 8, evening edition: 9.

———. 2012. "Rupo Hifuyūsō no Genjitsu [Close-Up on the Realities of the Nonwealthy]." December 9, morning edition: 1.

Tōkyōtochō. n.d. "Fūzoku Eigyōtō no Kisei oyobi Gyōmu no Tekiseikatō ni kansuru Hōritsu Shikō Jōrei [Regulations on Carrying Out the Revised Law Regulating Entertainment Businesses]." http://www.reiki.metro.tokyo.jp/reiki_honbun/ag10122141.html.

Trautmann, Thomas R. 1987. *Lewis Henry Morgan and the Invention of Kinship*. Berkeley: University of California Press.

Tsunoda, Yukiko. [2001] 2005. *Seisabetsu to Bōryoku: Zoku, Sei no Hōritsugaku* [Sexism and Violence: A Sequel to "Legal Studies of Sex"]. Tokyo: Yūhikaku.

———. 2010. "The Conditions of and Legal Controls on Prostitution in Japan." Paper presented at the Korean Association of Gender and Law International Conference, December 4.

Tsurumi, E. Patricia. 1990. *Factory Girls: Women in the Thread Mills of Meiji Japan*. Princeton, NJ: Princeton University Press.

United Nations. 2000. *Protocol to Prevent, Suppress and Punish Trafficking in Persons, Especially Women and Children, Supplementing the United Nations Convention Against Transnational Organized Crime*. G.A. Res. 55/25, Annex I, U.N. GAOR, 55th Session, November 15.

Uno, Kathleen S. 1991. "Women and Changes in the Household Division of Labor." In *Recreating Japanese Women, 1600–1945*, edited by Gail Lee Bernstein, 17–41. Berkeley: University of California Press.

Uretsky, Elanah. 2016. *Occupational Hazards: Sex, Business, and HIV in Post-Mao China*. Stanford, CA: Stanford University Press.

Utsunomiya, Yuji. 2003. "Tokyo Sets Up Security Task Force." *Japan Times*, August 2: 2.

Vance, Carole S. 2010. "Thinking Trafficking, Thinking Sex." *GLQ: A Journal of Lesbian and Gay Studies* 17 (1): 135–44.

———. 2011. "States of Contradiction: Twelve Ways to Do Nothing About Trafficking While Pretending To." *Social Research* 78 (3): 933–48.

Vogel, Ezra. 1963. *Japan's New Middle Class: The Salary Man and His Family in a Tokyo Suburb*. Berkeley: University of California Press.

Walkowitz, Judith R. 1980. *Prostitution and Victorian Society: Women, Class, and the State*. Cambridge: Cambridge University Press.

Walters, Kimberly. 2016a. "Humanitarian Trafficking: Violence of Rescue and (Mis) Calculation of Rehabilitation." *Economic and Political Weekly* 51 (44–45): 55–61.

———. 2016b. "The Stickiness of Sex Work: Pleasure, Habit, and Intersubstantiality in South India." *Signs: Journal of Women in Culture and Society* 42 (1): 99–121.

Wardlow, Holly. 2006. *Wayward Women: Sexuality and Agency in a New Guinea Society.* Berkeley: University of California Press.

Warner, Michael. 2002. *Publics and Counterpublics.* New York: Zone Books.

Warren, Kay B. 2010. "The Illusiveness of Counting 'Victims' and the Concreteness of Ranking Countries: Trafficking in Persons from Colombia to Japan." In *Sex, Drugs, and Body Counts: The Politics of Numbers in Global Crime and Conflict*, edited by Peter Andreas and Kelly M. Greenhill, 110–26. Ithaca, NY: Cornell University Press.

Weeks, Jeffrey. 1977. *Coming Out: Homosexual Politics in Britain, from the Nineteenth Century to the Present.* London: Quartet Books.

———. 1981. *Sex, Politics, and Society: The Regulation of Sexuality Since 1800.* New York: Longman.

Weeks, Kathi. 2007. "Life Within and Against Work: Affective Labor, Feminist Critique, and Post-Fordist Politics." *Ephemera* 7 (1): 233–49.

———. 2011. *The Problem with Work: Feminism, Marxism, Antiwork Politics, and Postwork Imaginaries.* Durham, NC: Duke University Press.

Weiner, Annette. 1976. *Women of Value, Men of Renown: New Perspectives in Trobriand Exchange.* Austin: University of Texas Press.

West, Mark. 2006. *Secrets, Sex, and Spectacle: The Rules of Scandal in Japan and the United States.* Chicago: University of Chicago Press.

Wilking, Anna. 2014. "Discourses of Subversion: Mothers Constructing Sex Work in Latin America." Paper presented at the Annual Meeting of the American Anthropological Association, Washington, DC, December 6.

Yagisawa, Takaaki. 2006. *Koganechō Maria: Yokohama Koganechō Rojō no Shōfutachi* [The Marias of Koganechō: Prostitutes on the Streets of Yokohama's Koganechō]. Tokyo: Mirion Shuppan.

Yamada, Masahiro. 2007. *Kibō Kakusa Shakai: "Makegumi" no Zetsubōkan ga Nihon o Hikisaku* [A Society with a Gap in Hope: The Despair of Being a "Loser" That Is Tearing Japan Apart]. Tokyo: Chikuma Shobō.

Yamaguchi, Tomomi. 2005. "Feminism, Timelines, and History-Making." In *A Companion to the Anthropology of Japan*, edited by Jennifer Robertson, 50–58. Malden, MA: Blackwell.

Yamazaki, Tomoko. [1972] 1999. *Sandakan Brothel No. 8: An Episode in the History of Lower-Class Japanese Women.* Translated by Karen Colligan-Taylor. Armonk, NY: M. E. Sharpe.

Yomiuri Shimbun. 2005. "Ihō Fūzokuten 'Itachi Gokko' Tomero [Stop the Cat-and-Mouse Game with Illegal Sex Industry Businesses]." October 9, Tokyo morning edition: 37.

———. 2008a. "'Fūzoku no Machi' Fusshoku e [Sweeping Away a "Sex Industry Town"]." May 22, Tokyo morning edition: 30.

———. 2008b. "Nishikawaguchi wa mō Fūzokugai Janai! [Nishi Kawaguchi Isn't a Sex Industry District Anymore!]." August 18, Tokyo morning edition: 31.

———. 2008c. "Shattāgai, Hanahiraita [Flowers Blossoming on a Shuttered Street]." January 20, Tokyo morning edition: 36.

———. 2018. "Joshi Jukensha o Ichiritsu Genten: Tōkyō Idai, Shi'iteki Sōsa [Female Test Takers Uniformly Marked Down: Arbitrary Manipulation by Tokyo Medical University]." August 2, Tokyo morning edition: 1.

Yoshida, Tsukasa. 2005. "Tōkyō Tochiji Ishihara Shintarō to iu Sakka no Shisō to no Taiji [Confronting the Ideology of Novelist and Tokyo Governor Ishihara Shintarō]." *NONFIX Nakkuruzu* 1: 52–59.

Yoshida, Yoko, ed. 2004. *Jinshin Baibai o Nakusu tame ni: Ukeiru Taikoku Nihon no Kadai* [Eliminating Human Trafficking: On the Major Destination Country Japan]. Tokyo: Akashi Shoten.

Yoshimi, Yoshiaki. [1995] 2000. *Comfort Women: Sexual Slavery in the Japanese Military During World War II*. Translated by Suzanne O'Brien. New York: Columbia University Press.

Zaloom, Caitlin. 2004. "The Productive Life of Risk." *Cultural Anthropology* 19 (3): 365–91.

Zelizer, Viviana A. 2005. *The Purchase of Intimacy*. Princeton, NJ: Princeton University Press.

———. 2010. "Caring Everywhere." In *Intimate Labors: Cultures, Technologies, and the Politics of Care*, edited by Eileen Boris and Rhacel Salazar Parreñas, 267–95. Stanford, CA: Stanford University Press.

Zheng, Tiantian. 2009. *Red Lights: The Lives of Sex Workers in Postsocialist China*. Minneapolis: University of Minnesota Press.

———, ed. 2010. *Sex Trafficking, Human Rights, and Social Justice*. New York: Routledge.

Index

Page numbers in italics refer to figures.

Lightning Source UK Ltd.
Milton Keynes UK
UKHW040614010922
408166UK00004B/381